Upgrading and Migrating to Sybase SQL Server 11

Library Congress Catalog Card Number
ISBN: 1-85032-861-7

For more information, contact:

International Thomson Computer Press
20 Park Plaza, 13th Floor
Boston, MA 02116
USA

International Thomson Publishing GmbH
Königswinterer Strasse 418
53227 Bonn
Germany

International Thomson Publishing Europe
Berkshire House
168–173 High Holborn
London WCIV 7AA
England

International Thomson Publishing Asia
221 Henderson Road #05-10
Henderson Building
Singapore 0315

Thomas Nelson Australia
102 Dodds Street
South Melbourne, 3205
Victoria
Australia

International Thomson Publishing Japan
Hirakawacho Kyowa Building, 3F
2-2-1 Hirakawacho
Chiyoda-ku, 102 Tokyo
Japan

Nelson Canada
1120 Birchmount Road
Scarborough, Ontario
Canada M1K 5G4

International Thomson Editores
Campos Eliseos 385, Piso 7
Col. Polanco
11560 Mexico D.F. Mexico

International Thomson Publishing Southern Africa
Bldg. 19, Constantia Park
239 Old Pretoria Road, P.O. Box 2459
Halfway House, 1685 South Africa

International Thomson Publishing France
1, rue st. Georges
75 009 Paris France

QEBFF 16 15 14 13 12 11 10 9 8 7 6 5 4 3 2
Library of Congress Cataloging-in-Publication Data

Publisher/Vice President: Jim DeWolf, ITCP/Boston
Manufacturing Manager: Sandra Sabathy Carr, ITCP/Boston
Contributing author: Mark Jonikas
Editor: John Pont

Project Director: Chris Grisonich/ITCP Boston
Marketing Manager: Kathleen Raftery, ITCP/Boston
Technical editor: Tarun Batra
Project Manager: Trudy Neuhaus

Production: mle design • 562 Milford Point Road • Milford, CT 06460

Upgrading and Migrating to Sybase SQL Server 11

Mitchell Gurspan

International Thomson Computer Press
I⊤P™ An International Thomson Publishing Company

London • Bonn • Boston • Johannesburg • Madrid • Melbourne • Mexico City • New York • Paris
Singapore • Tokyo • Toronto • Albany, NY • Belmont, CA • Cincinnati, OH • Detroit, MI

Table of Contents

Foreword

The release of a new product version often generates mixed emotions in the user community: excitement about the product's new features and capabilities, tempered by a certain amount of anxiety over the effort required to enjoy all of the potential benefits. And when a new version offers as much promise as does Sybase SQL Server 11™, those feelings can be particularly strong.

Compared to previous releases, SQL Server 11 provides tremendous gains in performance and scalability. In extensive benchmark testing by Sybase and, more importantly, by Sybase customers, the migration to SQL Server 11 has produced more than a fivefold improvement in the performance of some processes. (Of course, the magnitude of the performance gain depends on the particular environment—some tests have identified even greater improvements.) And SQL Server 11's scalability—its capability to take full advantage of multiprocessor hardware—creates the potential for dramatic improvements in throughput and response times.

Some of these improvements are free—in other words, they happen automatically when you upgrade to SQL Server 11. Others result from the skill with which you set up, tune, and administer SQL Server 11—for example, through your judicious use of the many new configuration options.

This book, *Upgrading and Migrating to Sybase SQL Server 11*, offers invaluable guidance for anyone making the move to SQL Server 11. For the many existing customers who plan to upgrade from a previous version—as well as those of you who are new to SQL Server—this book enables you to benefit from the experience and the expertise of skilled professionals who have already successfully deployed SQL Server 11.

Drawing on his experience as a consultant with Sybase's World Wide Professional Services, Mitchell Gurspan provides an insightful view into the new features, big and small, of SQL Server 11. He offers practical advice on how to achieve the best possible performance by using these new features, and he carefully details the options you have and the decisions you must make, during your migration to SQL Server 11. Mitchell guides you through each step in the migration process, serving up plenty of pertinent tips, references, and checklists to smooth your way. For DBAs, developers, and system administrators working in any type of environment, Mitchell offers the expert advice you need for successfully installing, monitoring, and tuning SQL Server 11 to achieve the performance you require.

Like any project, migrating a production environment to SQL Server 11—and taking advantage of SQL Server's many new features—requires careful planning and thorough attention to detail. From initial planning through fine-tuning of the installed system, this book will serve you as a concise reference, detailing the steps you must take and the pitfalls you must avoid, to successfully complete your migration to SQL Server 11. I encourage you to add this book to your collection of SQL Server 11 resources and begin enjoying the many benefits of the latest release of Sybase SQL Server.

Mitchell Kertzman
President and CEO, Sybase, Inc.

Acknowledgments

Have you ever wondered why a book's acknowledgments section lists so many people? Writing a book can be a long, arduous process, and having the right people to guide and assist you can make all the difference in the world.

I would like to thank several people for their help in creating this book. First, I would like to give special thanks to Carol McClendon of Waterside Productions, and Jose Cartagena and Sandy Emerson of Sybase Press. Without these people, this work would never have come to be. Their professionalism and friendly support throughout the development process was instrumental in producing this book. I would like to thank my publisher, James DeWolf of ITCP, for his support and for providing me with the opportunity to write this book. I would like to especially thank my editor, John Pont, for helping to shape my manuscript and for expertly guiding me through the entire process. His talents and professionalism greatly improved the final product. And I would like to thank Trudy Neuhaus for sharing her editorial and management skills and experience to help improve the book.

I would also like to thank the following people: John Lee and Tarun Batra, for their technical editing of the manuscript—their corrections and comments were extremely helpful; Susan Weiss, for offering spontaneous comma placement lessons, editing, and allowing me to wear out her laser printer; Sheldon and Michael Fried, for their expert legal advice; Kathleen Raftery, for her marketing expertise; and Lena Farberov, Rebecca Springer, and Craig Woods, for all their assistance.

I'd like to give a special mention and thanks to Mark Jonikas for writing Chapter 3, "Upgrading to SQL Server 11 in a Windows NT Environment." I put this chapter in Mark's capable hands because he is an expert on SQL Server in a Windows NT environment. Mark is the Competitive Assessment Manager at Sybase, and he has a great deal of experience benchmarking performance on Windows NT. Thanks, Mark, for a job well done.

I'd also like to give a special mention and thanks to Peter Thawley and Todd Ballinger of Sybase's Product Performance Group for their expert advice and for allowing me to use several of Peter's diagrams in my book. Peter is well known as Sybase's ultimate authority on performance and tuning, and the workshops that he and Todd present on SQL Server 11 migrations were invaluable during the writing of this book. If you have a chance to attend one of their workshops, I highly recommend doing so.

Finally, I would like to thank my family, my friends, and the management team at Sybase Professional Services (especially Robert Foster and Bruce MaGown) for their support and encouragement throughout this project.

Introduction

Welcome to *Upgrading and Migrating to Sybase SQL Server 11*, a practical, field-tested guide for migrating to Sybase SQL Server 11. Written primarily for current users of earlier releases of Sybase's SQL Server product (for example, SQL Server 4.9.2 or SQL Server 10.0.1), this book offers detailed information on how to prepare for and complete the migration process, in-depth explanations of SQL Server 11's new features and how to make use of them, and hands-on guidance for configuring and using SQL Server 11 to achieve a high-performance database system. If you currently use SQL Server 4.x or 10.x and you plan to upgrade to SQL Server 11, this book can help you ensure the success of your migration.

To help you decide whether this is the right book for your needs, here's a quick summary of this book's primary audience and intended uses:

- *SQL Server expertise*: Intermediate or advanced

- *Primary responsibilities*: Sybase DBA, developer, or project manager

- *Operating system*: UNIX and Windows NT

- *Intended uses*: Migration guide, detailed SQL Server 11 reference, performance and tuning guide

A Note for First-Time Users of Sybase SQL Server

If you plan to implement SQL Server 11 but you are not upgrading from a previous version, this book can still be of great help to your efforts. As long as you have a basic knowledge of relational database management systems (DBMSs), you will be able to apply most of the information provided in this book. If you are new to relational DBMSs, you may want to purchase an introductory book first, and then come back to this book after you gain the necessary experience.

How Does this Book Differ from other SQL Server 11 Books?

This book differs from other SQL Server books on the market in three important ways. First, instead of simply covering various topics related to SQL Server 11, this book concentrates on the entire migration process, from start to finish. Many books tell you all the great things that SQL Server 11 can do for you or how to use various commands, but they do not help you reach the point at which you can make use of that information. You may have a system with 20 GB of data stored in hundreds of tables, thousands of stored procedures to access that data, and dozens of front-end applications that use all the tables and procedures. This system may have been running on a previous release of SQL Server for several years, and your management expects it to keep on working. This book will help guide you through the entire migration effort, from the initial decision to migrate, through the process of learning everything you need to know about SQL Server 11, to monitoring and tuning the new system so its performance impresses your management team and gets you a well-deserved raise.

This book also differs from others on the market because it takes a practical technical approach. Most of the information in this book derives from experience in the field. Nothing can substitute for the insights you gain by actually performing a task. Each time you perform a task, you may encounter another issue that you must address. Conversely, the same issues may arise every time you perform the task. In either case, the experience of dealing with the same issues many times, under different circumstances, can provide a commonsense understanding of the task that you might not otherwise have. As much as possible, this book focuses on practical, field-tested information and thus allows you to benefit from the experiences of others. Although the migration task may be difficult, other Sybase SQL Server professionals have already successfully completed the move to SQL Server 11. Why not learn from their successes (and mistakes)?

Finally, this book differs from others because it is written by a Sybase employee. In writing this book, I have had the opportunity to work and speak with many of the people who have been involved in the development and support of SQL Server 11, since its inception. I have worked with SQL Server 11 since its first beta tests, and many of my questions have been answered by the engineers who wrote the software or the technicians who support it. With input from my colleagues at Sybase, I have been able to enhance this book with information that might not be otherwise available.

Who Should Read This Book?

This book is primarily intended for intermediate- and advanced-level users of the Sybase SQL Server DBMS. At the very least, the reader should have a basic knowledge of Sybase SQL Server as well as an understanding of fundamental database administrator or developer concepts. Although the book is geared toward current users of SQL Server 4.x and 10.x, first-time SQL Server users with DBMS skills will find it useful.

Conventions Used in This Book

I follow several conventions throughout this book. First, any keywords in a paragraph appear in italics. For example, you will see text that refers to the *sp_configure* command.

In a command, I use italics to identify information that the user must supply. For example, the user must include a valid user name when issuing the following command:

```
isql -Uusername
```

When I list the syntax for a command, I use the following conventions:

- Curly braces—{ }—indicate that you choose at least one of the enclosed options. Do not include the braces.

- Brackets—[ ]—indicate that you can choose one or more of the enclosed options, but doing so is optional. Do not include the brackets.

- A vertical bar—|—indicates that you choose only one of the options. Do not include the bar.

- Commas indicate that you may choose as many of the options as you like. When you issue the command, use commas to separate the options.

How This Book Is Organized

Upgrading and Migrating to Sybase SQL Server 11 covers three major topics:

- Understanding why and how you should migrate to SQL Server 11 (Chapters 1 through 4).

- Understanding and using all of SQL Server 11's new features and capabilities (Chapters 5 through 7).

- Monitoring and tuning SQL Server 11 to achieve high performance (Chapters 8 and 9).

Depending on your needs, you can either read the entire book from beginning to end, or simply use one section for a particular need. For example, once you have SQL Server 11 up and running, you may want to continually reference Chapter 8, "Monitoring SQL Server 11," and Chapter 9, "SQL Server 11 Performance and Tuning," while you fine-tune the system.

Here's a brief rundown on each chapter in the book:

- Chapter 1, "Preliminaries," helps you determine how much time and effort a migration requires, and then describes some useful UNIX tools and SQL queries, as well as field-tested advice and techniques for simplifying your migration.

- Chapter 2, "The Migration Process," presents a detailed plan for completing the six steps in a successful migration.

- Chapter 3, "Upgrading to SQL Server 11 in a Windows NT Environment," provides many useful tips for completing the physical upgrade process under Windows NT. This chapter was written by Mark Jonikas, a Windows NT expert who works on benchmarking system performance in the Sybase technical assessment center.

- Chapter 4, "Upgrading to SQL Server 11 in a UNIX Environment," covers the physical upgrade process for a UNIX-based system, guiding you through the *sybinit* process and showing you numerous tips for completing a successful upgrade or install of SQL Server 11.

- Chapter 5, "Configuring SQL Server 11," provides in-depth coverage of the new configuration system, with numerous examples showing the proper use of SQL Server 11's new configuration features.

- Chapter 6, "The Buffer Manager," offers a detailed explanation of the SQL Server 11 Buffer Manager system, named caches, buffer pools, and large I/O.

- Chapter 7, "SQL Server 11 Enhancements," explores the key new features found in SQL Server 11, with detailed analysis and explanations of the logging system, the locking system, table partitioning, and the housekeeper task.

- Chapter 8, "Monitoring SQL Server 11," describes all of the SQL Server 11 monitoring methods, including *sp_sysmon*, *dbcc traceon (302)*, *dbcc traceon (310)*, and *showplan*.

- Chapter 9, "SQL Server 11 Performance and Tuning," follows up on the monitoring topics covered in Chapter 8, by showing you how to fine-tune your SQL Server 11. This chapter covers such topics as choosing named caches and buffer pools, using *tcp no delay*, and using table partitioning to facilitate the use of multiple *bcp*s.

Upgrading and Migrating to Sybase SQL Server 11 also contains five appendixes:

- Sample Benchmark Results

- New Reserved Words, System Tables, and System Stored Procedures

- Configuration Groups (a complete listing of output from the *sp_configure* command)

- Command Reference

- SyBooks Installation Guide

The migration process and the subsequent maintenance of SQL Server 11 can be complex, challenging tasks. I hope this book helps to smooth the way for you, by sharing the experience and the advice of those who have already successfully made the move to SQL Server 11. When you perform a migration, remember to devise a plan before acting, and do not let deadlines force you into careless work. I wish you good luck in your endeavors.

1

Preliminaries

In This Chapter

- ◆ Understanding why you should migrate to SQL Server 11
- ◆ Determining how much time and effort a migration requires
- ◆ Using UNIX tools and SQL queries to help in your migration
- ◆ Using third-party tools and Sybase resources to help in your migration

Sybase SQL Server 11 is the most recent release of this well-known, highly acclaimed relational database management system (RDBMS). If you already use a previous version of Sybase SQL Server, you are probably wondering whether you should upgrade to this new version. This chapter describes the benefits of upgrading to SQL Server 11 as well as the effort this upgrade requires. This chapter also demonstrates several innovative techniques for simplifying the migration process by using basic UNIX tools such as *vi* and shell scripts. The chapter concludes with descriptions of currently available third-party tools—as well as tools and resources available from Sybase—that can facilitate both your migration effort and your daily use of SQL Server 11.

NOTE: Although this book focuses on providing guidance for readers who are upgrading to Sybase SQL Server 11, much of the information covered in this book also applies to first-time installations of SQL Server.

Why Migrate to SQL Server 11?

SQL Server 11 is primarily a performance release. In other words, SQL Server 11's main goal is to provide improved performance over previous releases. Benchmark tests for numerous scenarios show that SQL Server 11 offers significantly improved response times, compared to those of previous releases. These favorable results come from Sybase's official benchmark tests and, perhaps even more importantly, from customers who require high levels of performance from their applications.

To help you understand the potential performance gains that SQL Server 11 offers, Appendix A lists benchmark results from various test scenarios. Although not every site will experience significant performance gains in all of its applications, almost every user should see some improvement. In particular, upgrading to SQL Server 11 may help you to eliminate existing bottlenecks in your applications. Some users have reported as much as a fivefold increase in the performance of specific applications because SQL Server 11 enabled them to correct previously undetected problems in those applications.

Almost every application has room for improvement, and significant bottlenecks in an application often go undiscovered for years. For example, consider a stored procedure that creates temporary tables. If numerous users frequently execute this procedure, the locking of system tables can cause serious bottlenecks. When you create a temporary table, SQL Server inserts a row into the *sysobjects* table. This insert requires an exclusive lock, which causes all the other users to wait while you hold the lock. During the migration process, you can use the new monitoring tools available in SQL Server 11 to scrutinize your applications and thus find and eliminate these bottlenecks.

One of the most important new features of SQL Server 11 is its scalability—that is, its capability to leverage multiprocessor hardware. Symmetric multiprocessing (SMP) machines contain more than one CPU. Many of these new, powerful machines contain 16 or more CPUs. Unlike previous releases, SQL Server 11 takes full advantage of SMP hardware. As shown in Figure 1-1, using SQL Server 11 with an SMP machine offers the potential for significant performance gains over previous releases. This figure shows response time values for SQL Server 10.0 and SQL Server 11 using various packet sizes.

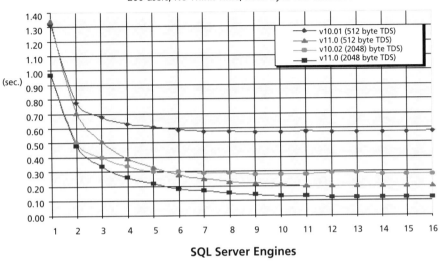

Figure 1-1: *With SQL Server 11, response time improves as you add engines. (Reprinted with permission from Peter Thawley and the Sybase Product Performance Group.)*

As detailed in subsequent chapters of this book, SQL Server 11 provides much greater performance and tuning capabilities than any previous release. In fact, the documentation for SQL Server 11 devotes an entire manual to performance and tuning. These performance and tuning capabilities are among the main strengths of SQL Server 11. For example, you can now place an important, frequently used table in its own data cache. By ensuring that this table always remains in memory, you eliminate time-consuming disk activity.

Other performance-enhancing features of SQL Server 11 include *large I/O* and *partitioning*. Large I/O allows you to manipulate data in much larger chunks than in previous releases. Table partitioning permits parallel disk writes. As shown in Figure 1-2, the use of large I/O and table partitioning can significantly improve performance. Chapter 6, "The Buffer Manager," discusses large I/O in more detail, and Chapter 7, "SQL Server 11 Enhancements," covers table partitioning.

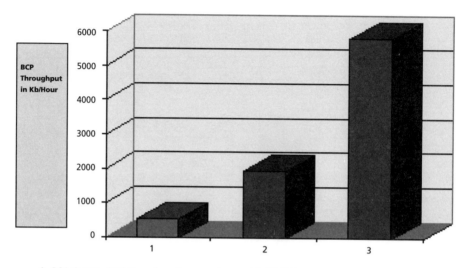

1. SQL Server 10.0.2 performing one bcp, with 2K I/O
2. SQL Server 11.0 performing one bcp, with 16K I/O
3. SQL Server 11.0 performing eight bcps, with eight slices and 2K I/O

Figure 1-2: For such tasks as a bulk copy (bcp) of data, SQL Server 11's support for large I/O
and table partitioning provide improved performance over previous releases. (Reprinted with
permission from Peter Thawley and the Sybase Product Performance Group.)

This book addresses the migration from two previous releases of Sybase SQL Server:

• SQL Server 10.x

• SQL Server 4.x

If you migrate from SQL Server 10.x to SQL Server 11, you benefit primarily from the
performance enhancements found in this new release. If you currently use SQL Server 4.x,
however, your migration to SQL Server 11 provides these performance benefits as well as
significantly improved functionality. SQL Server 10.x offered numerous enhancements to
SQL Server's basic functionality, and these capabilities carry over to SQL Server 11. The
enhancements include the use of cursors and thresholds as well as increased ANSI com-
pliance.

Although SQL Server 10.x offers greater functionality than SQL Server 4.x, that
upgrade did not provide any performance gains. In fact, the migration from SQL Server
4.x to SQL Server 10.x resulted in several instances of slightly decreased performance. For
this reason, some users never upgraded from SQL Server 4.x. to SQL Server 10.x. For

example, many Wall Street financial firms did not upgrade to SQL Server 10.x because their success depends on the performance of their real-time trading systems. A one-second delay in providing information from these systems can mean millions of dollars in losses. By upgrading to SQL Server 11, you can enjoy the benefits of improved performance and the added functionality that Sybase first introduced in SQL Server 10.x.

How Much Time and Effort Does a Migration Involve?

It is impossible to give precise numbers for the time and effort involved in a migration, because each case differs from all the others. For example, one company might have two SQL Servers and very few stored procedures while another company has 75 SQL Servers and thousands of stored procedures. One company might encounter only a few problems—for example, some conflicts with reserved words—and have lax procedures for bringing new applications into production. Another company might run into numerous problems and have strict standards requiring months of quality assurance (QA) testing before introducing new applications into production.

By considering the steps involved in a migration, you can come up with estimates of the time required for completing a migration. Table 1-1 lists the major tasks involved in a migration and the time required for completing each task. These estimates are for a simple migration of a single SQL Server.

Table 1-1: *Estimated Time for Completing Migration Tasks*

Task	Time to Complete
Analyze hardware requirements. Purchase more memory, if necessary, or a new SMP machine, if desired.	1 week to 1 month
Identify and resolve reserved word issues.	1 day to 1 month
Perform the upgrade.	3 days to 1 week
For SQL Server 4.x systems: Check for subqueries and other issues. Correct any problems.	2 weeks to 1 month
Create a test plan.	1 week
Test all applications in a test environment.	2 weeks to 1 month
Total	7 weeks to 4 months

Note that some tasks can overlap. For example, if you have to wait one month for new hardware, you can still perform many tasks on another machine. Also, certain tasks can be performed simultaneously—for example, database administrators and application developers can perform their respective tasks concurrently.

As Table 1-1 indicates, a migration requires approximately one to four staff months. However, you could have a test installation of SQL Server 11 up and running in two days. The remaining time permits the scrutiny necessary for a production system. Remember that the estimate of one to four months is stated in terms of *staff months*. Four people working on a four-month project should complete the migration in one calendar month.

Useful UNIX Tools and SQL Server Queries

The migration effort involves several labor-intensive tasks. For example, you may need to identify all the stored procedures and open client programs that use a certain reserved word. Or you may need to find all the queries that perform joins. This section demonstrates some tools you can use to simplify these tasks.

Remember that you can use the UNIX *man* command to find more information about a UNIX command. Similarly, you can use the SQL Server *sp_syntax* command to find the syntax of a SQL Server command. If the *sp_syntax* command is not installed on your system, you can install it by using the *ins_syn_sql* script, which you can find in the $SYBASE/scripts directory. (See the SQL Server 11 *Configuration and Installation Guide* for information on installing this script.)

TIP!   If you do not want to install the *sp_syntax* command (to save 2 MB of space in the *sybsystemprocs* database), you can still find the syntax for a command by using a text editor to search through the *ins_syn_sql* file. However, you must not make any changes in the *ins_syn_sql* file. Before you open this file with a text editor, make sure that write permission is not allowed. Because this book includes copy of the *SyBooks* CD, you probably will not need to open the *ins_syn_sql* file.

Outputting SQL Server Query Results to a File

Because many of your SQL Server queries will produce large amounts of output, you might want to create a query in a file and then run a simple command to produce an output file that contains the desired results. To accomplish this, you can create a shell script that runs *isql* and takes a file as its input. The following example shows *run_isql*:

```
isql -Uuser -Ppassword -Sservername -i$1 -o$1.out
```

The -i and -o flags simply specify an input file and an output file for the query. SQL Server 11 takes its input from the file specified with the -i flag, and sends its output to the file specified with the -o flag.

After you create this script, make it executable by using the UNIX *chmod* command:

```
chmod +x run_isql
```

You invoke this *run_isql* script with the name of your input file. The script produces an output file with the same name as the input file but with the *.out* extension. (Remember that your input file must end with the *go* command.) For example, you might create a file called *spdepend* which contains the following lines:

```
use pubs2
go
sp_depends titles
sp_depends authors
go
```

You can run *spdepend* by using your *run_isql* command:

```
run_isql spdepend
```

This produces the file *spdepend.out*, which contains the following information:

```
Things inside the current database that reference the object.
object                                   type
------------------------------------     ---------------------
dbo.deltitle                             trigger
dbo.history_proc                         stored procedure
dbo.title_proc                           stored procedure
dbo.titleid_proc                         stored procedure
dbo.titleview                            view
dbo.totalsales_trig                      trigger
(return status = 0)
Things inside the current database that reference the object.
object                                   type
------------------------------------     ---------------------
dbo.titleview                            view
(return status = 0)
```

You may want to add the -e or -w flags to your *run_isql* script. The -e flag repeats the input lines in the output file. This can be useful because you might otherwise lose track of your information. For example, if you create a file that contains the *sp_depends* output of 10 tables, you will not know which table corresponds to a particular line of output. With the -e flag, the output looks like this:

```
1> use pubs2
1> sp_depends titles
Things inside the current database that reference the object.
object                                     type
-----------------------------------        -----------------
dbo.deltitle                               trigger
dbo.history_proc                           stored procedure
dbo.title_proc                             stored procedure
dbo.titleid_proc                           stored procedure
dbo.titleview                              view
dbo.totalsales_trig                        trigger
(return status = 0)
1> sp_depends authors
Things inside the current database that reference the object.
object                                     type
-----------------------------------        -----------------
dbo.titleview                              view
(return status = 0)
```

Many commands produce lines of output wider than the 80-character default. The resulting output can cause confusion because one piece of data may appear on two or more lines. The -w flag changes the row width in the output file. For example, the flag -w150 specifies 150 characters per line.

You may want to create two scripts like *run_isql*: one to access SQL Server 11 and the other to access the old version of SQL Server. If you maintain both SQL Servers during the migration process, you may need to access both SQL Servers at various times.

Using *isql* from a Shell Script

It is sometimes useful to call the *isql* utility from within a shell script. The following shell script syntax runs the *isql* command and passes input to *isql* from the shell script file, until the EOF line is reached (note that EOF is an arbitrary choice of terminators):

```
echo $1
other shell commands
isql -Uuser -Ppassword -Sservername -ooutputfile <<EOF
use db1
go
select * from table1
go
EOF
echo "finished"
other shell commands
```

Timing SQL Statements

In many cases, you need to monitor how long SQL Server 11 takes to complete a stored procedure or a SQL query. You can accomplish this by using any of three methods. First, you can simply use the Sybase SQL Monitor product. One of Sybase SQL Monitor's screens displays the timing for each of the stored procedures that you execute. Second, you can use the T-SQL command *set statistics time on/off*. (For a complete discussion of this command, refer to Chapter 8, "Monitoring SQL Server 11.") Finally, you can use the *getdate* command and the *datediff* command. Because this method allows you to control the display of the timing information, it is particularly useful when you are writing scripts to benchmark SQL Server 11. (For complete information about the *getdate* command and the *datediff* command, refer to Volume 1 of the *SQL Server Reference Manual*.)

To time the stored procedure *sp_who*, use the following SQL commands:

```
declare @time1 datetime
declare @time2 datetime
select @time1=getdate()
exec sp_who
select @time2=getdate()
select "TIME",datediff( ms, @time1,@time2)
go
```

Executing these commands produces the following output:

```
(1 row affected)
spid    status      loginame    hostname blk    dbname    cmd
----    --------    --------    -------- ---    ------    --------
 1      running     sa          rolls    0      master    SELECT
 2      sleeping    NULL        rolls    0      master    NETWORK HANDLER
 3      sleeping    NULL        rolls    0      master    DEADLOCK TUNE
 4      sleeping    NULL        rolls    0      master    MIRROR HANDLER
 5      sleeping    NULL        rolls    0      master    HOUSEKEEPER
 6      sleeping    NULL        rolls    0      master    CHECKPOINT SLEEP
(6 rows affected, return status = 0)
(1 row affected)
----    ---------
TIME            13
```

Note that this method displays elapsed time—not CPU time—in milliseconds.

Using Editor Commands

The following sections discuss editor commands that you can use either interactively with the *vi* editor or as commands to the *sed* editor.

Making Global Substitutions

When modifying scripts or cleaning up output, you may need to perform a global substitution in the file. For example, assume that you have a script that runs the *sp_depends* command on 50 tables. You might want to modify the script to perform a *select* statement on the same tables. Or you might want to make your output files more readable by changing each tab character to a single space.

To perform a global substitution, you use the following command syntax:

```
s/pattern1/pattern2/g
```

where *pattern1* represents the text you want to replace and *pattern2* represents the replacement text.

In vi, press the Escape key to enter command mode and then type a colon, a percent sign, and the command you want to execute:

```
:%s/pattern1/pattern2/g
```

In *sed*, you simply enter the command as shown here:

```
sed "s/pattern1/pattern2/g" file1
```

TIP!   To change all the tabs in a file, simply press the tab key in place of *pattern1*.

Replacing the Beginning or the End of a Line

You often need to replace the beginning or the end of a line. For example, if a file you generate with the *sp_depends* command contains 50 table names, you might want to know the row count for each of those tables. To do this, you can replace the beginning of each line with the appropriate *select* statement. To perform this type of global substitution, you use the special characters ^ and $, which mean the beginning of a line and the end of a line, respectively.

Assume that the file *fnames* contains the following two lines:

```
titles
authors
```

Enter the following command:

```
:%s/^/select count(*) from /g
```

This produces the following output:

```
select count(*) from titles
select count(*) from authors
```

The following example shows how to add a *where* clause to the end of each row:

```
:%s/$/ where colname = 2/g
```

To add a new line containing the *go* command after each line, use the following command:

```
:%s/$/^V(ENTER)go/g
```

TIP! Note that ^V indicates that you press Control+V, and (ENTER) means to press the Enter key.

This command replaces the end of each line with a new-line character followed by the word *go*. The word *go* appears on the next line because it follows a new-line character. The *fnames* file now contains the following commands:

```
select count(*) from titles where colname = 2
go
select count(*) from authors where colname = 2
go
```

The *sp_depends* Command

The *sp_depends* command lists all of the objects that a specified object depends on as well as all the objects that depend on the specified object. The *sp_depends* command has the following syntax:

```
sp_depends objname
```

In place of *objname*, you can specify a table, a procedure, a trigger, or a view. For example, the following command lists all the objects that depend on the *titles* table:

```
sp_depends titles
```

The *defncopy* Command

When you work with stored procedures, you may prefer to work with text files and UNIX commands instead of searching system tables with SQL Server. If so, you can use the *defncopy* command to produce a UNIX file that contains the text of a stored procedure. By using the *defncopy* command, you can ensure that you use the correct version of a stored procedure. The *defncopy* command has the following syntax:

```
defncopy [-U username ][-P password ] [-S server ]
[-I interfaces_file ] [-a display_charset ] [-J client_charset ] [-z lan-
guage ] [-X] in filename dbname | out filename dbname
[ owner .] objectname [[ owner .] objectname ] …
```

The *grep* Command

To find lines in a UNIX file that contain a specified word, use the *grep* command. If necessary, use the case-insensitivity flag and quotation marks and spaces to help qualify a word. For example, if you need to search for the column called *executive* but your stored procedures also have columns called *executive_name* and *executive_id*, you can *grep* on " executive ".

The following example finds all occurrences of the name *auto_part* in the file *carnames*:

```
grep auto_part carnames
```

The *paste* Command

The *paste* command combines multiple files into one file with multiple columns. For example, assume that you have a list of 50 table names and you want to generate bulk copy (*bcp*) scripts for all of these tables. You need to use the table names twice in this script (once for the table and once for the file name) so that you can make a copy of the names file and paste the two files together:

```
cp file1 file2
```

Enter the following commands in *file1*:

```
:%s/^/bcp db1../g
:%s/$/ out /g
```

Next, paste *file1* and *file2* together, and redirect the combined file to *file3*:

```
paste file1 file2 > file3
```

In *file3*, enter the following line:

```
:%s/$/ -c -m2000 -F1 -L10000/g
```

The file *file3* now contains the *bcp* script for all the tables. (In a real *bcp* script, you may have to truncate the transaction log at some point because it might fill to capacity.)

Querying System Tables

You may find the following system tables useful during a migration:

- *sysobjects*
- *syscolumns*
- *syscomments*
- *systypes*

(For detailed descriptions of these tables, refer to the SQL Server 11 *Reference Supplement*.)

You will usually be interested in the name and id columns of these tables. To switch between names and IDs, use the following commands:

- select object_name(*id*). Use this command to get the name of an object when you have the object's ID.

- select object_id("*name*"). Use this command to get the ID of an object when you have the object's name. (Note the use of quotation marks in this command.)

By querying the *sysobjects* table, you can easily find all the user tables, procedures, or triggers in a database. (Remember that you must be in the correct database.) For example, the following query finds all the triggers in the *db1* database:

```
use db1
go
select name from sysobjects where type = "TR"
go
```

When specifying the type, you must use capital letters:

- For user tables, use **type = "U"**.

- For stored procedures, use **type = "P"**.

- For triggers, use **type = "TR"**.

The *syscolumns* table contains the names and the datatypes of the columns in a table. To get useful information, you must *join* the *syscolumns* table with the *sysobjects* table. To list all the columns in the *table1* table, use the following query:

```
use pubs2
go
select c.name, c.type, c.length from syscolumns c, sysobjects o
where
c.id = o.id
and o.name like "titles"
go
```

This query produces the following result:

```
name                            type    length
- - - - - - - - - - - - - - - - - - - -   - - - -   - - - - - -
title_id                         39        6
title                            39       80
type                             47       12
pub_id                           39        4
price                           110        8
advance                         110        8
total_sales                      38        4
notes                            39      200
pubdate                          61        8
contract                         50        1

(10 rows affected)
```

You can use the *syscomments* table to see the text of your procedures and triggers. You find this information in the text column of the *syscomments* table. The following example prints out the text of the *proc1* stored procedure in 255-byte chunks:

```
select text from syscomments where id = object_id("proc1")
go
```

You can use the *systypes* table to find the name of a datatype from the type field. For example, the previous query on the *syscolumns* table returns the datatype, which is not useful information because it is a number, not a name. You can convert this type id to the datatype name by looking up the type id in the *systypes* table:

```
select name from systypes where type = 39
go
```

The *awk* Command

The *awk* command is a complex, powerful command. This section demonstrates one simple use of the *awk* command. To separate columns of a file, use the following syntax:

```
awk '{print $1 $2}' filename
```

For example, to print out the first column (where columns are white space separated) of the *file1* file, issue the following command:

```
awk '{print $1}' file1 > file2
```

Assume that *file1* contains the following lines:

```
aaa bbb ccc
zzzzzz ddd tttttt
```

After you issue the *awk* command, *file2* contains the following information:

```
aaa
zzzzzz
```

The *sort* Command

When used with the *-u* flag (unique), the UNIX *sort* command sorts a file and removes duplicates. For example, assume that *file1* contains the following information:

```
titles
authors
titles
books
```

Issue the following command:

```
sort -u file1
```

This produces the following result:

```
authors
books
titles
```

Putting It All Together

The following scenario demonstrates how you might use several of the tools described in the preceding sections during your migration to SQL Server 11. While performing the reserved word check during a SQL Server 11 upgrade, you find that the reserved word *current* appears as a column name in both the *agents* table and the *brokers* table. You plan to change the names of these columns, but you must find all the procedures that reference those tables. To create a list of the stored procedures that you need to change, you create the following *find_depends* script:

```
use pubs2
go
sp_depends titles
go
sp_depends stores
go
```

You run this script by using your *run_isql* command:

```
run_isql find_depends
```

Running the *find_depends* script produces the following information:

```
Things inside the current database that reference the object.
object                                   type
---------------------------------------- ----------------
dbo.storeid_proc                         stored procedure
dbo.storename_proc                       stored procedure

(return status = 0)
Things inside the current database that reference the object.
object                                   type
---------------------------------------- ----------------
dbo.deltitle                             trigger
dbo.history_proc                         stored procedure
dbo.title_proc                           stored procedure
dbo.titleid_proc                         stored procedure
dbo.titleview                            view
dbo.totalsales_trig                      trigger

(return status = 0)
```

Next, you use the *grep* command, to identify the stored procedures in the *find_depends.out* file and place them in the *tmp1* file:

```
grep "stored procedure" find_depends.out > tmp1
```

The *tmp1* file now contains the following information:

```
dbo.storeid_proc                     stored procedure
dbo.storename_proc                   stored procedure
dbo.history_proc                     stored procedure
dbo.title_proc                       stored procedure
dbo.titleid_proc                     stored procedure
```

To write out the stored procedure names from the *tmp1* file and place them in a file called *tmp2*, issue the following command:

```
awk '{print $1}' tmp1 > tmp2
```

After you execute this command, the *tmp2* file contains the following information:

```
dbo.storeid_proc
dbo.storename_proc
dbo.history_proc
dbo.title_proc
dbo.titleid_proc
```

You use the following commands to edit the *tmp2* file so that only the names of the stored procedures remain:

```
:%s/dbo\.//g — removes 'dbo.'
:%s/ //g — removes any blank space from the file
```

Finally, you use the UNIX *sort* command, to remove any duplicate listings of procedure names:

```
sort -u tmp2 > tmp3
```

The *tmp3* file now contains a list of the stored procedures that you must check:

```
history_proc
storeid_proc
storename_proc
titleid_proc
title_proc
```

Useful Third-Party Tools

Several tools available from third-party vendors can be useful during your migration process, and new products continue to appear. (The information in this section is not meant as an endorsement or a recommendation of any of these products.) These tools may have uses in addition to those described in this section. For more information about a product, contact the vendor.

Cyrano Workbench®, from IMM Corp., is an application performance analyzer. This open server product captures performance information—about the SQL Server optimizer, for example—and stores that information in a SQL Server database or a file. You can use Cyrano Workbench to capture information from both your old version of SQL Server and your new installation of SQL Server 11. By comparing the performance of the two systems, you can identify any significant differences in optimization and performance as well as the transactions involved in the problem. For more information about Cyrano Workbench, call IMM Corp. or visit their Web site:

```
http://www.cyrano.com
```

During the migration process, you can use the Capture Server® and the Playback Server®—open server products from Context Integration Inc.—to capture and play back the Tabular Data Stream (TDS) packets from a SQL Server. (TDS is the proprietary protocol that Sybase uses for communication between servers.)

After capturing these TDS packets, Context Integration's servers can play them back on another SQL Server. This process serves two purposes. First, you can analyze the differences between your old version of SQL Server and your new installation of SQL Server 11. This allows you to identify any problems that might arise during the migration. Second, you can simulate an actual user load during QA tests on your new installation of SQL Server 11. This capability solves a significant problem in the testing of a newly migrated system: simulating the load that the system must handle once you put it into production. (After all, you cannot ask all of your users to spend a weekend testing your new application.) You can find more information about Context Integration by visiting the following Web site:

```
http://www.context.com
```

Many Sybase database administrators handle their dump and load activities by using SQL-BackTrack®, a tool from DataTools Inc. By providing a mechanism for object-by-object dumps and loads, SQL-BackTrack offers a safety net during your migrations.

When performing a migration, you must have a fallback plan—that is, you must know how to respond if your migration fails. SQL Server 11 can read a database dump made by SQL Server 10.x; however, SQL Server 4.x and SQL Server 10.x cannot read a database dump made by SQL Server 11. If you run SQL Server 11 for a week or two and then find that you must fall back to your older version of SQL Server, how do you get that two-week's worth of data into the fallback server? With SQL-BackTrack, you can do a dump of the SQL Server 11 database and load it into a pre-SQL Server 11 server.

For more information about SQL-BackTrack and DataTools Inc., check the Web site at the following address:

```
http://www.datatools.com
```

Migration Information Available from Sybase

Sybase offers the following migration material:

- The SQL Server 11 documentation set. In particular, you should review the manual entitled *What's New in Sybase SQL Server Release 11.0*.

- *The Migration Resource Guide*. This is a master index to all the migration resources available from Sybase.

- The Migration Kit. This kit contains white papers and other materials describing technical features of SQL Server 11.

- The Migration Web Site. Accessible from the Sybase home page (www.sybase.com), this site provides extensive references to migration materials.

- Sybase education classes. The Sybase education department offers several classes on SQL Server 11.

- Sybase Professional Services. Sybase offers consulting services to facilitate your migration to SQL Server 11.

- Sybase technology workshops. Sybase's technology workshops target experienced users and offer a wealth of advanced technical information.

With the exception of the documentation set (which comes with SQL Server 11), you can obtain these materials by contacting Sybase, Inc. or by visiting the Sybase Web site:

```
http://www.sybase.com
```

Summary

This chapter discusses the reasons for migrating to SQL Server 11 and offers a general analysis of the effort involved. The primary reason for migrating is to achieve improved system performance, especially by harnessing sophisticated multiprocessor hardware. The chapter also describes various tools and techniques to help your migration effort.

The following chapter details all the steps you must take to successfully migrate to SQL Server 11.

Migration Checklist

The following list summarizes the key migration tasks covered in this chapter:

- ◆ Determine the time frame required for your migration.

- ◆ Become familiar with the various tools and techniques you plan to use during your migration.

- ◆ Evaluate and purchase third-party tools to help in your migration.

2

The Migration Process

In This Chapter

- Understanding all the stages and steps in a successful migration
- Learning the details and some field-tested tricks that can simplify your migration
- Gathering information for the migration
- Performing the upgrade
- Analyzing the upgrade's effect on databases and applications and resolving any outstanding issues
- Testing the migration
- Monitoring and tuning SQL Server 11

Migrating to SQL Server 11 involves much more than simply installing your new software and running the *sybinit* utility. A successful migration requires careful planning. In all likelihood, your SQL Server 11 migration involves your company's core business data. Consequently, you must not underestimate the challenges that the migration process presents. Although a migration need not be difficult, the phrase *some assembly required* definitely applies to your new SQL Server 11.

In this chapter, you learn the details you need to consider and the potential pitfalls you must avoid, to ensure the success of your migration efforts. This chapter develops an orderly plan, based on Sybase's recommendations, and points out potential trouble spots and tricky details. You benefit from the knowledge, the experience, and the field-tested efforts of those who have already successfully completed the migration to SQL Server 11.

For the most part, the migration effort involves simple, straightforward steps. You map out your system resources and requirements, back up your current system, run the *sybinit* utility to bring up your new system, make any necessary changes to your applications, and then configure the new SQL Server 11 for high performance. The difference between a successful migration and one that results in serious post-installation problems rests in your attention to detail during the migration process. For example, consider the case of a migration in which the project team successfully upgrades the SQL Server but fails to update the directory paths on several client workstations. (In other words, the paths still point to the directories used by the previous release.) These clients might use some files from a previous version of SQL Server along with some of the newer, SQL Server 11 files. Although the clients might not immediately encounter problems, they will eventually experience unpredictable results.

Which Sections of This Chapter Should You Read?

To determine which topics in this chapter you should read, you need to answer the following questions:

- What role do you play in the migration process: database administrator (DBA), application developer, or both? In other words, do your responsibilities include such DBA activities as installing and configuring the server, or are you primarily responsible for such application development tasks as writing stored procedures and open client programs?

- Which version of SQL Server do you presently use: SQL Server 4.x or SQL Server 10.x?

Although the general structure of the migration process remains the same regardless of your answers to these questions, many tasks depend on your role in the process and the version from which you are upgrading. For example, the DBA's responsibilities do not include searching for potential query changes in open client code. And in a migration from SQL Server 10.x, you do not have to worry about most of the subquery changes, because the bulk of these changes occurred in the migration from SQL Server 4.x to SQL Server 10.x.

As you read this chapter, you might choose to skip sections that do not seem to apply to your responsibilities. However, the sections that address application developer responsibilities contain information that many DBAs and project managers may find important. In particular, a project manager should be familiar with all aspects of the migration process, because of the interplay between DBAs and application developers. For example, a DBA runs tests to find reserved word conflicts. If the DBA discovers that a column name is a reserved word, the DBA changes the column name and then the application developers must change any references to that name in their code.

TIP!   The upgrade from SQL Server 4.x to SQL Server 10.x included numerous enhancements that carry over to SQL Server 11. Consequently, an upgrade from SQL Server 4.x to SQL Server 11 involves substantially more work than an upgrade from SQL Server 10.x. However, this does not mean that current users of SQL Server 4.x should upgrade to SQL Server 10.x before upgrading to SQL Server 11. SQL Server 4.x users should upgrade directly to SQL Server 11.

Development Systems and Production Systems

Before you attempt to migrate a production system, you should complete the entire migration process on a development or test system and then carefully test the new system. Make sure that your stored procedures return the same results as they did with the old version, and verify that the performance of the new system is comparable to or better than that of the pre-SQL Server 11 system.

The test migration helps you identify problems you may encounter during the production migration. The test migration also helps you determine approximately how long the production migration will take—an important piece of information for planning the production migration, because your production system can be down for only a limited amount of time.

To determine the appropriate method for migrating to SQL Server 11, you must know how long your production system will be down. As detailed in the next section of this chapter, if you have a true 24-by-7 environment—that is, your SQL Server must be available 24 hours a day, seven days a week—you may need to use the *install method*, which involves using Replication Server during the migration. With the install method, you install a new, separate SQL Server 11 while your old server continues to run. You use Replication Server between the two servers, and cut over to the SQL Server 11 when the two servers are in sync. Because most companies do not have a true 24-by-7 need, you can usually avoid this complex method. You almost always have a window of acceptable downtime, even if it is only a few hours.

Methods for Upgrading a SQL Server

You can choose either of two methods for upgrading your SQL Server:

- The upgrade method
- The install method

The *upgrade method* uses the *sybinit* utility to upgrade an existing server. This method transforms a pre-SQL Server 11 server into a SQL Server 11 server. After the upgrade, the old server no longer exists. The upgrade method is simpler than the install method, but it offers less flexibility.

The *install method* creates a new SQL Server 11 server, separate from the existing server. In other words, this method leaves you with two servers. You then copy the objects and the data from the old server into the new, SQL Server 11 server.

TIP!   To use the install method, you must have enough space on the host machine for two SQL Servers.

With the install method, you must have scripts to recreate all the databases and then use *bcp* (Bulk Copy) to copy the data. If you are upgrading from SQL Server 10.x, you can use database dumps and loads instead of *bcp*.

SQL Server 11 can load database dumps that you create with SQL Server 10.x. Because of changes in the format of the log, however, SQL Server 11 cannot load database dumps that you create with SQL Server 4.x. In addition, SQL Server 4.x and 10.x cannot load dumps that you create with SQL Server 11. For database dumps and loads between SQL Server versions, you must use SQL Server 11 to read a SQL Server 10.x dump.

TIP!   The install method takes longer than the upgrade method because you must copy all the data from the old server to the new server. However, the install method does give you the flexibility to make changes to the new environment or to upgrade only part of the SQL Server.

Figure 2-1 shows the *sybinit* screen that lets you choose a method for upgrading a server. To use the install method, choose option 1, "Configure a new SQL Server." For the upgrade method, choose option 3, "Upgrade an existing SQL Server." For complete details about using *sybinit*, see Chapter 3, "Upgrading to SQL Server 11 in a Windows NT Environment," and Chapter 4, "Upgrading to SQL Server 11 in a UNIX Environment."

```
NEW OR EXISTING SQL SERVER

1.   Configure a new SQL Server
2.   Configure an existing SQL Server
3.   Upgrade an existing SQL Server
```

Figure 2-1: *The sybinit New or Existing SQL Server screen*

Contingency Plans

You must have a contingency plan for your migration. For example, what happens if the upgrade fails? Can you seamlessly fall back to your pre-upgrade SQL Server?

You need contingency plans for two possible scenarios:

- The upgrade fails.

- The upgrade succeeds, but you soon encounter problems and must back out of the upgrade.

In the first scenario, you may run into problems during the upgrade process and thus miss your window of opportunity for completing the upgrade. For example, you might plan to complete the upgrade during a weekend. If you have not successfully completed the upgrade by Sunday evening, you may need to fall back to the pre-SQL Server 11 production system. In the second scenario, you may successfully upgrade the SQL Server, but find a problem one week later. You need to prepare for both of these possibilities.

If you use the install method, you already have a fully functional server running a previous version of SQL Server. If the upgrade fails, you simply use the existing production system. Even if the upgrade succeeds, you may want to copy data to the old server for a few days, to keep it up to date. Depending on your business needs, you can *bcp* data from SQL Server 11 to the old server at the end of each day, or you may need to use Replication Server to maintain the old server with up-to-the-minute data.

If you use the upgrade method, ensure that you can recreate your pre-SQL Server 11 system in the event of a failure. Because the upgrade process permanently modifies your databases, you should back up all of your databases before upgrading the SQL Server. In addition to keeping scripts that can recreate your SQL Server, you should record such information as user logins and devices that the SQL Server uses.

The Migration Process

The migration process has six stages:

1. Information gathering.   *p.27*
2. The physical upgrade.   *p.38*
3. Analysis of the migration's effect on existing databases and applications and resolution of any outstanding issues.   *p.55*
4. Testing.   *p.66*
5. Monitoring.   *p.67*
6. Tuning.   *p.68*

These six stages represent the general, high-level tasks necessary for a successful migration. You should complete these tasks in the order shown, though some tasks overlap with others. In addition, you perform one step from stage three (the reserved word check) before you perform stage two, the physical upgrade.

Table 2-1 provides a master list of all the steps involved in each of the six stages in a successful migration. For each step, this table lists the responsible group: the DBA staff, the application development staff (DEV), or both.

Table 2-1: *The Migration Process*

Step	Description	Staff Involved
1.1	Read the documentation for your platform:	
	Installation and Configuration Guide	DBA
	Release Notes	DBA
	What's New in Sybase SQL Server Release 11	DBA, DEV
1.2	Analyze operating system and hardware requirements.	DBA
1.3	Install new hardware and operating systems, if necessary.	DBA
1.4	Gather information such as passwords, directories, and devices.	DBA
1.5	Complete the migration worksheet.	DBA
1.6	Make operating system changes such as creating directories or devices.	DBA
2.1	Run *dbcc checkdb*.	DBA
	Run *dbcc checkcatalog*.	DBA
	Run *dbcc checkalloc*.	DBA

(continues)

Table 2-1: *(continued)*

Step	Description	Staff Involved
2.2	Back up all databases.	DBA
2.3	Back up Sybase UNIX environment, if necessary.	DBA
2.4	Back up key system tables.	DBA
2.5	Bulk copy out all databases, if necessary.	DBA
2.6	Load SQL Server 11 software from media.	DBA
2.7	Perform the physical upgrade.	DBA
3.1	Perform a reserved word check.	DBA
3.2	Resolve reserved word conflicts.	DBA, DEV
3.3	Perform subquery checks.	DEV
3.4	Fix subquery issues, if necessary.	DEV
3.5	Drop and recreate stored procedures that contain subqueries.	DBA
3.6	Implement new DBA tasks, if necessary.	DBA
3.7	Learn new SQL Server 11 functionality.	DBA, DEV
4.1	Perform basic tests to ensure that all queries run.	DBA, DEV
4.2	Perform detailed test to ensure that all queries return the same results as the previous system.	DBA, DEV
4.3	Test all applications against the new SQL Server 11.	DBA, DEV
4.4	Ensure that performance matches or exceeds that of the previous system.	DBA, DEV
5.1	Monitor the new SQL Server 11.	DBA
5.2	Benchmark performance before and after the upgrade.	DBA
5.3	Identify performance trends and bottlenecks.	DBA
6.1	Tune SQL Server 11 for high performance.	DBA

Stage One: Information Gathering

p.26

To begin the migration process, you need to read the SQL Server 11 documentation, record information about your host and Sybase environments, and determine whether you need any new system resources—for example, more memory.

Reading the Documentation

The first step in a successful migration is to understand the process. Get familiar with the manuals, the documents, and the software you received and thoroughly read the *Release Notes* and the *Configuration and Installation Guide* for your platform.

Compared to previous releases, SQL Server 11 provides clearer, more detailed documentation. By carefully reading the *Release Notes* and the *Configuration and Installation Guide*, you can identify any tasks that you must complete before you begin the migration process.

Gathering the Necessary Information

After reviewing the documentation, make sure you have all the necessary information about your host system, the Sybase environment, and your system resources. For example, you should have at least the following information:

- The UNIX password for the *sybase* login
- The *sa* password for your existing SQL Server
- The release directory for the existing Sybase directory
- The directories in which you plan to install SQL Server 11
- The names of physical and logical devices
- The sizes of all databases

Verify that your system can use the media on which you received your SQL Server 11 software. Some upgrades have been delayed by several days simply because users received the SQL Server 11 software on a CD-ROM but they didn't have a CD-ROM drive.

As mentioned, the *Release Notes* point out some steps you may have to complete before you begin the migration. For example, you must verify that you have the correct operating system version and any required operating system patches, because certain earlier versions of your operating system may not support SQL Server 11. In particular, SunOS users must upgrade their machines to use Sun Solaris instead of SunOS. In addition, you may need to install operating system patches or set some parameters. Depending on your company's information technology (IT) policies and your operating system knowledge, you may need to have these steps completed by your UNIX system administrators.

TIP!   As you document your system while preparing for an upgrade, carefully note the correct paths for your old version of SQL Server and your new SQL Server 11 directory. For example, you might have the following path for your pre-SQL Server 11 directory: /home/sybase/sybase10. You might have the following path for your new SQL Server 11 directory: /home/sybase/sybase11.

Determining Memory Requirements

SQL Server 11 requires more memory (RAM) than previous versions. For example, the SQL Server kernel uses more memory than in previous releases and internal structures such as the new user log cache further increase the memory requirements. Compiled objects have grown in SQL Server 11 and they grew considerably in the upgrade from SQL Server 4.x to SQL Server 10. This means that the same number of database objects now take up more space in the procedure cache, so you may need to enlarge your procedure cache in order to maintain the performance levels you experienced with previous versions.

Before proceeding with the migration, you should determine whether you need to purchase more memory for your system. If you have been pushing the limits of your system's memory resources, you may need more memory. When evaluating memory requirements, remember that adding RAM to a system is one of the simplest means for obtaining substantial performance gains. For example, a *bcp* load of a 20-GB database was benchmarked (unofficially) on a Windows NT Server with two CPUs running at 100Mhz. Times were recorded for two scenarios. In one case, the machine running the SQL Server had 128 MB of RAM available. In the second case, the machine had 256 MB of RAM. The *bcp* performance on the system with 256 MB of RAM was approximately three times faster than that of the system with less memory.

It is important to note that adding memory can actually slow down a *bcp* if you do not make certain changes. Make sure that your buffer wash size is 60 percent to 70 percent of the memory for high *bcp* performance. Because adding memory can throw off this proportion, you need to make sure that you change this setting accordingly. By making the memory relatively small in comparison to the buffer wash size, you ensure that the buffers are continually flushed to disk instead of waiting for checkpoints or the end of the batch.

TIP!   If you do not allocate enough memory to the SQL Server, it will not start up. If you allocate too much memory (that is, more memory than is physically available), operating system page faults will cause an extreme degradation in performance.

When analyzing your memory requirements, you must consider three issues:

- Do you need to add more memory to meet the minimum requirements for SQL Server 11?

- Do you need to add more memory to maintain your pre-SQL Server 11 conditions?

- Do you want to add more memory to help improve SQL Server's performance?

Meeting the Minimum Memory Requirements for SQL Server 11. Although the minimum memory requirements for SQL Server 11 depend on your platform, SQL Server 11 generally needs at least 32 MB. For precise figures, check the *Configuration and Installation Guide* for your platform. You must realize that 32 MB represents the minimum for SQL Server 11 alone and does not take into account the operating system's requirements. Because most operating systems require at least 32 MB, the host machine should contain at least 64 MB of memory.

Keep in mind that using the minimum amount of memory will not give you optimal performance on your SQL Server 11. You may experience acceptable performance with light use, but you can improve performance by adding RAM to the machine that runs SQL Server 11. In other words, you cannot have too much RAM available on your machine. (Of course, you eventually reach a point of diminishing returns.)

Most major corporations run their production SQL Server 11 on a machine with at least 256 MB of memory, and many have as much as 1 GB of memory available. You can use these figures as a point of reference.

Adding Memory to Maintain pre-SQL Server 11 Conditions. After upgrading to SQL Server 11, you will have less memory allocated to certain areas of the SQL Server. Because the SQL Server 11 kernel and many of its internal structures use more memory than in previous releases, you need to allocate more memory by using the *total memory* configuration parameter and you may need to reconfigure the procedure cache percentage parameters to bring them back up to their pre-SQL Server 11 settings. As shown in Figure 2-2, compiled objects have grown larger in SQL Server 11. Because the same number of database objects now take up more space in the procedure cache, you may need to enlarge your procedure cache in order to maintain the same amount of memory as it had in previous releases.

Increase your procedure cache by increasing the total memory available to the server. (You do this by setting the *total memory* parameter.) Do not try to increase the procedure cache by increasing the *procedure cache size* parameter, because doing so decreases the data cache size. Remember that the procedure cache size and the data cache size depend on one another. After allocating memory to all of its internal structures, the SQL Server divides the remaining available memory between the procedure cache and the data cache. SQL Server determines the correct proportions by using the *procedure cache size* parameter. For example, if you set the *procedure cache size* to 20 and the server has 50 MB of memory left, the data cache gets 80 percent, or 40 MB, and the procedure cache gets 20 percent, or 10 MB. Because you don't want to take valuable memory away from the data cache, you should enlarge the procedure cache by increasing the *total memory* available to the server.

Table 2-2 provides some rules of thumb to help you set up your new SQL Server 11 environment. Once you have your new SQL Server 11 up and running, you can fine-tune these settings.

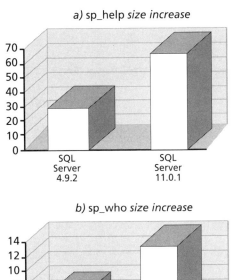

a) sp_help *size increase*

b) sp_who *size increase*

Figure 2-2: *The* **sp_help** *procedure and the* **sp_who** *procedure have grown in size from previous releases.*

Table 2-2: *Approximate Memory Increases for SQL Server 11*

	Increase from 4.x	**Increase from 10.x**
Stored procedures	75%	25%
User connections	30K per connection	15K per connection
Executable code size and internal structures	5 MB	5 MB

Use the chart in Table 2-2 and the memory checklist in Table 2-3 to determine whether you need to install more memory before migrating to SQL Server 11. With this method, you analyze your current SQL Server's memory use and then estimate the increased needs of SQL Server 11. The memory checklist provides approximate values for those areas of the SQL Server that have easily determined memory use. Some of the memory use fields in this checklist are blank because these values depend on your particular environment.

Table 2-3: *Approximate Memory Use Increases for SQL Server 11*

SQL Server Field	Approximate Memory Use
Operating system	
Other processes on the operating system	
SQL Server executable	4 MB
Kernel and internal structures	3 MB
Overhead	3 MB
Procedure cache	
Data cache	
Additional network memory	
Number of user connections	75K per connection
Number of open databases	17K per database
Number of locks	72K per 1,000 locks

If you want greater accuracy than these approximations provide, you can use one of the following two methods to resize SQL Server's procedure cache values.

Resizing the Procedure Cache. Examine the errorlog of your pre-SQL Server 11 server and write down the values for the following entries:

- *Number of buffers in buffer cache.* This value specifies the amount of memory available for the data cache. It is given in 2K pages (4K on Stratus).

- *Number of proc buffers allocated.* This value identifies the number of compiled objects that can reside simultaneously in the procedure cache.

- *Number of blocks left for proc headers.* This value defines the amount of memory available to the procedure cache. It is given in 2K pages (4K on Stratus).

These three values from your pre-SQL Server 11 errorlog determine the sizes of that SQL Server's data cache and procedure cache. As the following example demonstrates, you can use these values to calculate the increase in memory needed to compensate for the decreased procedure cache size.

Assume that your pre-SQL Server 11 errorlog contains the following lines:

```
Number of buffers in buffer cache: 20514
Number of proc buffers allocated: 6632
Number of blocks left for proc headers: 7507
```

These values show that your pre-SQL Server 11 server has a 40-MB data cache (20,514 x 2,048) and a 14.5-MB procedure cache (7,507 x 2,048) that can contain no more than 6,632 compiled objects at the same time.

The following list summarizes this cache size information for your pre-SQL Server 11 server:

- Data cache: 40 MB

- Procedure cache: 14.5 MB

- Maximum number of objects in procedure cache: 6,632

The errorlog for your new SQL Server 11 server contains the following information:

```
Number of proc buffers allocated:  4632
Number of blocks left for proc headers:  5120
Memory allocated for the default data cache cache: 32768 Kb     (=32×1024)
```

NOTE: Notice that the SQL Server 11 errorlog does not contain an entry for *Number of buffers in buffer cache*, but it does add a new entry for *Memory allocated for the default data cache*. This entry clearly identifies the amount of memory allocated to the data cache. The errorlog contains one such line for each data cache in the system.

Based on this information, the following list summarizes the cache size settings for your SQL Server 11 server:

- Data cache: 32.0 MB

- Procedure cache: 9.5 MB   (see p.34)

- Maximum number of objects in procedure cache: 4,632

Your new SQL Server 11 has a 32-MB data cache (32,768/1,024) and your old server has a 40-MB data cache, so you want to increase the data cache size by 8 MB. With the *procedure cache size* parameter set to 20, 80 percent of any memory you add goes to the data cache and 20 percent goes to the procedure cache. To increase the data cache size by 8 MB, you must increase the SQL Server 11's total memory by 10 MB.

To continue this example, your new SQL Server 11 can have only 4,632 compiled objects in the procedure cache. You want to regain the functionality of your old SQL Server, which could have as many as 6,632 objects in its procedure cache. To determine how much memory you must add to the server to achieve this goal, you need to perform several calculations.

The total size of the procedure cache is simply the sum of the memory allocated to the proc buffers plus the memory allocated to the proc header:

```
procedure cache size = proc buffer memory + proc header memory
```

The errorlog lists the number of proc headers in units of 2K pages, so you do not need to convert that value to another unit of measure. However, the errorlog lists the number of proc buffers in units of buffers (not pages), so you need to convert the proc buffers value to pages, as follows. First, because a single proc buffer is 76 bytes, you can convert buffers to bytes:

old #

```
(6,632 buffers) x (76 bytes per buffer) = 504,032 bytes
```
proc. buffers

Then convert this value to pages (note that this calculation rounds up to the nearest page boundary):

```
(504,032 bytes) x (1 page per 2,048 bytes) = 247 pages
```
½₀₄₈ ¹⁄2048

Finally, determine the amount of memory the procedure cache uses (note that 512 2K pages = 1 MB):

```
4,632 pages + 247 pages = 4,879 pages = 9.5 MB
```
proc. buffers headers

To allow SQL Server 11 to have as many compiled objects in the procedure cache as the old SQL Server does, you must increase the procedure cache size by 5 MB (14.5 MB from pre-SQL Server 11 minus the 9.5 MB available now). Because the procedure cache in this example gets 20 percent of the cache memory, you must increase SQL Server 11's total memory by 25 MB. (5/0.2 = 5x5=25)

Resizing the Caches (A Simpler Method). For a simple alternative to the numerous calculations described in the preceding section, you can keep track of the procedure and data cache sizes before the upgrade, and then calculate the size differences after the upgrade. This tells you how much additional memory your new SQL Server 11 requires. Just follow these steps:

1. Record the data cache and procedure cache values from the errorlog:

```
Number of buffers in buffer cache: 20514
Number of proc buffers allocated: 6632
Number of blocks left for proc headers: 7507
```

2. If necessary, free up memory for upgrading the server by resetting some configuration parameters to their default values. Table 2-4 lists the parameters that you might need to change. Before you do so, however, be sure to record the values of these parameters in the *Current Value* column of Table 2-4. In this way, you can easily set them back to your original values in SQL Server 11.

Table 2-4: *Memory-Consuming Parameters*

Configuration Parameter	Current Value	Default Value
user connections		25
locks		5,000
open objects		500
memory		at least 7,680 (15 MB)

You can set these parameters to their defaults by using the *sp_configure* command. For example, you can reset the *user connections* parameter to its default value by issuing the following command:

```
sp_configure "user connections",25
go
```

3. Restart the SQL Server and record the new procedure and data cache values. You need to compare these values with the SQL Server 11 values.

4. Start your SQL Server 11 server, record the procedure and data cache values from the errorlog, and subtract these values from the pre-SQL Server 11 values. The result—the memory difference between SQL Server 11 and the previous version—shows how much additional memory you need to configure in SQL Server 11.

Adding Memory to Improve the Performance of SQL Server 11. Adding memory is one of the simplest, most powerful methods for increasing performance. Chapter 8, "Monitoring SQL Server 11," and Chapter 9, "SQL Server 11 Performance and Tuning," describe techniques that can help you determine whether you should add memory to increase SQL Server 11's performance.

Determining Whether You Need New Hardware

You may want to purchase an SMP machine for running SQL Server 11 because SMP hardware allows you to take full advantage of SQL Server 11's power. The significant performance gains you can achieve with SQL Server 11 result from the system's scalability. Of course, you must make a trade-off: greatly enhanced performance at the expense of purchasing new hardware. Chapter 5, "Configuring SQL Server 11," provides details about this performance increase.

Making Room for the *sybsystemprocs* Database

If you plan to migrate from SQL Server 4.x, you need a new device for *sybsystemprocs,* the system database that contains all system stored procedures. SQL Server 4.x stores these procedures in the *master* database. As of SQL Server 10.x, the system stores these procedures in their own database called *sybsystemprocs*.

If you migrate from SQL Server 10.x, you need to enlarge your *sybsystemprocs* database to make room for the new system stored procedures. Check your *SQL Server Installation and Configuration Guide* to find the correct size, and alter *sybsystemprocs* before you begin the upgrade. If you do not set *sybsystemprocs* to the correct size, *sybinit* will fail.

In general, you should make *sybsystemprocs* 16 MB to 24 MB in size. Remember that any of your own stored procedures that you store in *sybsystemprocs* will become larger in SQL Server 11, and keep in mind that the new *sp_sysmon* stored procedure takes lots of space.

NOTE: If the *sybsystemprocs* database is too small, the upgrade will fail.

During an upgrade from SQL Server 10 to SQL Server 11, the system drops all system stored procedures from *sybsystemprocs* and then recreates the system stored procedures. If you have customized any of your system stored procedures, you will lose the customizations when this happens. If you want to save customizations to any system stored procedures, you should rename them before the upgrade. If you do not rename them, you have to recustomize them after the upgrade, because the upgrade process overwrites them with the default procedures.

Special Considerations for SunOS Users

The SunOS operating system does not support SQL Server 11. If you currently run the SunOS operating system, you must migrate your UNIX operating system to Solaris 2.4 or later, before you migrate to Sybase SQL Server 11. The *Sybase SQL Server Installation and Configuration Guide for Sun Solaris 2.x* details the procedure for migrating a SQL Server on SunOS. This procedure requires a person with UNIX system administration experience, and you must have a Sun Solaris copy of SQL Server at the same release level as your SunOS SQL Server.

You must reinstall the pre-SQL Server 11 server on Sun Solaris before you can upgrade to SQL Server 11. The SunOS pre-SQL Server 11 server will not work with Sun Solaris. For example, if you upgrade from SQL Server 4.9.2, you need to acquire SQL Server 4.9.2 for Sun Solaris. Upgrade SunOS to Sun Solaris and then install the SQL Server 4.9.2 on Sun Solaris. You can then upgrade from SQL Server 4.9.2 to SQL Server 11.

If You Have Replication Server

If you are upgrading a SQL Server that uses Replication Server, you must take some special steps prior to the upgrade. You must disable and drain the transaction logs, because SQL Server 11 transaction logs are not compatible with those of previous releases. For a complete description of the necessary steps, refer to the *Configuration and Installation Guide*.

Directory Placement

The directory placement for your new SQL Server 11 can cause confusion and, in some cases, serious and hard-to-diagnose problems. You should create a separate, entirely new directory path for SQL Server 11. Do not make it a subdirectory of the existing, pre-SQL Server 11 directory, and do not confuse the two directory paths when you upgrade to the new system, or later, when you use the new system.

In many cases, an organization successfully upgrades to SQL Server 11, only to have users encounter strange, occasional problems a few weeks after the upgrade. The cause of these problems often involves a path or a $SYBASE environmental variable that points to the old Sybase directory structure instead of the new SQL Server 11 path. In such cases, a user might pick up an old version of *bcp* or an old *db-lib* library and mix it in with the SQL Server 11 server.

> ***TIP!***   Be careful to set the $SYBASE environmental variable to the *new* SQL Server
> 11 directory and not the older, pre-SQL Server 11 directory. For example, the
> old SQL Server installation might use the following directory structure:
> /home/sybase/sybase10. And you might install SQL Server 11 in
> /home/sybase/sybase11/. In this case, you should set $SYBASE to
> /home/sybase/sybase11.   ⟵*new*

Most Sybase executables—for example, *sybinit, bcp,* and *isql*—have a *-v* option, which lists the executable's version number. As shown in the following examples, this helps you to ensure that you use the correct version of the executable:

```
bcp -v
go
bcp/10.0.2/P/sun_svr4/SPARC Solaris 2.3/1/Mon Oct 31 22:07:42 PST 1994
isql -v
go
isql/10.0.2/P/sun_svr4/SPARC Solaris 2.3/1/Mon Oct 31 22:08:21 PST 1994
```

You can also ensure that you use the right copy of an executable, by using the UNIX *which* command.

> ***TIP!***   Make sure you change the paths for any front-end applications, to pick up
> the sybase11 libraries and executables.

Complete the Migration Worksheet

At the end of the first chapter of your *Installation and Configuration Guide*, you can find a worksheet that's designed to help you organize all the system information you need. You should make a copy of this worksheet and fill it out, before you begin the upgrade process. You perform the system upgrade by running *sybinit.* (In versions prior to SQL Server 10.x, *sybconfig* performs this task.) For details about using *sybinit*, refer to Chapter 3, "Upgrading to SQL Server 11 in a Windows NT Environment," and Chapter 4, "Upgrading to SQL Server 11 in a UNIX Environment."

Stage Two: The Physical Upgrade

The second stage in the migration process involves backing up your current system and databases, installing new system resources (if necessary), loading the new software, and performing the SQL Server upgrade.

Ensuring Database Integrity by Running **dbcc** *Commands*

Before you back up your existing databases and perform the upgrade, you should check the consistency of all databases (including *master* and *model*) by using the *dbcc checkalloc*, *checkdb*, and *checkcatalog* commands. These commands find any problems that you must correct in your databases before you can continue the upgrade. Specifically, you need to find any reports of *suspect* or *read only*, as well as any errors in a database. Do not worry about row and database corrections from *checkdb*; these are not errors. For details about the *dbcc* commands, refer to Chapter 17 in the *System Administration Guide*.

The *dbcc checkalloc* command has the following syntax:

```
dbcc checkalloc [( database_name [, fix | nofix] )]
```

The *database_name* parameter specifies the name of the database that you want to check. If you issue the command without a *database_name*, the command checks the current database.

The *dbcc checkalloc* command uses nofix as its default mode. If you specify fix on the command line, the command fixes the errors it finds.

The following example runs the *dbcc checkalloc* command on the *pubs2* database:

```
dbcc checkalloc(pubs2)
go
```

The following sample output does not report any errors, so the migration can continue:

```
Checking pubs2
**********************************************************
TABLE: sysobjects   OBJID = 1
INDID=1   FIRST=1   ROOT=8   SORT=0
 Data level: 1.   3 Data   Pages in 1 extents.
 Indid    : 1.   1 Index Pages in 1 extents.
INDID=2   FIRST=16   ROOT=16   SORT=0
 Indid    : 2.   1 Index Pages in 1 extents.
TOTAL # of extents = 3
**********************************************************
TABLE: sysindexes   OBJID = 2
INDID=1   FIRST=24   ROOT=32   SORT=0
 Data level: 1.   5 Data   Pages in 1 extents.
 Indid    : 1.   1 Index Pages in 1 extents.
TOTAL # of extents = 2
**********************************************************
...
**********************************************************
Processed 50 entries in the sysindexes for dbid 6.
```

```
Alloc page 0 (# of extent=32 used pages=91 ref pages=81)
Alloc page 256 (# of extent=32 used pages=95 ref pages=85)
Alloc page 512 (# of extent=32 used pages=182 ref pages=182)
Alloc page 768 (# of extent=2 used pages=16 ref pages=12)
Total (# of extent=98 used pages=384 ref pages=360) in this database
DBCC execution completed. If DBCC printed error messages, contact a user
with System Administrator (SA) role.
```

The *dbcc checkdb* command has the following syntax:

```
dbcc checkdb [( database_name [, skip_ncindex]) ]
```

Again, the *database_name* parameter specifies the name of the database that you want to check. If you do not specify a *database_name*, the command checks the current database.

If you specify the optional *skip_ncindex* mode, *dbcc checkdb* does not check any of the nonclustered indexes on user tables in the database.

The following example runs the *dbcc checkdb* command on the *pubs2* database:

```
dbcc checkdb(pubs2)
go
```

This command produces the following output:

```
Checking 1
The total number of data pages in this table is 3.
Table has 49 data rows.
Checking 2
The total number of data pages in this table is 5.
Table has 51 data rows.
...
Checking 336004228
The total number of data pages in this table is 1.
The total number of TEXT/IMAGE pages in this table is 6.
Table has 6 data rows.
DBCC execution completed. If DBCC printed error messages, contact a user
with System Administrator (SA) role.
```

The *dbcc checkcatalog* command has the following syntax:

```
dbcc checkcatalog [( database_name )]
```

The *database_name* parameter specifies the name of the database that you want to check. If you do not specify a *database_name*, this command checks the current database.

The following example uses the *dbcc checkcatalog* command on the *pubs2* database:

```
dbcc checkcatalog(pubs2)
go
```

This command produces the following output:

```
Checking pubs2
The following segments have been defined for database 6 (database name
pubs2).

virtual start addr  size    segments
------------------  ----    --------
5636                1024
                            0
                            1
                            2

DBCC execution completed. If DBCC printed error messages, contact a user
with System Administrator (SA) role.
```

Backing Up All Databases

You cannot be too careful with the data contained in your SQL Server. Before you upgrade to SQL Server 11, you must back up all of your databases. The upgrade process permanently modifies your databases. If the upgrade fails, you need your backups for restoring your databases. You can back up your databases by using your existing backup procedures.

TIP!   The upgrade process permanently modifies your databases. Back up all databases before performing the upgrade, so that you can restore them if the upgrade fails.

You must be prepared for all contingencies, because you cannot predict beforehand everything that might go wrong during an upgrade. In addition to backing up your databases, you should make sure that you have scripts to recreate all objects, such as tables, triggers, and stored procedures. Although your environment should already include these scripts, you need to ensure that you have up-to-date scripts. Many sites needlessly add two to three weeks to their upgrade by failing to keep their environments up to date.

TIP!   During the upgrade process, you will probably see reports of errors on some stored procedures. After much investigation, you may find that the errors have nothing to do with the upgrade to SQL Server 11—that is, they would have occurred the next time you recompiled the stored procedure, regardless of whether you upgraded to SQL Server 11. For example, you might change a column in an underlying table of a stored procedure but still refer to the old column structure in the stored procedure. If you have the scripts available, you can easily check and correct these types of problems.

Backing Up the UNIX Sybase Environment

Before loading the new SQL Server 11 software, you should back up the current directory structure. If you need to recreate your old environment, this simple step can save you lots of trouble. You can simply recreate the entire environment, overwriting any changes you made by installing the new software.

Backing Up Key System Tables

You should *bcp* out the data from some of the main system tables. System tables such as *sysusers*, *syslogins*, *sysconfigures*, *sysdevices*, *sysdatabases*, and *sysusages* contain crucial data that you should retain, because you may need this information for certain fallback situations. For example, if you try to load a dump from an old SQL Server to a new one, you may need to recreate the user logins. The *syslogins* table contains this information.

BCP All Data, If Necessary

If you use the install method and you are migrating from SQL Server 4.x, you must *bcp* out all of the data from your current SQL Server. If you migrate from SQL Server 4.x, this is the only way you can populate the new SQL Server 11. If you migrate from SQL Server 10.x, however, you can populate the new SQL Server 11 by using a database *load* (or *bcp*). The data that *bcp* copies also provides the means for falling back to the original system if the migration fails. You can easily create scripts to *bcp* in and out all of your tables by using the methods described in Chapter 1, "Preliminaries." For easy reference, create a separate file with each table's data.

Loading the Software

To load the SQL Server 11 software onto your system from the distribution media, you use the *sybload* utility. Your SQL Server 11 *Installation and Configuration Guide* provides step-by-step instructions for completing this straightforward process.

Remember to set the $SYBASE environmental variable to the new SQL Server 11 directory. Make sure that the Sybase home directory exists and has enough free disk space. Although you can use any valid path name for the Sybase home directory, you should choose a meaningful name that you won't confuse with the path names for previous or future releases of Sybase SQL Server.

The following example creates a new directory for SQL Server 11, assigns this directory to the $SYBASE variable, and displays the variable:

```
cd /home/sybase
mkdir sybase11
```

```
setenv SYBASE /home/sybase/sybase11
echo $SYBASE
```

For the C shell, you set the $SYBASE variable to the proper value by issuing the following command:

```
setenv SYBASE /home/sybase/sybase11
```

For the Bourne shell or the Korn shell, you issue the following command:

```
SYBASE="/home/sybase/sybase11"; export SYBASE
```

Make sure that all appropriate shell initialization files include a line that sets this variable. In other words, all users who need to access SQL Server 11 must have one of these commands in their shell initialization files. If they use the C shell, the *.cshrc* file must include the appropriate command. If they use the Bourne shell or the Korn shell, the command must be in the *.profile* file.

To create the Sybase home directory and run *sybload*, you should be the UNIX user *sybase*. You must also ensure that the user *sybase* has read, write, and execute privileges for the Sybase directories. Do not try to use *root* or some other user for creating the Sybase home directory and running *sybload*; use the *sybase* account for these tasks.

After you run *sybload*, your SQL Server 11 directory contains the full SQL Server 11 directory tree. Figure 2-3 presents a diagram of this directory tree.

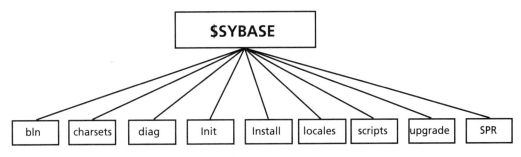

Figure 2-3: *The $SYBASE directory structure*

Checking for Reserved Words

A successful migration to SQL Server 11 requires a careful check for reserved words. Reserved words are keywords that the SQL Server uses and thus, they have special meanings. The term *reserved* means that you cannot use these words as object names. Any object names—for example, the names of tables and columns—that use these reserved words must be changed. For example, if your SQL Server 4.x server has a table named *widget_table* that contains a column named *current*, you must rename that column.

When you need to rename objects that use reserved words, the challenge rests in finding all the references to the reserved word and changing each instance to the new name. In the preceding example, you might have 20 stored procedures that perform queries on the column *current*, as well as a front-end GUI application that contains two hard-coded references to that column.

The upgrade from SQL Server 10.x involves only a few new reserved words. If you are upgrading from SQL Server 4.x, however, you must check for many new reserved words. When checking for reserved words, you need to search the following objects:

- Database names
- Table names
- View names
- Stored procedure names
- Log names
- Rule names
- Default names
- Trigger names
- Constraint names
- Referential constraint names
- Server names
- Device names
- Segment names
- User-defined datatypes
- User names
- Login names
- Remote login names

By running the *sp_checkreswords* system stored procedure, you can check for all of the objects in this list except for stored procedures and triggers. After you identify reserved words by using *sp_checkreswords*, you must manually search for references to those reserved words in all of your stored procedures, triggers, open client code, and front-end code.

TIP!   The *sp_checkreswords* system stored procedure does not check stored procedures and triggers. If you suspect that any of these objects reference any reserved words, you must search them manually.

How to Check for Reserved Words. SQL Server 11 provides a stored procedure called *sp_checkreswords*. By running *sp_checkreswords* on your existing SQL Server, you can check for any names that you need to change before upgrading to SQL Server 11.

The *sp_checkreswords* stored procedure searches each database and prints a report of the reserved words that it finds. The *sybinit* utility can run *sp_checkreswords* for you during a *sybinit* session, or you can load *sp_checkreswords* into your existing server and run it manually. You should load the procedure and run it manually, because the *sybinit* session fails if *sp_checkreswords* finds any reserved words while running from *sybinit*.

Use the following procedure to load *sp_checkreswords* into your existing (pre-SQL Server 11) SQL Server:

1. If you have not already done so, load the SQL Server 11 software into your new SQL Server 11 directory structure by using *sybload*.

2. Run the *installupgrade* script, which you can find in the $SYBASE/scripts directory ($SYBASE represents the new SQL Server 11 directory). You run this script by issuing the following command:

```
isql -Usa -Ppassword -Sserver_name < $SYBASE/scripts/installupgrade
go
```
pre-11   *new*

The environmental variable $SYBASE represents the *new* SQL Server 11 directory. For the *server_name* parameter, you specify the name of your existing server—that is, the pre-SQL Server 11 server. Do not confuse the directories and server names for your old server and your new SQL Server 11 server. You run this script from the new SQL Server 11 directory, but you run it against your existing (pre-SQL Server 11) server.

If you are upgrading from SQL Server 10.x, you may already have a version of *sp_checkreswords* on your SQL Server. SQL Server 10.x installs this procedure during the upgrade from SQL Server 4.x. Do not use the SQL Server 10.x version of the *sp_check-*

reswords stored procedure, because that version recognizes only the SQL Server 10.x reserved words. It does not recognize the new SQL Server 11 reserved words. Although SQL Server 11 introduces only a few new reserved words, you must test for them. In short, even if you see an *sp_checkreswords* procedure on your SQL Server, you should still run the *installupgrade* script.

TIP!   Run the *installupgrade* script even if you already have a version of the *sp_checkreswords* procedure on your SQL Server, because older versions of that procedure do not recognize SQL Server 11 reserved words.

After you load the *sp_checkreswords* stored procedure on your existing (pre-SQL Server 11) server, run this stored procedure in every database—including *master*—on your server. The following example runs *sp_checkreswords* on two databases:

```
use database_name1
go
sp_checkreswords
go
use database_name2
go
sp_checkreswords
go
```

For easy access to the reserved word report that *sp_checkreswords* creates, redirect the output of this command to a file. Create an input file to pipe into the SQL Server, and redirect the output from *sp_checkreswords* to a file. For example, assume that the file *test_res_words* contains the following commands:

```
use master
go
sp_checkreswords
go
use database1
go
sp_checkreswords
go
use database2
go
sp_checkreswords
go
```

You can run the commands in this file by issuing the following command:

```
isql -Usa -Ppassword -Sserver_name -itest_res_words -oreserve_word_report
```

For the *server_name* parameter, you specify the name of your pre-SQL Server 11 server. When you run this command, SQL Server creates the file *reserve_word_report*, which contains a listing of all the reserved words that *sp_checkreswords* finds.

What to Do If You Find Reserved Words. If you find any reserved words in your database, you must change them. The section, "Preparing for Future Reserved Words," later in this chapter, provides guidelines for choosing new names.

If you find reserved words in a table, a view, or a column, you can use the *quoted_identifier* option of the set command, as an alternative to changing those words. To use this method, you enclose the words in question with quotation marks and then make sure that you access those objects with the *quoted_identifier* option turned on. Because use of the *quoted_identifier* method can lead to confusion and inconsistencies, however, you should avoid this method. If you try to access an object but forget to turn on the *quoted_identifier* option, errors will result. (For details about the *quoted_identifier* method, refer to the *sp_checkreswords* section and the set command section in the *SQL Server Reference Manual*.)

Changing Reserved Words by Using System Stored Procedures. The method you use for changing an object's name depends on the object's type. Depending on which type of object you need to change, you use one of the following methods:

- *sp_rename*
- *sp_renamedb*
- Drop and recreate

As an alternative to *sp_rename* and *sp_renamedb*, you may want to change your object names by using scripts. The next section of this chapter, "Changing Reserved Words by Using Scripts," describes this option.

You can use *sp_rename* for renaming the following types of objects:

- Tables
- Indexes
- Views
- Procedures
- Triggers

- Rules

- Defaults

- User-defined datatypes

- Columns

The *sp_rename* command has the following syntax:

```
sp_rename objname , newname
```

In place of *objname*, you specify the object's current name. The *newname* parameter represents the object's new name. To rename a column or an index, you must specify the object's name in the form *table.column* or *table.index*.

Note that you can only rename an object in the current database and you must own the object. If you have any scripts that create the object that you plan to rename, you must remember to change the name in those scripts. If you use *sp_rename* to change an object's name and then use an unchanged script to recreate that object, you will encounter reserved word problems.

The following example uses the *sp_rename* command to change the table named *current* to a table named *bn_current_tab*:

```
sp_rename current, bn_current_tab
go
```

The following command changes the column named *user* in the table *bn_user_ids* to a column named *bn_user_id*:

```
sp_rename "bn_user_ids.user", bn_user_id
go
```

As its name suggests, you use the *sp_renamedb* command to change the names of databases. The *sp_renamedb* command has the following syntax:

```
sp_renamedb dbname , newname
```

In place of *dbname*, you specify the original name of the database. The *newname* parameter represents the new name for the database.

TIP!   Before you run the *sp_renamedb* command, you must place a database in single-user mode. After you rename the database, remember to put it back into multi-user mode.

The following example renames the database named *work* as *workdb*:

```
sp_dboption work, single, true
go
use work
go
checkpoint
go
sp_renamedb work, workdb
go
use master
go
sp_dboption workdb, single, false
go
use workdb
go
checkpoint
go
```

Be aware that *sp_renamedb* fails if any tables in the database have foreign or primary constraints. If *sp_renamedb* fails for this reason, you can drop the cross-table constraints by using the *alter table* command and then rerun *sp_renamedb*. For complete details, see the *sp_renamedb* entry in the *SQL Server Reference Manual*.

TIP!   When you change an object's name, any procedures, views, and triggers that depend on that object continue to work until SQL Server recompiles them. They do not recognize the new name until SQL Server recompiles them. Because recompilation can occur at any time and without warning to the user, you must remember to change the object's name in all procedures, views, and triggers and then drop and recreate those procedures, views, and triggers.

You can use commands to drop and recreate for the following types of object names:

- Character set and language names

- Device names

- Login names

- Remote server names

- Segment names

- User names

The following example shows how to change a user name from *work* to *bob*. The user *work* is a user in the *db1* and *db2* databases.

First, check and record the user's permissions in each database:

```
use db1
go
sp_helprotect
go
use db2
go
sp_helprotect
go
```

Next, drop the user from each database:

```
use db1
go
sp_dropuser work
go
use db2
go
sp_dropuser work
go
```

Then, drop the login:

```
sp_droplogin work
go
```

Add the new login, add the user to the two databases, and restore the user's permissions:

```
sp_addlogin bob,bobpasswd
go
use db1
go
sp_adduser bob
go
grant all on db1 to bob
go
use db2
go
sp_adduser bob
go
grant all on db2 to bob
go
```

Note that in this example, the user *work* does not own any objects. If a user owns objects, you cannot drop that user until you drop all of its objects.

If you cannot drop some of your objects that are reserved words, you can try the following method as a last resort: Change the system tables relating to that object. However, manipulating system tables is dangerous and you should avoid this method. If you believe that you must use this method, thoroughly read the section on *sp_checkreswords* in the *SQL Server Reference Manual* and then call Sybase technical support to help walk you through the procedure. Do not try to change system tables without help from technical support, because you can cause serious, permanent damage to your SQL Server.

Changing Reserved Words by Using Scripts. Instead of using *sp_rename* and *sp_renamedb*, you may prefer to manually drop and recreate the objects. Although the use of scripts offers a simple, straightforward method for changing object names that use reserved words, the changes do not occur in real time and you must take care of any data that belongs to the objects. This method involves searching all of your scripts that create the objects in question, changing the objects' names, and then dropping the objects from the database and recreating them with the new scripts.

This method's advantage rests on the fact that you must change these scripts at some point, and by doing so at this stage in the migration you ensure consistency between your scripts and your database. As mentioned, however, you must also take care of any data that belongs to the objects. For example, if you must change the name of a column in a table, you have to *bcp* out the data or *select* the data *into* the new table before you drop the table.

Checking for Reserved Words in Dependent Objects. Once you change the names of all objects that use reserved words, you must find all references to those objects and change them to reflect the new names. In other words, you must change any stored procedures, triggers, code, or scripts that reference the objects that you have changed. For example, if you change a column in *table1*, you must find and check all of the stored procedures that use *table1*.

This part of the reserved words task can be time consuming, and you need to take a structured, orderly approach. Use the *sp_depends* stored procedure as the starting point for this task. By using the output from *sp_checkreswords*, you can create a file that lists the names of any tables, stored procedures, or triggers that contain reserved words. Run *sp_depends* against the objects in this file. This produces a list of objects that may reference the tables, stored procedures, or triggers that contain a reserved word. Remember to check open client code, front-end GUI code, scripts, and anything else that might contain references to database objects.

The *sp_depends* command has the following, simple syntax:

```
sp_depends objname
```

In place of *objname*, you specify the name of a table, a view, a stored procedure, or a trigger that you want to examine for dependencies.

For example, to find the database dependencies of the *titleview* table, use the following command:

```
sp_depends titleview
go
```

This command produces the following information:

```
Things that the object references in the current database.
     object        type            updated   selected
 -------------- ------------    -------   --------
dbo.authors      user table   no        no
dbo.titleauthor user table   no        no
dbo.titles       user table   no        no
Things inside the current database that reference the object.
object            type
 ----------    --------------
dbo.tview2        view
```

The following example finds the dependent procedures for tables in the *db1* database. Here's the output from the *sp_checkreswords* test:

```
Reserved Words Used as Database Object Names for Database db1
Upgrade renames sysobjects schema to sysobjects.schemacnt.
Owner
 -------------------------------
benjy
Table               Reserved Word     Column Names
 --------------    --------------    ------------
cursor_tab          current
tran_tab            current
user_key            identity
```

This output shows that *sp_checkreswords* found two reserved words in three tables.

Next, you need to find any objects that depend on these tables. To do this, create the following file, named *find_depends*:

```
use db1
go
```

```
sp_depends cursor_tab
go
sp_depends tran_tab
go
sp_depends user_key
go
```

Now run this script, to find the dependencies:

```
isql -Uuser -Ppassword -Sserver -ifind_depends -odepends.out
```

After you run the script, *depends.out* contains the following information:

```
Things that the object references in the current database.
object          type              updated   selected
-------------   --------------    -------   --------
dbo.get_user    userprocedure     no        no
dbo.show_user   userprocedure     no        no
dbo.get_key     userprocedure     no        no
Things inside the current database that reference the object.
object          type
-------------   --------------
dbo.view1       view
Things that the object references in the current database.
object          type              updated   selected
-------------   --------------    -------   --------
dbo.get_user    user procedure    no        no
dbo.show_user   user procedure    no        no
dbo.get_tran    user procedure    no        no
```

The following command generates a unique list of dependent procedures. The -l flag to *grep* prints the filename instead of a line from the file, and the -i flag makes the search case-insensitive:

```
grep -li "procedure" depends.out | sort -u > depends.list
```

When you edit *depends.list*, you can remove the *dbo.* prefixes from the procedure names. This leaves you with a list of four procedures that you need to check for the reserved words *current* and *identity*:

```
get_user
show_user
get_key
get_tran
```

The following example uses the UNIX *grep* command to search for a reserved word in a piece of open client code:

```
grep -i "current" *.c
```
└ *insenstive*

This finds the following line in the file *sel_cur.c*:

```
sel_cur.c: dbcmd(dbproc, "select current from table1");
```

When you find a reserved word, you must replace all references to that word with a new name. For example, you may decide to rename all instances of the reserved word *current* to *current_nm*. The following example shows the new line of open client code:

```
dbcmd(dbproc, "select current_nm from table1");
```

Preparing for Future Reserved Words

P.47

During the migration process, reserved word conflicts can create a tremendously time-consuming task. To avoid this problem during future upgrades, devise some rules for renaming columns and choosing names in new projects.

By adopting some form of naming convention, you can simplify the process of choosing names for objects and variables in your projects. Even an informal convention can make life much simpler. Choose prefixes and suffixes for the names so you can immediately identify the projects and the tasks involved. For example, if you have a column called *user* that represents the user id of an account in your widget order system, you might change the column name to wid_userid. By using names of this type and avoiding less-descriptive names such as *user* and *time*, you can ensure that you avoid reserved word problems in the future.

Turning off Database Options

To prepare your databases for the upgrade, you must turn off all database options except for the *select into/bulkcopy* option. If you leave any other options turned on in any of the databases, the upgrade will fail.

Use the *sp_helpdb* command to display database options that you have set, and use the *sp_dboption* command to change a database's options. After changing a database's options, you must run the *checkpoint* command in that database. The *checkpoint* command causes the changed options to take effect, and it synchronizes the databases and the transaction logs. Remember that you must be in the *master* database to change a database's options by using *sp_dboption*.

The following example uses the *sp_helpdb* command to check which database options are set in *data1*:

```
sp_helpdb data1
go
```

This command produces the following information:

```
name    db_size    owner   dbid    created     status
-----   --------   -----   -----   --------    ------
data1   20.0MB     sa      40029   Nov 23,1995 trunc log on chkpt
```

The following commands turn off the *trunc log on chkpt* option in the *data1* database:

```
use master
go
sp_dboption data1, "trunc log on chkpt", false
go
```

To put the previous option changes into effect, the following commands run the *checkpoint* command in *data1*:

```
use data1
go
checkpoint
go
```

Performing the Upgrade by Using Sybinit

After you complete the preupgrade tasks—for example, filling out the migration work-sheet and checking for reserved words—you can perform the upgrade of the SQL Server. p.38 Chapter 3 describes the upgrade procedure for Windows NT-based SQL Servers, and Chapter 4 details the procedure for UNIX-based SQL Servers.

3/6

Stage Three: Database and Application Impact Analysis and Resolution

p.26

This stage involves testing queries, code, and databases for reserved word issues and other potential problems. After identifying these issues, you make the necessary changes to your applications and databases.

Subquery Tests

If you used the upgrade method to migrate your SQL Server, you should drop and recreate any stored procedures that contain subqueries. Subquery processing has changed significantly in SQL Server 11, and most subqueries perform better if they use the new processing mode. However, procedures that contain subqueries do not automatically use SQL Server 11's new processing mode, because they were originally compiled to work with the pre-SQL Server 11 mode. By dropping and then recreating these procedures, you force them to use the new mode. You do not need to perform this task if you used the install method, because the procedures in this method are initially created in SQL Server 11. In the following sections of this chapter, you learn how to determine which procedures contain subqueries, and how to determine whether they have been recompiled.

At this point in the migration process, you need to complete only one more analysis task before you have a fully functional SQL Server 11 server: analyzing your code for changes that were made to certain types of queries. SQL Server 11 processes certain queries differently than SQL Server 10.x. These queries might not return the same results in SQL Server 11 as they did in previous releases. This analysis is easy if you are upgrading from SQL Server 10.x, but may require a significant amount of work if you are upgrading from SQL Server 4.x.

TIP!   Upon completion of this task, you have a fully functional SQL Server 11 server. However, you still need to configure the server to fine-tune its performance.

Understanding Why You Must Analyze Queries. In addition to adding functionality or increasing performance, new releases of SQL Server fix bugs from previous releases and correct noncompliance to the ANSI standard. Consequently, when you run certain queries in SQL Server 11, your results may differ from those of your pre-SQL Server 11 queries. This happens only if your applications somehow depend on the incorrect behavior of the previous release. In SQL Server 4.x, for example, you can specify the values in a *between* statement in any order. In SQL Server 10.x, on the other hand, the second value listed must always be greater than the first value listed.

Consider the following *where* clause:

```
"where colx between val1 and val2"
```

Prior to SQL Server 10.x, val1 could be less than or greater than val2. In SQL Server 10.x and later releases, val2 must be greater than val1 in all *between* statements. With this in mind, you must check all pre-SQL Server 10.x code to make sure you don't have any statements like the following example:

```
"where colx between 10 and 5"
```

In SQL Server 4.x, if colx contains the values 1, 2, 3, 4, 5, 6, 7, 8, 9, 10, this query returns (5, 6, 7, 8, 9, 10). Once you upgrade from SQL Server 4.x to SQL Server 11, this query does not return any values.

Learning How to Test for Subqueries. To help you find and deal with subqueries, SQL Server 11 provides a new system stored procedure called *sp_procqmode*. The *sp_procqmode* stored procedure performs two somewhat unrelated tasks. First, it displays the query processing mode of a procedure, a trigger, or a view. The *query processing mode* informs you whether the object was created on a SQL Server 11 server or a server running a previous version of SQL Server.

Because subqueries created in versions prior to SQL Server 11 use a different processing mode and generally perform slower than those created on a SQL Server 11, you should run this *sp_procqmode* procedure on all your procedures, triggers, and views after upgrading. The upgrade process does not change the processing mode of the subqueries; you must drop and recreate those objects that require the faster processing mode.

In addition to displaying the query processing mode, *sp_procqmode* can test an object to determine whether it contains a subquery. By using this procedure, you can compile a list of procedures, triggers, and views that you need to test for subquery behavior changes.

TIP!   At the time of this writing, *sp_procqmode* has a minor bug on some platforms, such as Solaris 2.4. (Sybase will probably have the bug fixed by the time you read this.) Because of this bug, *sp_procqmode* does not always find all of the objects that contain subqueries. The *SPR* subdirectory of your *$SYBASE* directory contains a listing of known problem reports for your platform. To find out whether this bug affects your system, use the UNIX *grep* command to search for the keyword *"sp_procqmode"* in the files in the *SPR* directory. If this bug in *sp_procqmode* affects your platform, contact Sybase technical support to ask for a fix or a workaround for this problem. Even with this bug, *sp_procqmode* finds almost all of the subqueries.

As an alternative to using *sp_procqmode*, you can use UNIX commands such as *grep* to search for variants of *"(select"*, because all subqueries are introduced in this way. However, you may encounter spaces or lines between parts of this construct. Consequently, you may have to search manually through all your procedures, triggers, and views, to ensure that you find all subqueries.

Using sp_procqmode to Test for Subqueries. The *sp_procqmode* command has the following syntax:

```
sp_procqmode [ object_name [, detail]]
```

In place of *object_name*, you specify the name of a procedure, a trigger, or a view for which you want to examine the query processing mode. If you do not provide an *object_name*, *sp_procqmode* provides information on all procedures, triggers, and views in the current database.

If you use *sp_procqmode* with the *detail* parameter, *sp_procqmode* tells you whether the object contains a subquery, as well as whether the *syscomments* table for this object contains any text.

The following example runs the *sp_procqmode* command:

```
sp_procqmode
```

This returns the following results:

```
Object Owner.name  Object Type      Processing Mode
-----------------  -----------      ---------------
dbo.au_info        stored procedure  pre-System 11
dbo.titleview      view              System 11 or later
```

The next example displays the query processing mode of the stored procedure *old_sproc*, reports whether *old_sproc* contains any subqueries, and reports whether *syscomments* has information about *old_sproc*:

```
sp_procqmode old_sproc, detail
```

This command produces the following information:

```
Object Owner.Name  Object Type      Processing Mode Subq  Text
-----------------  ---------------  --------------- ----  ----
dbo.old_sproc      stored procedure  pre-System 11   no    yes
```

For a detailed report on all objects in the database, use *sp_procqmode* with the following parameters:

```
sp_procqmode null, detail
```

Using either *sp_procqmode* or some other method, compile a listing of procedures, triggers, and views that contain subqueries in each of your databases.

Subquery Tests for SQL Server 10.x Conversions. When migrating from SQL Server 10.x to SQL Server 11, you must test for only one scenario: an update with a correlated expression subquery in its set clause. (Recall that a correlated subquery is simply a subquery that depends on the outer query for its values. You can easily identify a correlated subquery because it cannot function independently.) Prior to SQL Server 11, if no rows match the query, this type of command incorrectly returns 0 instead of NULL. In this case, SQL Server executes the subquery repeatedly, once for each row selected by the outer query.

Search through all your code to find any subqueries that are part of an *update* statement. If you find any queries that contain a correlated expression subquery in the *set* statement, you must analyze them to determine whether they depend on the pre-SQL Server 11 behavior. Remember that in versions prior to SQL Server 11, this type of query returns 0 when it finds no matching rows. In SQL Server 11, however, it returns NULL.

The following excerpt from a trigger demonstrates how your queries might depend on the incorrect behavior of previous versions:

```
update tbl1
set col1 = (select max(col1) from inserted where tbl1.col2 =
inserted.col2)
```

If col1 of tbl1 does not allow NULLs, the *update* statement fails in SQL Server 11, because it tries to insert a NULL value into a column that does not allow NULLs.

To correct this situation, you must rewrite the trigger as follows:

```
update tbl1
set col1 = (select isnull(max(col1), 0) from inserted where tbl1.col2 =
inserted.col2)
```

By adding the *isnull* statement, you force SQL Server to update col1 with the value 0 instead of NULL when no rows are returned.

TIP! Remember to check subquery changes carefully, because you may not see any error messages with the new behavior—only different results. Be sure to check stored procedures and triggers as well as open client code and front-end code.

Subquery Tests for SQL Server 4.x Conversions. Because Sybase made numerous corrections in SQL Server 10.x that still apply in SQL Server 11, migrations from SQL Server 4.x require analysis of several other types of subqueries in addition to the type mentioned in the preceding section. Using the methods described in the preceding sections of this chapter, search for and analyze the subquery types listed in this section. If you find a query that depends on the SQL Server 4.x behavior, you must rewrite that query.

TIP! For more details as well as examples of these subqueries, be sure to read the section, "Changes That May Affect Existing Applications," at the end of Chapter 3 in your _What's New in Sybase SQL Server 11_ reference manual.

You need to analyze the following types of subqueries:

1 • Subqueries using *not in,* when the subqueries return NULL values.

2 • *in* and *any* subqueries, when combined with *or.*

3 • >all and <all with subqueries that return no rows.

4 • Subqueries that suppress duplicate values from the outer query.

5 • Aggregate queries with *exists,* when there are duplicate values.

6 • Correlated subqueries with *distinct,* when used with *in.*

7 • Correlated subqueries that use *in* or *any.*

In SQL Server 4.x, a query with a correlated subquery that uses *in* or *any* returns duplicates if the subquery returns duplicates. Consider the following example:

```
select pub_name
from publishers where pub_id in
(select pub_id
from titles)
```

In SQL Server 4.x, this query returns the following information:

```
pub_name
--------------------
New Age Books
New Age Books
New Age Books
New Age Books
New Age Books
Binnet & Hardley
Binnet & Hardley
Binnet & Hardley
Binnet & Hardley
Binnet & Hardley
Binnet & Hardley
```

```
Binnet & Hardley
Algodata Infosystems
Algodata Infosystems
Algodata Infosystems
Algodata Infosystems
Algodata Infosystems
Algodata Infosystems
```

In SQL Server 11, this query returns the following information:

```
pub_name
--------------------
New Age Books
Binnet & Hardley
Algodata Infosystems
```

If your application depends on duplicate rows, you can rewrite this query as a join:

```
select pub_name from publishers p, titles t
  where
    p.pub_id = t.pub_id
```

Additional Tests for SQL Server 4.x Conversions

If you are migrating from SQL Server 4.x, you must test for several other scenarios. Like subqueries, these scenarios involve changes to the SQL Server that might affect the results of your queries. You cannot use the *sp_procqmode* procedure to find instances of these scenarios, but you can use simple UNIX tools such as *grep* to help find the keywords associated with these scenarios.

You should search all of your code for the following scenarios:

- Use of the *between* predicate. In SQL Server 4.x, you can specify the values in a *between* statement in any order. In SQL Server 10.x and SQL Server 11, the second value listed must be greater than the first value listed.

- Use of comments. SQL Server now supports standard-style comments, which begin with two minus signs (- -). SQL Server ignores any characters after the pair of minus signs. If you have any code that subtracts a negative number but does not use parentheses, it may return different results after you upgrade from SQL Server 4.x. For example, the following query returns 9 in SQL Server 4.x, but it returns 6 in SQL Server 10.x and SQL Server 11:

```
select 6- -3
```

SQL Server 10.x and SQL Server 11 interpret the pair of minus signs as a comment indicator. Use parentheses to correct this problem:

```
select 6-(-3)
```

- Floating-point to character conversions. In SQL Server 4.x, some conversions from float to character may allow truncation without generating an error message. In SQL Server 10.x and SQL Server 11, the conversion succeeds only if no digits are lost. For example, if you set a float variable to 1556.0125 and then convert it to a character variable with a length of 3, the conversion fails. To solve this potential problem, use a target character string of at least 25 characters.

- Integer to character conversions. If a conversion from integer to character results in an overflow, the SQL Server no longer fills the integer with asterisks. Instead, the attempted conversion produces an overflow error. You must check any conversions of this type to ensure that the integer's maximum value will not overflow the character string.

In addition to these scenarios, you may want to search for several other minor changes. Depending on your environment, you may need to consider such issues as datatype hierarchy and numeric-to-numeric truncation. For details about these and other issues, refer to Chapter 3 in the *What's New in Sybase SQL Server 11* reference manual.

Ensuring that Your Objects Use the New SQL Server 11 Processing Mode

After upgrading to SQL Server 11, you should drop and recreate all stored procedures, triggers, and views that contain subqueries, so that those objects can take advantage of SQL Server 11's new, faster processing mode. To find out which objects you need to drop and recreate, use the new system stored procedure *sp_procqmode*. For complete information about this procedure, see the section, "Learning How to Test for Subqueries," earlier in this chapter.

Once you drop and recreate an object in SQL Server 11, you cannot go back to the pre-SQL Server 11 processing mode. Before you upgrade, you may want to create copies of any procedures, triggers, and views that contain subqueries. Use *sp_rename* to copy the original, and create a new copy. After dropping and recreating one copy of each object, you can compare each object's performance under the old processing mode and the new SQL Server 11 processing mode.

Becoming Familiar with New Functionality in SQL Server 11

When you migrate your system to SQL Server 11, you need to become familiar with the new features available in this release. The remaining chapters in this book focus on showing you how to use these new features. In particular, you can find in-depth coverage of the new SQL Server 11 features in the following chapters:

- Chapter 5, "Configuring SQL Server 11"

- Chapter 6, "The Buffer Manager"

- Chapter 7, "SQL Server 11 Enhancements"

Becoming Familiar with New Functionality Introduced in SQL Server 10.x

For users who are migrating their systems from SQL Server 4.x, this section describes the major functional enhancements that Sybase introduced in SQL Server 10.x. You need to be familiar with this information because the SQL Server 10.x features carry over to SQL Server 11. This section covers only the major enhancements. To become completely familiar with all the new features, you should review the documentation or attend one of Sybase's education classes. (For a detailed list of all the new features, read the *What's New in SQL Server Release 11* manual.)

This section covers the following topics:

- The backup server

- Thresholds

- The *sybsystemprocs* database

- New security features

- Cursors

- Name changes

The Backup Server. As of SQL Server 10.x, every SQL Server installation comes with a new server known as the *backup server*. When you use the *load* and *dump* commands to back up databases, these tasks are handled by the backup server, not the SQL Server.

You install the backup server by using the *sybinit* utility, in much the same way as you install SQL Server. The default name for a backup server is SYB_BACKUP, and you must assign a port number to the backup server in the interfaces file. (You do this by using *sybinit*.) If you check the processes running on your host machine, you can see the backup server running as a separate process. You can also see the backup server by using the *showserver* command:

```
showserver
```

The following example shows the output of the *showserver* command. You can see both the SQL Server (*dataserver*) and the backup server:

```
USER      PID %CPU %MEM  SZ  RSS  TT    S START  TIME    COMMAND
mitchell  795 77.7  1.2  340 ?    R      Aug 11 910:32 bin/dataserver
mitchell 6947  0.3  1.5 5560 456 pts/1 S 13:22:01 0:00 bin/backupserver
```

The *dump* and *load* commands automatically use the backup server, but you must maintain this server. You start the backup server with a runfile that *sybinit* creates, and you can bring down the backup server by issuing the *shutdown* command. To shut down the backup server, you logon to the SQL Server (not the backup server) and issue the *shut-down* command followed by the name of the backup server. For example, to shut down the SYB_BACKUP backup server, logon to the SQL Server and issue the following command:

```
shutdown SYB_BACKUP
go
```

Remember that you use the SQL Server to shutdown the backup server. Because the backup server does not have a language handler, it cannot parse and understand instructions it receives.

If you have scripts that handle dumps and loads, you must modify them to accommodate the new backup system.

Thresholds. *Thresholds* are used to monitor free space on database devices. SQL Server places databases on devices and assigns a finite amount of space to each database. A database can fill up all of its assigned space. If a database device runs out of space at an inopportune time, you can run into serious trouble. Thresholds allow you to monitor and automatically free up space when the device reaches a certain point. The threshold accomplishes this by kicking off its associated stored procedure when the device reaches the threshold size. You can write the stored procedure to take whatever actions you deem appropriate.

SQL Server has two types of thresholds. The first type—a *last-chance threshold*—automatically exists whenever a database's transaction log is stored on a separate segment. This *last-chance threshold* is kicked off whenever the remaining space in the log segment falls below the threshold. You can add the second type of threshold—a general *free space threshold*—to monitor any database segment.

For a detailed discussion of thresholds and their related commands, refer to the *SQL Server System Administration Guide* and the *SQL Server Reference Manual, Volume 2*.

The sybsystemprocs Database. SQL Server 10.x and SQL Server 11 include a new system database—the *sybsystemprocs* database—that stores all system stored procedures. Previous versions store these stored procedures in the *master* database. SQL Server 10.x and SQL Server 11 have many more system stored procedures than previous versions, and these procedures take up much more space than those of previous versions. For this and other reasons, Sybase created the *sybsystemprocs* database.

When you migrate from SQL Server 4.x, you must create a device for storing the *sybsystemprocs* database. Like the *master* database, *sybsystemprocs* requires its own device. This device must be at least 16 MB, but you should make it larger than that. You may find yourself customizing system stored procedures or adding your own procedures to this database. By making this device larger than the 16-MB minimum, you also prepare for the next upgrade to your SQL Server, which may require an even larger device for *sybsystemprocs*. If you have the space available, you might make *sybsystemprocs* as large as 24 MB.

If you have any scripts or procedures that include hard-coded calls to system stored procedures, you must change these calls to reference the *sybsystemprocs* database.

New Security Features. SQL Server 10.x introduced two important new security features. Sybase added these features—along with several other security implementations—to comply with Department of Defense security criteria. SQL Server 10.x complies with class C2 criteria for security. (The Secure SQL Server product complies with class B1 criteria.)

Passwords must now be at least six bytes long and SQL Server stores them in encrypted form. The upgrade process does not change existing passwords that are less than six bytes, but any new passwords you create must be at least six bytes long.

For added security, SQL Server 10.x and SQL Server 11 use the concept of *roles*. *Roles* provide accountability for system administration and security-related tasks. Previous versions of SQL Server support just one system administrator (sa) login. Any person who logs into the SQL Server with that account has full system administration permissions. In SQL Server 10.x and SQL Server 11, you can grant certain permissions to a user by assigning different roles. By using the *sp_role* command, you can give a user one or more of three roles:

- System administrator

- System security officer

- Operator

Following the upgrade, one of the DBA's first tasks is to assign roles to certain users who need the proper permissions. For example, only a user with the *operator* role can perform system dumps and loads. The *Security Administration Guide for SQL Server* provides the details about roles.

⁵/₆ **Cursors.** With SQL Server 10.x, Sybase added cursors to the T-SQL command language. Cursors allow you to step through a result set, one row at a time. They provide you with greater flexibility when you write code and they can simplify the process of writing high-performance applications. You should analyze your current applications to determine whether you can improve them by replacing certain sections with cursors. You may also want to use cursors in new applications that you create. Familiarize yourself with cursors by reading the *Sybase SQL Server Transact-SQL User's Guide* and attending Sybase education classes, such as "Fast Track to Sybase SQL Server."

⁶/₆ **Name Changes.** You should be aware of two simple name changes that Sybase made in SQL Server 10.x. In SQL Server 4.x, you configure SQL Server products by using the *sybconfig* utility. In SQL Server 10.x and SQL Server 11, you use the *sybinit* utility.

In SQL Server 4.x, the default runfile that you use for starting SQL Server is called *RUNSERVER*. This file is now called *RUN_SYBASE*. If you have a file called RUNSERVER, *sybinit* automatically changes this file's name to RUN_SYBASE. If you have any scripts that automatically start the SQL Server—for example, a *startserver* script or a system startup UNIX file—you must change these to reference RUN_SYBASE.

Note that RUN_SYBASE is simply a default name. You can choose any name for the runserver file, but you should use the convention of RUN_*name,* where *name* represents the SQL Server's name. For example, the runserver file for a SQL Server named PROD1 should be RUN_PROD1.

⁴/₆ ## Stage Four: Testing

p.26

Once you complete the migration of your development or test system, you must thoroughly test your new SQL Server 11 server. You should test the system for several weeks before you attempt to upgrade your production systems.

You should already have rigorous quality assurance procedures in place. At a minimum, you should test the results of all queries to verify that they return the same results as the old system, and you should benchmark performance to ensure that the new system provides at least comparable performance. Remember to simulate a multi-user environment. Although you can perform initial testing with single instances of queries, you must realize that SQL Server 11 will perform differently under a heavy user load. By testing this type of scenario, you can accurately simulate a production environment.

Unfortunately, you cannot easily simulate a multi-user environment. Ideally, you should arrange to have multiple users stress test the system. If that's not possible, you can try to simulate user loads by using third-party tools or UNIX scripts.

In addition to testing to ensure that applications return the correct results, you should benchmark the new system's performance by using the techniques described in Chapter 8, "Monitoring SQL Server 11." In this way, you can ensure that SQL Server 11 performs at least as well as your previous system. Remember that the performance may not be significantly better at this point because you have not yet tuned the system. In all likelihood, however, you will see performance gains at this point.

You can run multiple scripts simultaneously by using the UNIX *at* and *cron* commands. In this way, you can simulate heavy user loads on SQL Server 11. You can queue up commands on different queues by using the *at -q* command, which allows you to run numerous scripts at exactly the same time. For example, if you have a stored procedure named *st_proc1* that your application normally calls many times, you should simulate its simultaneous use by multiple users. In this way, you can simulate locking, caching, and time-slicing loads that you might not otherwise see. Using the techniques described in Chapter 1, "Preliminaries," create scripts that run *st_proc1* on SQL Server 11. Use the *at* command to run numerous instances of the scripts simultaneously, and study the system performance by using a monitoring tool such as Sybase SQL Server Monitor.

5/6 Stage Five: Monitoring   )²⁶

SQL Server 11 provides tools to monitor and analyze your system in great detail. In stage five of the migration process, you use these tools to obtain the information necessary for properly configuring the new SQL Server 11. You also monitor the system to find ways to increase performance.

You have two main resources for monitoring your SQL Server 11: the stored procedure *sp_sysmon* and the Sybase SQL Server Monitor product. At the time of this writing, you must purchase Sybase SQL Server Monitor as a separate product, but this small investment is worthwhile. SQL Server 11 includes the powerful new *sp_sysmon* stored procedure. If you do not have this stored procedure, you can find it on the Answerbase CD or you can obtain it from Sybase. Chapter 8 provides in-depth coverage of SQL Server 11 monitoring.

Stage Six: Tuning

p. 26

In the final stage of the migration process, you use the information gathered in the monitoring stage to fine-tune your SQL Server 11, the host operating system, and your hardware for the fastest possible performance. Improved performance is the primary reason for migrating to SQL Server 11, so you should invest the necessary time experimenting with different configuration settings and benchmarking performance. Chapter 9, "SQL Server 11 Performance and Tuning," details the necessary steps for tuning your new SQL Server 11.

Summary

This chapter presents a comprehensive plan for migrating to SQL Server 11. After reading the chapter, you can use it as a reference throughout your migration process. In particular, you may want to refer to Table 2-1 during your migration. The remaining chapters in this book elaborate on some of the main tasks that this chapter describes.

Command Reference

sp_addlogin

Syntax

```
sp_addlogin loginame,passwd,[,defdb [,deflang [,fullname]]]
```

Example

```
sp_addlogin david, davidpw, db1
```

sp_adduser

Syntax

```
sp_adduser loginame [,name_in_db [,groupname]]
```

Example

```
sp_adduser lucyd, lucy, grp1
```

sp_checkreswords

Syntax

```
sp_checkreswords [ username ]
```

Example

```
use db1
sp_checkreswords
```

sp_dboption

Syntax

```
sp_dboption [dbname, optname, {true | false}]
```

Example

```
use master
go
sp_dboption pubs2, "select into", true
go
use pubs2
go
checkpoint
go
```

sp_depends

Syntax

```
sp_depends objname
```

Example

```
sp_depends title
```

sp_droplogin

Syntax

```
sp_droplogin loginame
```

Example

```
sp_droplogin mitchell
```

sp_dropuser

Syntax

```
sp_dropuser name_in_db
```

Example

```
sp_dropuser david
```

sp_helpdb

Syntax

```
sp_helpdb [dbname]
```

Example

```
sp_helpdb db1
```

sp_helprotect

Syntax

```
sp_helprotect [name [,username [,"grant"]]]
```

Example

```
sp_helprotect titles
```

sp_procqmode

Syntax

```
sp_procqmode [objname [,detail]]
```

Example

```
sp_procqmode null, detail
```

sp_rename

Syntax

```
sp_rename objname, newname
```

Example

```
sp_rename "books.title", newbkname
```

sp_renamedb

Syntax

```
sp_renamedb dbname, newname
```

Example

```
sp_renamedb db1, newdbname
```

3

Upgrading to SQL Server 11 in a Windows NT Environment

In This Chapter

◆ Comparing your current hardware with the hardware requirements for running SQL Server 11 on Windows NT

◆ Completing the necessary preliminary steps before installing or upgrading to SQL Server 11 on Windows NT

◆ Handling problems you may encounter during the installation process

◆ Setting up the Windows NT interfaces file by using *SQLEDIT*

◆ Learning about alternative ways to run SQL Server 11 on Windows NT

◆ Setting SQL Server 11 configuration parameters on Windows NT

◆ Using the Windows NT Performance Monitor

◆ Using SQL Central, the new graphical tool for administering SQL Server

This chapter describes the process of upgrading from SQL Server 10.x to SQL Server 11 on the Windows NT operating system. The chapter examines the hardware requirements for running SQL Server 11 in the Windows NT environment, and identifies hardware choices that can improve your system's performance. The chapter then reviews the key tasks in the installation and upgrade process.

Reviewing Your Server Hardware

Before you upgrade to SQL Server 11 on Windows NT, you should review your hardware configuration to ensure that it can support your current and future database needs. SQL Server 11's hardware requirements vary depending on the profile of your application load, and later in this chapter you learn about some Windows NT tools that can help you identify bottlenecks and areas in which you can improve performance. First, the following sections describe how each hardware component affects database performance.

Memory

To ensure good performance from your database applications, you must verify that your system has sufficient memory. Regardless of the profile of your database applications, adding memory to your system invariably improves throughput or response time. Because memory is an expensive server component, however, you must be prepared to justify the amount you request.

TIP!   Memory is one of your server's most expensive components. Although you may find better prices for memory through alternate suppliers, you must ensure that the memory you purchase is compatible with your system and its currently installed memory modules.

Both Windows NT 3.51 and NT 4.0 have a minimum memory requirement of 16 MB. SQL Server 11 requires a minimum of 16 MB of RAM. Consequently, a SQL Server 11 installation under Windows NT has a minimum total memory requirement of 32 MB. In addition to this minimum amount, you need memory for each user connection and other overhead associated with your transactions. Installing other Sybase products further increases your memory requirements. On a typical system, you probably would not run SQL Server 11 with less than 64 MB of RAM. The Technology Assessment labs at Sybase—which run tests with 60 or more clients—use systems with at least 128 MB of memory. Some systems now support as much as 2 GB of RAM. For more details on calculating your memory requirements, refer to the *System Administration Guide*.

Processor

Your Intel-based system should have a Pentium™ or a Pentium Pro™ processor. In addition to its advanced architecture, the Pentium Pro offers integrated second level cache, which accelerates most transactions.

The processor speed plays an important role in improving database performance. A database application that saturates a Pentium processor operating at 66 MHz may not be processor-bound on a 133-MHz processor. The Pentium Pro offers speeds in excess of 166 MHz.

Because SQL Server handles queries by issuing multiple threads that the system can spread over multiple processors, you can almost certainly improve the system's performance by adding a second CPU. For processor-intensive applications, you should seriously consider the purchase of additional CPUs. SMP systems offered by Compaq and Hewlett-Packard support as many as four processors, and Windows NT automatically supports configurations with as many as four processors. To determine how much you could gain by adding processors, you should run the Windows NT Performance Monitor on your system. For details about this tool, see the section, "Using the Windows NT Performance Monitor," later in this chapter.

The I/O System

Once your system has sufficient processors, the performance bottleneck shifts to the I/O system. If possible, you should select a system that uses a PCI (Peripheral Component Interface) bus architecture rather than one with an EISA (Extended Industry Standard Architecture) bus. With its 33-MHz clock, the PCI bus allows for internal data transfer rates of 132 MB/sec; EISA, with its 8-MHz clock, achieves 33 MB/sec. The only disadvantage to using PCI is that a system is normally limited to four PCI slots. If your requirements exceed that limit, higher range systems offered by Compaq and Hewlett-Packard offer a dual PCI bus, which these systems implement by means of a PCI-to-PCI bridge. Less expensive solutions include a mixture of PCI slots and EISA slots for less time-critical components.

TIP! Choose a system with a PCI bus architecture rather than using an EISA-based system.

When planning your I/O system, carefully consider your disk controllers and your disk drives. Ensure that the disk controller you choose supports the number of drives and the level of RAID (Redundant Array of Inexpensive Disks) that you intend to use. For a mission-critical database application, decide whether you plan to use mirroring with a dual set of drives or RAID 5, a less expensive option. If you decide to use mirroring, consider using dual controllers for further safety. Although the hardware costs for mirroring exceed those for RAID 5, you pay a smaller performance penalty for this form of redundancy. In particular, RAID 5 exacts a significant toll on performance when SQL Server retrieves larger pieces of data, such as images, from the database. For redundancy and optimal performance, the best—and most expensive—solution is mirroring striped drives, sometimes referred to as RAID 0+1.

TIP!	Make sure your system has enough slots for attaching all of the peripherals, such as network cards, tape backup systems, and uninterruptible power supplies (UPSs).

For best performance, your disk controller should support a 32-bit Fast Wide SCSI-2 interface. Check whether your disk controller has a cache, and determine whether it is a read cache, a write cache, or a mixed cache.

Your application profile determines the usefulness of controller cache. If most of your system's workload involves decision support and includes aggregate queries that require lots of sorting, disk controller cache can help performance considerably. For OLTP applications, the benefits of disk controller cache are less obvious. And for applications that execute only random reads, the cache search overhead can degrade performance. OLTP workloads with inserts or updates can benefit from write-through cache for writes to the log. In this case, either make sure the controller has battery backup or use a UPS to ensure log write consistency in case of a power outage.

TIP!	Disk controller cache is useful primarily for certain decision support applications. It offers limited utility in an OLTP environment, especially if the majority of queries are read-only. You should run benchmarks on your typical transaction load to measure performance with controller cache switched on and off.

Ensure that you have enough disk space for your current and near-future needs, including a separate physical drive for the log. On most systems, the disk drives constitute the major bottleneck to optimal system performance. You may want to consider purchasing additional drives. Larger capacity drives usually offer faster seek times, and you need to balance this consideration against the advantage of spreading tables over several spindles.

If you are considering RAID striping, you can choose either hardware striping or NT software striping. Hardware striping gives you slightly better performance, but the setup is usually more complicated.

SQL Server 11 on Windows NT allows you to use either NTFS file partitions or raw file partitions for your database files. Either form of partitioning preserves your disk caching coherency in the event of a system crash. Using raw file partitions usually gives you slightly better performance but NTFS partitions are easier to manage, particularly if you intend to do full system backups on the Operating System level. For security and performance reasons, you should not use FAT partitions.

The Network Interface

Network throughput usually does not present a problem for database systems, unless your system transfers lots of text or images (Binary Large Objects, or BLOBs) to numerous users. In that case, you might want to spread your users over several network segments that talk to a separate network card on your server. You might also improve performance by using a router or a network switch. Finally, consider using the faster 100 Mbit/sec network cards, if your hubs and routers can support this speed.

TIP!   Avoid putting SQL Server on the primary domain controller, the default gateway, the primary WINS server, the secondary WINS server, or the Domain Name Service (DNS) server.

Before You Upgrade

The booklet *Installing Sybase SQL Server for Windows NT*—which comes with your installation CD—contains an outline of products available with the installation. This booklet also provides detailed information about system requirements and describes how to perform the installation. Rather than repeat all of the information in that booklet, this section focuses on only a few key issues.

It is important to read the Release Bulletins that you find on the installation CD-ROM. In File Manager, double-click on *\release\rebul.hlp*. This file contains last-minute information that did not make it into the printed documentation. The file *\release\install.spr* documents known installation and product problems.

TIP!   You should be running the latest Service Pack for Windows NT. Service Pack recommendations should be confirmed with Sybase technical support.

Check with Microsoft for the latest version of Service Pack for your current version of Windows NT, and make sure you have the correct version installed. To verify the Service Pack version you are currently running:

- *For Windows NT 3.51*: In Program Manager, choose Help | About Program Manager.

- *For Windows NT 4.x:* In the Control Panel, choose System and then click on the General tab.

You should back up your original database. If you encounter a problem during the upgrade, you can restore your original database and reinstall SQL Server.

If your server is replicated, you must follow the guidelines set out for installing SQL Server on replicated servers; otherwise, the installation might fail. The *Installing Sybase SQL Server* booklet details the correct methodology for installing SQL Server on replicated servers.

TIP!   Check the size of your *sybsystemprocs* database.

The SQL Server 11 installation presupposes that your *sybsystemprocs* database is at least 16 MB. You can check the current size of *sybsystemprocs* by issuing the following command:

```
sp_helpdb sybsystemprocs
```

If this is set to the System 10 default of 12 MB, you must increase it to at least 16 MB; otherwise, the installation will fail. Again, the *Installing Sybase SQL Server* booklet describes the procedure for checking this information and, if necessary, increasing the database size.

Upgrading Your System

The Sybase SQL Server installation pack contains two CDs: the SQL Server installation CD and the Workplace Infobase. The Workplace Infobase provides online information about SQL Server for Windows NT in a user-friendly format.

To begin the installation, insert the SQL Server installation CD in your server's CD-ROM drive. Choose File Manager and the drive corresponding to your server's CD-ROM drive. In the CD-ROM's root directory, double-click on *setup.exe*.

Each window that the installation process displays has a button that allows you to backtrack to the previous window. In this way, you can change parameters you may have entered by mistake. Each window also has a Help button, which lets you access extensive online help concerning each stage of the installation process.

The first window displayed during the installation process prompts you for your Customer Authorization String, which is printed on the back of your SQL Server installation pack. Next, the installation process asks for the directory in which you want to install

SQL Server 11. If you already have SQL Server 10 installed, the install program detects SQL Server 10's current installation directory and enters this in the prompt. Unless you want to run both SQL Server 10 and SQL Server 11 on the same system (say, for performance evaluation on a test system), you should accept this value and click on Continue. If you need to run both versions of SQL Server, you need to change the SQL Server Registry keys for your original server. The *Configuring and Administering Sybase SQL Server for Windows NT* manual describes the methodology for changing the SQL Server Registry keys.

The Product Set Selection window gives you the choice of installing either 16- or 32-bit applications. During server installation, you should select the 32-bit Windows NT applications.

The 16-bit applications consist of the Language Modules and the Open Client. The Language Modules contain localization and sort order support. The Open Client application contains all the connectivity libraries, the interactive *sql* program and the *bulk copy* utility for loading ASCII data into a database. If you need these 16-bit applications, you can also select them in the next window displayed during the installation process: the Product Selection window. As shown in Figure 3-1, you use the Product Selection window to specify which applications you want to install.

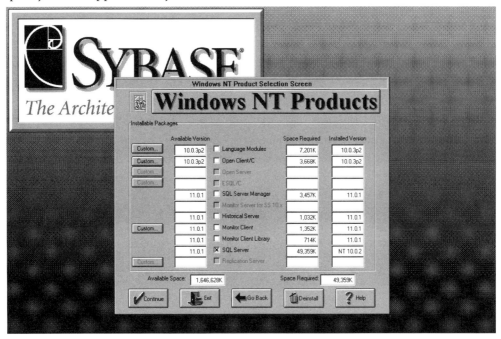

FIGURE 3-1: *The Product Selection window*

TIP! You do not need to install the 16-bit Open Client to get *isql* or *bcp*, because
the 32-bit Open Client also contains these applications. You only need to
install the 16-bit Open Client on Windows NT if you plan to run a 16-bit
application on the NT machine.

This window lists the size and the version number of each application that you want
to install. If you selected the 32-bit applications in the Product Set Selection window, SQL
Server 11 is automatically selected in the Product Selection window. You may also want to
select some of the other applications that the Product Selection window lists:

- SQL Server Manager: You can administer SQL Server by using this graphical tool.
  Note that starting with SQL Server 11.0.2, the SQL Central application replaces
  SQL Server Manager.

- SQL Server Monitor: This application obtains statistics on SQL Server performance by monitoring SQL Server shared memory.

- SQL Server Historical Server: This program records past SQL Server Monitor statistics for comparison with subsequent statistics. Do not install this application on
  the same system as the SQL Server that you want to monitor.

- SQL Server Monitor Client: This graphical performance monitoring tool for SQL
  Server can help you to analyze performance problems.

- SQL Server Monitor Client Library: This library contains application program-
  ming interface (API) calls that provide access to all SQL Server performance
  counters.

In addition to these tools, SQL Server 11.0.2 offers the following applications:

- SQL Central: This application offers an alternative to SQL Server Manager, and it
  allows you to administer any SQL Anywhere databases on your network.

- NetImpact Dynamo: The latest tool from Sybase supports requests for data from
  SQL Server via a Web browser.

After you complete the Product Selection window, the system decompresses the applications you selected. As shown in Figure 3-2, the next window displayed by the installation process offers to set up SQL.INI, your Windows NT interfaces file. This SQL.INI
dialog box asks whether you want to run *SQLEDIT* to create an interfaces file, import an
existing interfaces file, or defer the setup of the interfaces file. The next section in this
chapter, "Configuring SQL.INI: The Windows NT Interfaces File," covers the setup of the
interfaces file.

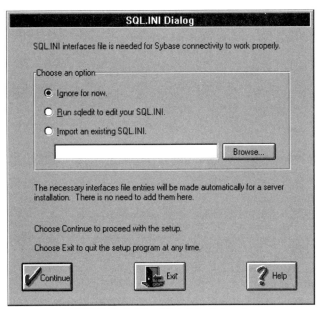

FIGURE 3-2: *The SQL.INI dialog box*

The install process sets up the new SQL Server icons on the desktop and then announces that the first part of the installation process is complete.

The installation process then asks you for the path of the earlier installation of SQL Server and the name of the server that you want to upgrade. You are asked to login as system administrator. If the SQL Server is not currently running (and it won't be), the installation process offers to start it for you.

The installation process then performs the preupgrade eligibility test. The installation log lists any problems identified during this step. You can find the installation log in the SQL Server directory *sybase\init\logs*. The following example from a failed preupgrade test indicates a problem with the size of the *sybsystemprocs* database:

```
07/03/96 10:08:37 PM BEGIN ENVIRONMENT INFORMATION

USER ENVIRONMENT
--------------------------------------------
current directory:              D:\
character set:                  cp850
language:                       us_english
sybinit release directory:      C:\SYSTEM10
working release directory:      C:\SYSTEM10

DSQUERY:                        TITANIC10
```

```
DSLISTEN:                        TITANIC10

07/03/96 10:08:37 PM END ENVIRONMENT INFORMATION
07/03/96 10:08:48 PM Calling the shell with 'C:\SYSTEM10\bin\sqlsrvr.exe
                  -dC:\SYSTEM10\data\master.dat -sTITANIC10
                  -eC:\SYSTEM10\install\errorlog -iC:\SYSTEM10\ini
                  -MC:\SYSTEM10'.
07/03/96 10:08:48 PM waiting for server 'TITANIC10' to boot...
07/03/96 10:11:10 PM Calling the shell with 'C:\SYSTEM10\upgrade\preup-
grd.exe
                  -STITANIC10 -P -N '.
07/03/96 10:11:20 PM Calling the shell with '2}"Œ~„ = return code.'.
07/03/96 10:11:20 PM Done
07/03/96 10:11:20 PM Begin output from 'preupgrd':
    Starting preupgrade of SQL Server
    Checking status in all existing databases.
    Sybsystemprocs has size of 12 MB. It requires 16 MB for release 11.0.1.
07/03/96 10:11:20 PM End output from 'preupgrd'.
07/03/96 10:13:00 PM Server 'TITANIC10' failed preupgrade eligibility
test.  See log for more information.
```

If your installation fails, you should immediately check the installation log for clues as to reason for the failure.

To complete the installation process, the SQL Server upgrade installs the system stored procedures.

Configuring SQL.INI: The Windows NT Interfaces File

The interfaces file contains the information that SQL Server uses for connecting with clients. Windows NT calls this file SQL.INI and stores it in the Sybase directory \sybase\ini\. The *SQLEDIT* utility offers the simplest means for setting up this file. If necessary, you can manually edit this ASCII file, although this is not recommended. Figure 3-3 shows the user interface for the *SQLEDIT* utility.

If you let the system set up your SQL.INI file, it creates master and query entries for both WinSock and Named Pipes connections for SQL Server. WinSock is Microsoft's implementation of TCP/IP protocol support on Windows NT, and Named Pipes is Microsoft's proprietary network protocol based on NetBEUI. If you select Backup Server and Monitor Server during the installation, *SQLEDIT* also sets up entries for these servers.

If you use multiple protocols or multiple network cards to access the database server, you may need to edit, add, or delete connectivity entries. To do so, highlight a server entry or enter a new one in the Input Server Name box and then choose Add or Update. Then, select a Connection Service Entry or create a new one by selecting the master or query service type, the appropriate platform, and the type of Network Library Driver. *SQLEDIT* supports DECnet, Named Pipes, NetWare, and WinSock Network Library Drivers. If you use a custom driver, you can enter it by using the Edit Platform & Net-Library Driver button. *SQLEDIT* stores the Net-Library Driver information in the *libctl.cfg* file, which you can also edit manually (again, however, this is not recommended).

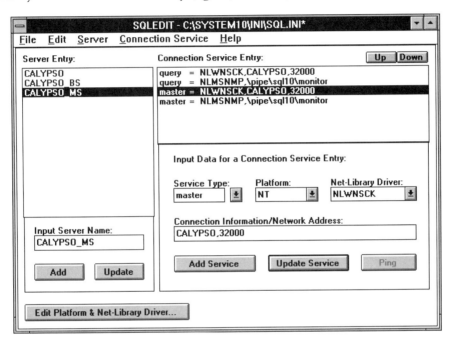

FIGURE 3-3: *The **SQLEDIT** utility*

TIP!   Most Windows NT-based servers use DNS to locate a TCP/IP host. To obtain the host name of the local server, open the Control Panel, click on Network, and then click on Installed Network Software. To display the host name of the server, choose TCPIP, Configure, DNS Configure. Select Advanced, and verify that the option Enable DNS for Windows Name Resolution is set.

The connection information for the WinSock entry for TCP/IP connectivity corresponds to a network interface name and a unique port number. For name resolution, you can use the *hosts* file, which defines a name for each network card available on the system. Alternatively, you can use the explicit IP address for each network interface. You find the *hosts* file in the following location:

```
C:\WINNT35\SYSTEM32\DRIVERS\ETC\HOSTS
```

The path *C:\WINNT35* represents the location of the Windows NT operating system. (This may differ from the path name on your machine, depending on how you set up the operating system.)

TIP!   Make sure that each SQL Server has a unique port number. In particular, if you share the system with an Internet server that has its own port number, ensure that your SQL Server port numbers do not conflict with the port number of the Internet server.

You should start up the server and *ping* each query interface you define. You can also do this by using the *SYBPING* utility. When you finish editing the *SQLEDIT* entries, save the configuration.

Running SQL Server 11

You can run SQL Server by using the Services Manager traffic light icon. Choose the service and the corresponding server and then double-click on the green light. The server names that appear in the Services Manager icon correspond with Sybase SQL Server entries in the Registry. If you need to change them for any reason, you have to edit the Registry entries by using the *regedt32* application. The *Installing SQL Server for Windows NT* booklet provides instructions for doing this.

As an alternative, you can run the server from a batch file in a DOS Command Prompt window and thus have direct access to the errorlog on your console screen. This is particularly useful when you run SQL Server with a *dbcc trace* and you want to follow the trace interactively on the screen. If you start SQL Server from a batch file in a DOS window, however, you must not close the window before shutting down the SQL Server via shutdown. If you close the DOS window, the SQL Server process terminates abnormally.

TIP!   If you run SQL Server from a batch file in a DOS window, you should increase the screen buffer size to allow you to scroll through the entire output of your SQL Server log. You do this by clicking on the square at the top left of the window and selecting Properties. On Windows NT 3.51, choose the Screen Size tab and set the Screen Buffer Size to a very high value, such as 9999. On Windows NT 5.x, choose the Options tab and set the Buffer size to 9999.

By default, SQL Server appends the errorlog to the errorlog file in the *\sybase\install* directory. If you run the server from the icon, you have to reopen the errorlog file each time you want to consult it.

The installation process creates a batch file named RUN_*servername* (in the following example, RUN_CALYPSO) and stores this file in the *\sybase\install* directory. You can edit this batch file to serve your needs. The following listing shows an example of this batch file:

```
C:\SYBASE\bin\sqlsrvr.exe -dC:\SYBASE\DATA\MASTER.DAT -sCALYPSO
-eC:\SYBASE\install\errorlog -iC:\SYBASE\ini -MC:\SYBASE
```

Table 3-1 explains the parameters used in this batch file.

Table 3-1: *Parameters Used by the RUN_***servername** *Batch File*

Parameter	Description
-d	Specifies the location of *master.dat*, the master database file
-s	Specifies the server name
-e	Specifies the location of the errorlog file
-I	Specifies the location of the interfaces file
-M	Specifies the location of the configuration file
-P	Runs the process at the highest priority

TIP! To ensure the best performance, edit the batch file to include the -P parameter, which runs SQL Server as the highest priority process on your system. Also set the system to run with *Best Foreground Application Response Time* option. To set this parameter on Windows NT 3.51, open the Control Panel in the Program Manager, start up the System icon, and in the window that's displayed, select Tasking and then set this option.

Optimizing SQL Server 11 Performance on Windows NT

The process of optimizing a system's performance has many elements. Complete coverage of these elements is beyond the scope of this chapter. However, the following sections point out some helpful ideas and useful performance-tuning features specific to SQL Server 11 on Windows NT.

Using the *sp_configure* Command

SQL Server 11 offers numerous options for optimizing database performance. You can set these options by using the *sp_configure* database command and other configuration-related stored procedures. This section examines specific aspects of *sp_configure* as they apply to Windows NT. For more details on the *sp_configure* parameters, refer to Chapter 5, "Configuring SQL Server 11."

Whenever you reset these parameters, SQL Server 11 writes them to a *Servername*.cfg file (for example, CALYPSO.cfg). SQL Server reads this file each time you restart the server. Each time you use *sp_configure*, SQL Server saves the previous version of the configuration file. SQL Server saves these old configuration files with filenames that have numerically increasing suffixes—for example, CALYPSO.001, CALYPSO.002.

TIP!   In some cases, you may prefer to edit the configuration file directly rather than execute the appropriate stored procedures for setting the desired options. These changes do not take effect until you restart your server. (This holds true for certain parameters regardless of which method you use for changing their settings).

The stored procedure *sp_cacheconfig* and other stored procedures required to set up a named cache are particularly cumbersome to execute using SQL. After noting how SQL Server records these settings in the configuration file, you may prefer to change these settings by editing the configuration file directly. You can also set these parameters by using SQL Central, the new server administration tool.

TIP!   By experimenting, you will determine useful configuration files for specific situations. Save these configurations with meaningful names, such as CALYPSO.NIGHTBATCH.CFG. (Windows NT allows you to use filenames longer than eight characters.) Write batch files to reinstate these parameters when you need them.

SQL Server 11's use of configuration files can save you from being locked out of your server. This sometimes occurs on older versions of SQL Server because a DBA has set *sp_configure* parameters incompatible with the system hardware (for example, allocating more memory than the system has available). If SQL Server 11 detects configuration parameters incompatible with the system configuration, it resets the parameters to their default values and writes them to the configuration file. SQL Server stores the configuration files in the *\sybase* directory.

The following listing shows a sample configuration file:

```
###########################################################################
#
#          Configuration File for the Sybase SQL Server
#
#          Please read the System Administration Guide (SAG)
#          before changing any of the values in this file.
#
###########################################################################
[Configuration Options]

[General Information]

[Backup/Recovery]
     recovery interval in minutes = 20
     print recovery information = DEFAULT
     tape retention in days = DEFAULT

[Cache Manager]
     number of oam trips = DEFAULT
     number of index trips = 3
     procedure cache percent = 5
     memory alignment boundary = DEFAULT

[Named Cache:default data cache]
     cache size = DEFAULT
     cache status = default data cache

[16K I/O Buffer Pool]
     pool size = 5M
     wash size = DEFAULT

[Disk I/O]
     allow sql server async i/o = DEFAULT
     disk i/o structures = DEFAULT
     page utilization percent = DEFAULT
     number of devices = 50
     disable character set conversions = DEFAULT

[Network Communication]
     default network packet size = DEFAULT
     max network packet size = 16384
     remote server pre-read packets = DEFAULT
     number of remote connections = DEFAULT
     allow remote access = DEFAULT
     number of remote logins = DEFAULT
     number of remote sites = DEFAULT
     max number network listeners = DEFAULT
     tcp no delay = DEFAULT
     allow sendmsg = DEFAULT
     syb_sendmsg port number = DEFAULT
```

```
[O/S Resources]
    max async i/os per engine = DEFAULT
    max async i/os per server = DEFAULT

[Physical Resources]

[Physical Memory]
    total memory = 48000
    additional network memory = 3999744
    lock shared memory = DEFAULT
    shared memory starting address = DEFAULT

[Processors]
    max online engines = 1
    min online engines = DEFAULT

[SQL Server Administration]
    number of open objects = DEFAULT
    number of open databases = DEFAULT
    audit queue size = DEFAULT
    default database size = DEFAULT
    identity burning set factor = DEFAULT
    allow nested triggers = DEFAULT
    allow updates to system tables = DEFAULT
    print deadlock information = DEFAULT
    default fill factor percent = DEFAULT
    number of mailboxes = DEFAULT
    number of messages = DEFAULT
    number of alarms = DEFAULT
    number of pre-allocated extents = DEFAULT
    event buffers per engine = DEFAULT
    cpu accounting flush interval = DEFAULT
    i/o accounting flush interval = DEFAULT
    sql server clock tick length = DEFAULT
    runnable process search count = 2000
    i/o polling process count = DEFAULT
    time slice = DEFAULT
    deadlock retries = DEFAULT
    cpu grace time = DEFAULT
    number of sort buffers = DEFAULT
    sort page count = DEFAULT
    number of extent i/o buffers = 150
    size of auto identity column = DEFAULT
    identity grab size = DEFAULT
    lock promotion HWM = DEFAULT
    lock promotion LWM = DEFAULT
    lock promotion PCT = DEFAULT
    housekeeper free write percent = DEFAULT
    partition groups = DEFAULT
    partition spinlock ratio = DEFAULT
```

```
[User Environment]
    number of user connections = 150
    stack size = DEFAULT
    stack guard size = DEFAULT
    systemwide password expiration = DEFAULT
    permission cache entries = DEFAULT
    user log cache size = DEFAULT
    user log cache spinlock ratio = DEFAULT

[Lock Manager]
    number of locks = DEFAULT
    deadlock checking period = DEFAULT
    freelock transfer block size = DEFAULT
    max engine freelocks = DEFAULT
    address lock spinlock ratio = DEFAULT
    page lock spinlock ratio = DEFAULT
    table lock spinlock ratio = DEFAULT
```

TIP!   When you edit your configuration file, use comments liberally to document your changes. Comments are preceded by a hash sign (#).

Before changing any of these parameters, consult the *Systems Administration Guide* and the *Performance and Tuning Guide*. If used incorrectly, some of these parameters can degrade your system's performance.

Using the Windows NT Performance Monitor

This section describes some performance tuning ideas specific to Windows NT. (For more details about tuning SQL Server 11, refer to Chapter 9, "SQL Server 11 Performance and Tuning.") Keep in mind that a correct approach to tuning involves many different levels (database design, query coding, and so on) before you should consider system tuning.

First, observe which transactions or transaction mixes cause performance problems. SQL Central can help you track transactions with possible problems. Try to isolate which transactions cause a bottleneck. Analyze the code for those transactions to see which tables they access. Determine which drives physically store these tables. Once you verify that you cannot resolve the problem on the application level, you can explore system or hardware factors that might be affecting performance.

Learn to use the Performance Monitor tool supplied with Windows NT, to see which aspects of the system are adversely affected. The *Microsoft Windows NT Resource Kit* includes documentation for the Performance Monitor. Look at the CPU and disk utilization counters. If you have not yet looked at disk utilization, you must enable it by running the following command from the command line and rebooting your system:

```
diskperf -y
```

By logging your performance counters to another machine on the network, you can examine them at a later stage in the tuning process. For performance reasons, you should disable *diskperf* after you obtain the disk statistics:

```
diskperf -n
```

Once you identify the bottlenecks, you can start to experiment with database tuning parameters to alleviate the situation. In most cases, bottlenecks relate to I/O, which is usually the slowest element of your system. A particularly useful new configuration option in SQL Server 11 allows you to set I/O buffer pools to sizes larger than 2K (the default I/O size). Using a 16K I/O buffer pool gives an immediate performance boost to any query involving large quantities of data (for example, a sort). You can assign a 16K buffer pool to the default data cache, and SQL Server will use it whenever the larger buffer pool proves useful for a particular query. For more complex situations, you should use a named cache so that a decision support query does not interfere with OLTP transactions. The *SQL Server Performance and Tuning Guide* provides in-depth coverage of named cache configuration.

TIP!   For more information on tuning SQL Server 11 using the Performance
Monitor, refer to the Sybase white paper, *Tuning and Measuring Performance of Sybase SQL Server 11 on Windows NT,* by Ed Bueche.

Using SQL Central

SQL Server 11.0.2 contains a new utility called SQL Central. Figure 3-4 shows this new tool, which replaces SQL Server Manager.

SQL Central is a Windows tool for managing both Sybase SQL Server 11 and SQL Anywhere databases. It will also manage NetImpact Dynamo, the new Sybase Web/Database interface tool. SQL Central allows the DBA to manage the objects within the database (creation and editing of tables, procedures, and so on). It also helps the DBA perform common database-wide tasks such as starting up databases and backing them up.

SQL Central is organized in a hierarchical manner. It shows the databases within your domain as well as the status of each database. By using SQL Central, you can start up a database, look at any object within a database, and change parameters associated with that object. You can track and analyze the processes running on each database displayed. SQL Central also includes a code editor for displaying and editing code for triggers, procedures, and views. By using SQL Central's formatting and Data Definition Language (DDL) formulation capabilities, DBAs can easily generate and change code. To help you with more complicated tasks, SQL Central provides wizards, which walk you through a task, step by step.

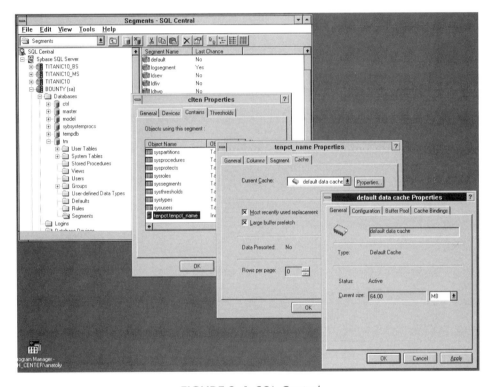

FIGURE 3-4: *SQL Central*

Summary

This chapter details the steps you take to prepare for and complete the migration to SQL Server 11 in a Windows NT environment. The chapter also introduces various tools that can help you monitor, tune, and administer SQL Server 11 on Windows NT. In the following chapter, you learn the necessary steps for migrating to SQL Server 11 in a UNIX environment.

Migration Checklist

The following list summarizes the key migration tasks covered in this chapter:

♦ Review your hardware to determine whether it is adequate for current and near-future capacity and performance requirements.

♦ Make sure you are running the latest Service Pack for Windows NT.

♦ Check the size of your *sybsystemprocs* database.

♦ Follow the installation instructions in the booklet, *Installing Sybase SQL Server for Windows NT.*

♦ Check the installation log for any errors encountered during the installation.

♦ Edit the SQL.INI file for your specific connectivity requirements, making sure that each port has a unique number.

♦ Decide whether you plan to run the server by using the icon or from a command line by using a batch command. You can create a series of batch commands with different configuration files for different workloads.

♦ Use the Windows NT Performance Monitor to identify system bottlenecks and to help you tune the SQL Server.

4

Upgrading to SQL Server 11 in a UNIX Environment

In This Chapter

◆ Configuring the *sybsystemprocs* and *master* devices

◆ Turning off database options

◆ Choosing port numbers

◆ Upgrading a SQL Server by using *sybinit*

◆ Installing a SQL Server 11 by using *sybinit*

◆ Using *sybinit's* resource files

This chapter introduces you to the steps you take and the pitfalls you must avoid, when you perform a SQL Server 11 upgrade or install in a UNIX environment. You learn how to use the *sybinit* process to perform the physical upgrade. This chapter assumes that you have already performed any necessary steps outlined in previous chapters—for example, completing the migration worksheet, assigning directories and devices, loading the software, and conducting the reserved word checks.

What Is sybinit?

The SQL Server 11 software includes an executable UNIX process called *sybinit*. When you run *sybload* to load the SQL Server 11 software, *sybload* deposits *sybinit* in the $SYBASE/install directory. Sybase first included *sybinit* with SQL Server 10.x; previous versions of SQL Server use a process known as *sybconfig*. The *sybinit* process is simply a new, more modern version of *sybconfig*.

When you use *sybinit*, you can take two approaches to upgrading a SQL Server: the upgrade method or the install method. With the *upgrade* method, you upgrade a server from a previous version to SQL Server 11. Once you complete the upgrade, you no longer have a pre-SQL Server 11 server, just the new, SQL Server 11 server.

The *install* method installs a new, separate SQL Server 11 server. When you complete the installation, you have two SQL Servers: the original (pre-SQL Server 11) server and the new, SQL Server 11 server. You must then transfer all data and structures to the SQL Server 11 server (because it is an empty SQL Server at this point). Chapter 2, "The Migration Process," describes the decisions you make when choosing whether to use the upgrade method or the install method.

TIP!   Before proceeding with either method, you should read the entire *Installation and Configuration Guide* and the *Release Bulletin* for your system. Then, make sure you have the correct settings for environmental variables and logins. In particular, ensure that you use the UNIX *sybase* login, and verify that the $SYBASE variable points to the *new* SQL Server 11 directory. Add the SQL Server 11 directory to your UNIX path variable, and include the new path and variables in the shell initialization file.

½ *Using the Upgrade Method*

As mentioned in the preceding section, you upgrade or install a SQL Server 11 server by running *sybinit*. If you choose the upgrade method, you must complete two tasks before you run *sybinit*. You must check the size of your *sybsystemprocs* database and ensure that you turn off most database options.

½ Checking *sybsystemprocs*

If you are migrating from SQL Server 4.x, you must create a raw device that is at least 16 MB to 24 MB in size. Be sure to record the device's name in your migration worksheet. Try to obtain a raw disk partition for this device. If you do not have a raw partition, you can use an operating system file as a last resort, but this is not recommended.

If you are migrating from SQL Server 10.x, check the size of your *sybsystemprocs* database and device. If *sybsystemprocs* is smaller than 16 MB (double-check the required size in your *Installation and Configuration Guide*), you need to increase its size before upgrading. If *sybsystemprocs* is too small, the upgrade will fail. Even if *sybsystemprocs* is exactly

16 MB in size, you may want to increase its size by a few megabytes, to provide space for your own system stored procedures, *sp_sysmon*, and any future *sybsystemprocs* needs.

You increase the size of *sybsystemprocs* on its device or another raw device by using the *alter database* command. First, however, you need to check the size of *sybsystemprocs*:

```
sp_helpdb sybsystemprocs
go
```

SQL Server responds with the following information:

```
name                db_size   owner  dbid   created        status
----------------    -------   -----  ----   ------------   -------------------
sybsystemprocs      12.0 MB   sa        4   Aug 30, 1996   trunc log on chkpt
device_fragments      size           usage                free kbytes
----------------    ---------      --------------------    -----------
sysprocsdev           12.0 MB      data and log               3728
(return status = 0)
```

Next, you need to make sure the device has enough room for the new size you want to specify for *sybsystemprocs*:

```
sp_helpdevice sysprocsdev
go
```

SQL Server displays information about the device:

```
device_name    physical_name description   status cntrltype     device_number
low    high
----------------------------------------------------
sysprocsdev /home/usr/u/man1/devices/MAN1_1_procs.dat special, physical
disk, 20.00 MB 2 0 1 16777216 16787455
(1 row affected, return status = 0)
```

After verifying that the device has sufficient space, you increase the size of *sybsystemprocs* by using the *alter database* command:

```
use master
go
alter database sybsystemprocs on sysprocsdev = 6
go
```

SQL Server confirms the change:

```
Extending database by 3072 pages on disk sysprocsdev
```

To display the new size of the *sybsystemprocs* database, issue the *sp_helpdb* command:

```
sp_helpdb sybsystemprocs
go
```

SQL Server displays the new size:

name	db_size	owner	dbid	created	status
sybsystemprocs	18.0 MB	sa	4	Aug 30, 1996	no options set

device_fragments	size	usage	free kbytes
sysprocsdev	6.0 MB	data and log	6144
sysprocsdev	12.0 MB	data and log	3728

½ Checking the Database Options

Remember to check all the database options before starting *sybinit*, because any database options (other than *select into/bulkcopy*) cause *sybinit* to fail. The following example shows how you check all the database options for all the databases and then turn off the appropriate options. You check the database options by issuing the *sp_helpdb* command:

```
sp_helpdb
go
```

SQL Server responds by displaying the current status for all database options:

name	db_size	owner	dbid	Created	status
master	8.0 MB	sa	1	Jan 01, 1900	no options set
model	2.0 MB	sa	3	Jan 01, 1900	no options set
pubs2	3.0 MB	sa	6	Aug 30, 1996	no options set
sybsecurity	5.0 MB	sa	5	Aug 30, 1996	trunc log on chkpt
sybsystemprocs	12.0 MB	sa	4	Aug 30, 1996	trunc log on chkpt
tempdb	2.0 MB	sa	2	Sep 04, 1996	select into/bulkcopy

```
(return status = 0)
```

This output shows that both *sybsystemprocs* and *sybsecurity* have the *trunc log on chkpt* option turned on. To turn off this option, issue the following commands:

```
use master
go
sp_dboption sybsystemprocs, "trunc log on chkpt", false
go
sp_dboption sybsecurity, "trunc log on chkpt", false
```

```
go
use sybsystemprocs
go
checkpoint
go
use sybsecurity
go
checkpoint
go
```

Running *sybinit*

To start the *sybinit* process, go to the $SYBASE/install SQL Server 11 directory and then enter the following command:

```
sybinit
```

If *sybinit* is not found, make sure you added the SQL Server 11 directories to your path. You can also use the UNIX *which* or *whereis* commands to locate the *sybinit* executable file. When *sybinit* starts, you see the menu shown in Figure 4-1.

```
SYBINIT

1.  Release Directory: /usr/u/sybase
2.  Edit / View Interfaces File
3.  Configure a server product
4.  Configure an Open Client/server product

ctrl-a Accept and Continue, ctrl-x Exit Screen, ? Help.
```

*Figure 4-1: The **sybinit** main menu*

The *sybinit* process offers a simple, straightforward interface. You simply type the number of the menu option you want to use and then press Enter. Type the appropriate information for that option and then press Ctrl-a (that is, press the Control key while you type the letter *a*) to accept the information. At any time, you can exit the current screen and return to the previous screen, by pressing Ctrl-x. You can end the *sybinit* session by pressing Ctrl-c. However, you should not do this during a process—for example, during an eligibility test. If you exit by pressing Ctrl-c, you must start from the beginning the next time you use *sybinit*.

From the *sybinit* main menu, use option 1 to set the release directory to the new SQL Server 11 directory. Then, choose option 2 to edit the interfaces file.

Adding an Entry to the Interfaces File

The interfaces file contains the information SQL Server uses for its client-server connectivity. SQL Server uses this file as a lookup table to find such information as the host names and the port numbers used by various servers. Without the proper entries in this file, you cannot make use of SQL Server or its clients.

You can add entries for SQL Server 11 and the backup server by using *sybinit*, or you can manually enter this information into the interfaces file. In either case, the key is to pick appropriate port numbers and correctly specify the *master* and *query* lines in the interfaces file. If you are not familiar with interfaces files, enter the port numbers by using the *sybinit* process.

Many SQL Server users mistakenly believe that the interfaces file must include the number 2025, because this number appears in numerous examples throughout the documentation for previous versions of SQL Server. In reality, you can use any port number in the interfaces file as long as it meets the following requirements:

- It must be an integer between 1,025 and 65,535.

- It must not be used for any other purpose.

You can make sure that you choose a unique port number by using either of two methods. First, you can check your system's */etc/services* file. This file should have records of all port numbers currently in use. You cannot rely on this file, however, because it must be maintained manually. In all likelihood, this file does not list all of the currently used ports.

The second method for choosing a unique port number requires the use of UNIX tools such as the *netstat* command. This command lists all of the currently used ports. Choose port numbers for SQL Server 11 and the backup server, and then use the *netstat* command to verify that those numbers are not in use. For example, the following command searches for the port numbers 3091 and 3092:

```
netstat -a | grep 3092
netstat -a | grep 3091
```

The following output indicates that some process already uses 3091, so you cannot use that port number for SQL Server 11:

```
tcp   0   0  edman1.3091        *.*           LISTEN
```

Once you choose appropriate port numbers, enter them in the interfaces file by choosing *sybinit* menu option 2, "Edit/View Interfaces File." As shown in Figure 4-2, *sybinit* displays the Server Interfaces File Entry screen.

```
SERVER INTERFACES FILE ENTRY SCREEN

1. Retry Count: 0
2. Retry Delay: 0

3. Add a new listener service
```

Figure 4-2: *The Server Interfaces File Entry screen*

Choose option 3, "Add a new listener service." As shown in Figure 4-3, *sybinit* displays the Edit TCP Service screen.

```
EDIT TCP SERVICE

1. Hostname/Address: harpo
2. Port:
3. Name Alias:

4. Delete this service from the interfaces entry
```

Figure 4-3: *The Edit TCP Service screen*

Use option 1 of this screen to enter the host name of the machine you plan to use for running SQL Server 11, and use option 2 to enter the port number. By returning to the Server Interfaces File Entry screen, you can then enter values for the retry count and the retry delay. In most cases, however, you can use the default values for these options.

Configuring a Server Product

Once you finish with the interfaces section of *sybinit*, return to the main menu, which is shown in Figure 4-4. Choose option 3, "Configure a Server product." As shown in Figure 4-5, *sybinit* displays the "Configure Server Products" screen.

```
SYBINIT

   1.  Release Directory: /usr/u/sybase
   2.  Edit / View Interfaces File
→  3.  Configure a server product
   4.  Configure an open client/server product

ctrl-a Accept and continue, ctrl-x Exit screen, ? Help.
```

*Figure 4-4: The **sybinit** main menu*

```
CONFIGURE SERVER PRODUCTS

   Product            Date Installed      Date Configure
→  1.  SQL Server     Dec 16 95 16:33
```

Figure 4-5: The Configure Server Products screen lists the Sybase products available for configuration.

Choose a SQL Server product, and then choose "Upgrade an existing SQL Server," from the New or Existing SQL Server screen, shown in Figure 4-6.

```
NEW OR EXISTING SQL SERVER

   1.  Configure a new SQL Server

   2.  Configure an existing SQL Server

→  3.  Upgrade an existing SQL Server
```

Figure 4-6: The New or Existing SQL Server screen

As shown in Figure 4-7, the s*ybinit* utility displays a list of SQL Servers, which it finds by looking in the interfaces file. Choose the existing (pre-SQL Server 11) server that you want to upgrade.

```
CONFIGURE EXISTING SQL SERVER

1.  PUB

2.  MARKET

3.  SYBASE_492
```

Figure 4-7: *When you choose the "Upgrade an existing Server" option,* **sybinit** *displays a list of the SQL Servers that you can upgrade.*

TIP!   Any problems you encounter at this point in the *sybinit* process may indicate that *sybinit* cannot find the interfaces file. Make sure your path includes the directory that contains the interfaces file (the $SYBASE directory) and verify that the interfaces file has read and write permissions set for the *sybase* user. If you need to change either of these settings, you must exit *sybinit* by pressing Ctrl-c, make the necessary changes, and then restart *sybinit*.

After you choose the existing server that you want to upgrade, *sybinit* displays the SQL Server Upgrade window, shown in Figure 4-8.

```
SQL SERVER UPGRADE

1.  Test SQL Server upgrade eligibility now

2.  Check for reserved word conflicts

3.  sybsystemprocs databse configuration

4.  Upgrade SQL Server now
```

Figure 4-8: *The SQL Server Upgrade window*

Run the tests listed in the Upgrade window, in the order shown. For thoroughness, you should run the check for reserved word conflicts, even though you have already identified and resolved any reserved word issues. If you encounter any problems during this stage, take appropriate actions based on the error messages and the log messages that *sybinit* displays. For example, the following *sybinit* output shows that an error occurred during an eligibility test:

```
Testing SQL Server 'MAN1_1' for eligibility to upgrade to release
'11.0.1'.
.Done
Server 'MAN1_1' failed preupgrade eligibility test.  See log for more
information.
Press <return> to continue.
```

Using *sybinit* Log Files

You find logs in the $SYBASE/init/logs directory. You can tell which log to examine by checking the log's name, which indicates the month and day the log was created. The log's filename extension indicates the number of times *sybinit* was run for a given day. For example, the third time you start *sybinit* on January 12th, *sybinit* creates the log named log0112.003.

The following excerpt from the log elaborates on the eligibility test error mentioned in the preceding section of this chapter:

```
09/05/96 01:46:41 PM Testing SQL Server 'MAN1_1' for eligibility to
upgrade to release '11.0.1'.
09/05/96 01:46:42 PM Done
09/05/96 01:46:42 PM Begin output from 'preupgrade':
Starting preupgrade of SQL Server
Checking status in all existing databases.
** Database 'sybsecurity' is marked 'trunc. log on chkpt.'.
** You must reset this via sp_dboption before upgrade can continue.
Upgrade of SQL Server to 11.0.1 aborted.
09/05/96 01:46:42 PM End output from 'preupgrade'.
```

The log clearly identifies the problem. To solve this problem, simply exit *sybinit*, turn off the database option, and start a new *sybinit* session.

Unlike previous releases, *sybinit* now creates just one log during the upgrade process. This simplifies the process of finding information about any problems you may encounter. In addition to the log, *sybinit* generates various temporary files in the *init/logs* directory. These files come and go as the upgrade process continues, and they no longer exist once you complete the upgrade. If you run into a problem during an upgrade, however, you can check the temporary file (if one exists) for more details about the problem. The *sybinit* utility names this temporary file *tmp*.

If the upgrade fails after trying to boot the new SQL Server 11, you may find additional useful troubleshooting information in SQL Server 11's errorlog.

If the upgrade runs successfully, you see the following messages during the *sybinit* session:

```
Running task: upgrade the SQL Server.
Testing SQL Server 'MAN1_1' for eligibility to upgrade to release
'11.0.1'.
....Done
Server 'MAN1_1' passed preupgrade eligibility test.  Proceeding.
Checkpointing all databases.
...Done
```

```
The log file for sp_checkreswords output is
'/work1/home/man1/sybase11/init/logs/checkres.dmp'.
Running script '/work1/home/man1/sybase11/upgrade/usage.sql' to save
Database segment information
Successfully saved database segment information
Shutting down the SQL Server 'MAN1_1'
..Done! All databases recovered.
Upgrading SQL Server MAN1_1 from release 10.0.2 to release 11.0.1
.................................................Done
Upgrade of server 'MAN1_1' to release '11.0.1' succeeded.
Task succeeded: upgrade the SQL Server.
Running task: update the SQL Server runserver file.
Task succeeded: update the SQL Server runserver file.
Running task: boot the SQL Server.
Task succeeded: boot the SQL Server.
Running task: install system stored procedures.
.............................................................
Task succeeded: install system stored procedures.
Running task: set permissions for the 'model' database.
Done
Task succeeded: set permissions for the 'model' database.

Configuration completed successfully.
Press <return> to continue.
```

At this point, your new SQL Server 11 is up and running and the old SQL Server no longer exists. You can make sure SQL Server 11 is running by using the *showserver* command, which you can find in the $SYBASE/install directory, or the UNIX *ps* command. You can also check the errorlog to determine when SQL Server 11 has finished its startup process. The following lines in the errorlog indicate that SQL Server has completed the startup process and should be up and running:

```
00:96/09/04 10:52:56.82 server   Recovery complete.
00:96/09/04 10:52:56.82 server   SQL Server's default sort order is:
```

Because the errorlog is cumulative, you may see several occurrences of these lines from previous days. Make sure the lines you see begin with the correct date.

You have now completed the upgrade process and you can use your new SQL Server 11. If you run into serious problems during the *sybinit* process, Appendix A of the *Sybase SQL Server Installation and Configuration Guide* provides solutions for many common problems.

²⁄₂ *Using the <u>Install Method</u>*

When you use the install method, you install a new SQL Server 11 rather than upgrade your current SQL Server. To use the install method, you must have enough disk space for the second SQL Server and enough memory to run two SQL Servers on one machine.

Even though you plan to use the install method, you should read the preceding section of this chapter, "Using the Upgrade Method." That section covers topics that you need to understand—for example, choosing port numbers and configuring devices.

Because the install method creates a new SQL Server 11, you must have raw devices that you can use for the *master* database and the *sybsystemprocs* database. The section, "Checking *sybsystemprocs*," earlier in this chapter, shows you how to set up the raw device for *sybsystemprocs*. Repeat that procedure for the *master* device. The *master* device must be at least 21 MB (for exact numbers, check the *Sybase SQL Server Installation and Configuration Guide*).

Choose port numbers and record them in your migration worksheet. You can manually create the appropriate entries in the interfaces file or you can enter the port information by using *sybinit*.

Running *sybinit*

To start the *sybinit* process, go to the $SYBASE/install SQL Server 11 directory and issue the following command:

```
sybinit
```

If *sybinit* is not found, make sure you added the SQL Server 11 directories to your path. When *sybinit* starts, you see the main menu, shown in Figure 4-9.

```
SYBINIT
1.  Release Directory: /usr/u/sybase
2.  Edit / View Interfaces File
3.  Configure a Server product
4.  Configure an Open Client/Server product
ctrl-a Accept and Continue, ctrl-x Exit Screen, ? Help.
```

*Figure 4-9: The **sybinit** main menu*

Choose menu option 3, "Configure a Server product." In the next window, choose "SQL Server." Finally, choose "Configure a New SQL Server." The *sybinit* utility displays the SQL Server Configuration window.

Configuring a New SQL Server 11

As shown in Figure 4-10, the SQL Server Configuration menu offers several options for configuring different elements of SQL Server. To fully configure the new SQL Server 11, you must complete all of the steps listed in this menu. In most cases, you can choose the default values for language, character sets, and sort order, and you can leave auditing inactive.

```
SQL SERVER CONFIGURATION
1.   CONFIGURE SERVER'S INTERFACES FILE ENTRY        Incomplete
2.   MASTER DEVICE CONFIGURATION                     Incomplete
3.   SYBSYSTEMPROCS DATABASE CONFIGURATION           Incomplete
4.   SET ERRORLOG LOCATION                           Incomplete
5.   CONFIGURE DEFAULT BACKUP SERVER                 Incomplete
6.   CONFIGURE LANGUAGES                             Incomplete
7.   CONFIGURE CHARACTER SETS                        Incomplete
8.   CONFIGURE SORT ORDER                            Incomplete
9.   ACTIVATE AUDITING                               Incomplete
```

Figure 4-10: *The SQL Server Configuration menu*

Figure 4-11 shows an example of the *sybsystemprocs* Database Configuration screen. If you have already created the new device, enter *no* for option 3, "create new device for the sybsystemprocs database."

```
SYBSYSTEMPROCS DATABASE CONFIGURATION

1.  sybsystemprocs database size (Meg): 16

2.  sybsystemprocs logical device name: sysprocsdev

3.  create new device for the sybsystemprocs database: yes

4.  physical name of new device: /usr/u/sybase/sysprocs.dat

5.  size of the new device (Meg): 16
```

Figure 4-11: *The **sybsystemprocs** Database Configuration screen*

If you try to increase the size of the database by using option 1, "sybsystemprocs database size," you might receive the following error message:

```
'sybsystemprocs' database size ('18' megabytes) is larger than the size of
the device on which it is to be placed ('16' megabytes).
Press <return> to continue.
```

If this happens, simply increase the size of the device by using option 5, "size of the new device," before you increase the value in option 1. Of course, this assumes that you specified the correct size for the UNIX device. You should also keep in mind that a device is exclusively reserved. If you have a 100-MB device for your *master* device and you use *sybinit* to allocate 25 MB for the *master* device, the remaining 75 MB cannot be used by any other device.

Once you complete all the options of the SQL Server Configuration menu, you can start the configuration process by pressing Ctrl-a. If you have successfully completed all the menu options, *sybinit* asks whether you want to start the configuration process. Enter *yes*, and *sybinit* configures and initializes the new SQL Server 11. If you did not complete all of the configuration options, *sybinit* does not allow you to continue. You must first complete the SQL Server Configuration menu.

When *sybinit* finishes, you see the following message:

```
Configuration Completed Successfully.
```

TIP!   As with the upgrade method, you can look for any problems by checking the upgrade logs and the SQL Server 11 errorlog.

Setting the *sa* Password

At this point in the installation process, SQL Server 11 has an *sa* user account with a null password. For a null password, just press Return key at the password prompt or leave the password blank on the command line. You should log onto SQL Server 11 with this *sa* account and change the password. Remember that passwords must be least six characters long in SQL Server 11. You change the password by using the *sp_password* command. This command has the following syntax:

```
sp_password old_password, new_password, <login>
```

The following example logs onto SQL Server 11 immediately after installation and sets the *sa* password to *abC3kmit*:

```
isql -Usa -P -Sserver_name
sp_password null, abC3kmit, sa
go
```

Using Resource Files

If you are upgrading or installing more than one SQL Server 11, you may want to use *sybinit*'s resource file facility. This facility allows you to generate a file that contains all the information you enter during a *sybinit* session. You can use this file (with slight changes) to install another SQL Server. If you use resource files, you do not have to interactively complete all the steps in the *sybinit* process. Instead, you simply start *sybinit* with the resource file and it automatically completes the task.

To generate a resource file from your *sybinit* session, simply press Ctrl-w at the end of the *sybinit* session, just before you exit *sybinit*. By pressing Ctrl-w, you generate a resource file named *resource.dmp* in the $SYBASE/init/logs directory. At the prompt that *sybinit* displays, you can choose a different name for the resource file.

You can also use basic templates as resource files. You edit these templates and add the appropriate values by using a text editor. You can find the templates in the $SYBASE/init/sqlsrv directory. The install template is named *new.rs* and the upgrade template is named *upgrade.rs*.

TIP!   On some platforms, you cannot use the generated resource file directly. You must copy its information into one of the templates. For details, see your *Sybase SQL Server Installation and Configuration Guide*.

The following example shows a few lines from a resource file:

```
sybinit.charset: roman8
sybinit.language: us_english
sybinit.release_directory: /work1/home/man1/sybase11
sybinit.boot_directory: /work1/home/man1/sybase11
# -END_ATTRIBUTES-
```

Before starting *sybinit* with a resource file, make sure you make any necessary changes to the resource file. For example, make sure you change the device names, because you cannot reuse the same device.

To use *sybinit* with a resource file, start it with the -r flag. This command has the following syntax:

```
sybinit -r resource_file_name [-option] [parameter]
```

TIP!   For a complete list of options and parameters, refer to Appendix B in the *Sybase SQL Server Installation and Configuration Guide*.

You may want to consider using the -T IGNORE_WARNINGS flag. The *sybinit* utility generates warnings for many reasons—for example, using an operating system file for the *master* device. Without this IGNORE_WARNINGS flag, *sybinit* terminates if any warnings are generated.

The following command starts *sybinit* with the *resource.dmp* file and the IGNORE_WARNINGS flag:

```
sybinit -r resource.dmp -T IGNORE_WARNINGS
```

Summary

This chapter describes the process of upgrading a SQL Server in a UNIX environment. You use *sybinit* to upgrade an existing SQL Server or install a new SQL Server. Careful planning—including gathering the necessary information and completing your migration worksheet—provides the key to a successful migration. The next three chapters describe the new features of SQL Server 11, and give a detailed account of how to use them.

Migration Checklist

The following list summarizes the key migration tasks covered in this chapter:

- Complete your migration worksheet by recording such information as port numbers and devices.
- Decide whether you want to use the upgrade method or the install method.
- Use *sybinit* to configure and install SQL Server 11.
- Change the *sa* password.

Command Reference

sp_password

Syntax

```
sp_password old_password, new_password
```

Example

```
sp_password 123456, aj5Gh1
```

sybinit

Syntax

```
sybinit -r resource_file_name [-option] [parameter]
```

Example

```
sybinit -r resource.dmp -T IGNORE_WARNING
```

5

Configuring SQL Server 11

In This Chapter

- ◆ Understanding configuration parameters

- ◆ Displaying and setting configuration parameters

- ◆ Learning about the changes to the *sp_configure* command and its output

- ◆ Using *sp_configure*'s *read*, *write*, *verify*, and *restore* subcommands

- ◆ Editing the configuration file

- ◆ Learning about new configuration parameters

- ◆ Working with configuration groups

- ◆ Using display levels and the *sp_displaylevel* command

- ◆ Using the *reconfigure* command

- ◆ Resolving configuration management issues

SQL Server 11 includes many changes to and improvements over previous releases—the most noticeable of these changes involve server configuration. Compared to previous versions, configuration management in SQL Server 11 offers a new look and feel, greater flexibility, and enhanced features. With these improvements, SQL Server 11 provides simpler, yet more powerful, capabilities for server administration and performance and tuning than in previous versions.

In this chapter, you learn how to configure SQL Server 11 and you find out how this process has changed from previous releases. You explore all of the new configuration features and you see examples of their proper use. Throughout this and other chapters, you also learn how to configure SQL Server 11 to achieve maximum performance for specific situations.

How Has Configuration Changed in SQL Server 11?

To improve your control over SQL Server configuration, Sybase has modified the *sp_configure* command, added new functionality to the system, and more than doubled the number of parameters available for modifying the system's behavior. SQL Server 11 contains more than 100 user-definable parameters. Previous releases of SQL Server hide the configuration parameters in the first 2K block of the master device. SQL Server 11 simplifies configuration management by making all of the parameters readily available and viewable in the *configuration file*.

Although these parameters have default values, you will sometimes need to change them, to administer SQL Server 11 and to optimize its performance. You set these parameters by using the *sp_configure* command or by editing the configuration file, which provides a single, straightforward point of access for all server configuration tasks. You no longer need to use the buildmaster -y or -r commands or the *dbcc tune* command. In fact, Sybase has eliminated the buildmaster -y and -r commands, which you used to configure previous versions of SQL Server under certain circumstances.

Previous versions of SQL Server include numerous obscure, but useful, trace flags. In SQL Server 11, many of these are just simple configuration parameters. A *trace flag* is a command line parameter that you can use when you start SQL Server. In previous versions of SQL Server, you pass these parameters when you invoke the *dataserver* executable to start SQL Server. The -T flag identifies parameters that SQL Server considers to be trace flags. For example, the following command starts SQL Server 10.x with the *tcp no delay* trace flag (that is, trace flag 1610):

```
dataserver -d/dev/devicename -T1610
```

Don't worry if you are not familiar with trace flags. Sybase created configuration parameters to replace useful trace flags such as *tcp no delay* because most people are not familiar with trace flags. With SQL Server 11, you simply set the *tcp no delay* configuration parameter to make use of this high-performance feature. (Chapter 9, "SQL Server 11 Performance and Tuning," discusses *tcp no delay* in detail.)

What Are Configuration Parameters?

A *configuration parameter* is a setting that SQL Server uses to control some aspect of its behavior. SQL Server 11 maintains more than 100 of these user-definable settings, more than twice as many as in previous releases.

A user (usually the Database Administrator) can change these parameters to customize SQL Server 11. For example, the configuration parameter *number of open databases* specifies the maximum number of databases that can be open simultaneously. Setting this value too low might prevent a user from opening a needed database, while setting it too high might take valuable memory resources away from other parts of SQL Server. As shown in Figure 5-1, the use of memory for the user configuration parameters can take memory away from other parts of SQL Server.

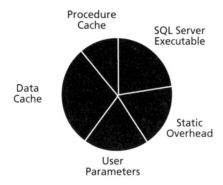

Figure 5-1: *SQL Server memory allocation*

A configuration parameter can be either dynamic or static. *Dynamic* parameters take effect as soon as you change their values. They require no further action from the user other than simply changing the values. On the other hand, changes to *static* parameters do not take effect until you restart the SQL Server. Static parameters reallocate internal memory structures in the SQL Server and this cannot occur until you restart the SQL Server.

Displaying and Setting Configuration Parameters

As in previous releases, you can display or set configuration parameters by using the *sp_configure* command. Although the basic use of this command has not changed with the release of SQL Server 11, *sp_configure* now offers additional functionality. In versions prior to SQL Server 11, the *sp_configure* command has the following syntax:

```
sp_configure [parameter[, value] ]
```

For example, in versions prior to SQL Server 11, you display information about the *open databases* parameter by entering the following command:

```
sp_configure "open databases"
go
```

When you execute this command, SQL Server displays the following information:

```
name             minimum   maximum      config_value   run_value
- - - - - - - -   - - - -   - - - - -    - - - - - -    - - - - -
open databases         5   2147483647            30           30
```

The following example shows how you set the *open databases* parameter in versions prior to SQL Server 11:

```
sp_configure "open databases", 25
go
```

When you execute this command, SQL Server displays the following information:

```
name             minimum   maximum      config_value   run_value
- - - - - - - -   - - - -   - - - - -    - - - - - -    - - - - -
open databases         5   2147483647            25           30
```

In SQL Server 11, the *sp_configure* command serves two major purposes. First, *sp_configure* allows you to interactively set or display a *configuration parameter*. This works in the same way as in previous releases, except that you can now specify either a single parameter or a group of related parameters. (The section "Configuration Groups," later in this chapter, explains the concept of groups.) To interactively set or display configuration parameters, you use the following syntax:

```
sp_configure [parameter [value] | group_name | non_unique_parameter_fragment]
```

The *sp_configure* command also allows you to manage the configuration file. (You learn about the details of the configuration file in the next section of this chapter.) For this purpose, you use the following syntax:

```
sp_configure "configuration file", 0, {"write" | "read" | "verify" |
"restore"} "file_name"
```

Understanding the Configuration File

SQL Server 11 makes use of a new feature known as the *configuration file*. This ASCII text file contains the values for all of the configuration parameters. You can display or edit the configuration file by using your text editor. This mechanism helps make all configuration parameters readily available and is useful for storing different sets of configurations or for replicating a specific configuration to numerous servers.

The following listing shows a sample configuration file:

```
############################################################################
#
#          Configuration File for the Sybase SQL Server
#
#          Please read the System Administration Guide (SAG)
#          before changing any of the values in this file.
#
############################################################################

[Configuration Options]

[General Information]

[Backup/Recovery]
     recovery interval in minutes = 1
     print recovery information = DEFAULT
     tape retention in days = DEFAULT

[Cache Manager]
     number of oam trips = DEFAULT
     number of index trips = DEFAULT
     procedure cache percent = 5
     memory alignment boundary = DEFAULT

[Named Cache:default data cache]
     cache size = DEFAULT
     cache status = default data cache

[4K I/O Buffer Pool]
     pool size = 5.0000M
     wash size = DEFAULT

[16K I/O Buffer Pool]
     pool size = 40.0000M
     wash size = DEFAULT

[Disk I/O]
     allow sql server async i/o = DEFAULT
     disk i/o structures = 200
```

```
    page utilization percent = DEFAULT
    number of devices = 80
    disable character set conversions = DEFAULT

[Network Communication]
    default network packet size = DEFAULT
    max network packet size = DEFAULT
    remote server pre-read packets = DEFAULT
    number of remote connections = DEFAULT
    allow remote access = DEFAULT
    number of remote logins = DEFAULT
    number of remote sites = DEFAULT
    max number network listeners = DEFAULT
    tcp no delay = DEFAULT
    allow sendmsg = DEFAULT
    syb_sendmsg port number = DEFAULT

[O/S Resources]
    max async i/os per engine = 200
    max async i/os per server = DEFAULT

[Physical Resources]

[Physical Memory]
    total memory = 102400
    additional network memory = DEFAULT
    lock shared memory = DEFAULT
    shared memory starting address = DEFAULT

[Processors]
    max online engines = 2
    min online engines = DEFAULT

[SQL Server Administration]
    number of open objects = 2000
    number of open databases = 50
    audit queue size = DEFAULT
    default database size = DEFAULT
    identity burning set factor = 500
    allow nested triggers = DEFAULT
    allow updates to system tables = DEFAULT
    print deadlock information = 1
    default fill factor percent = DEFAULT
    number of mailboxes = DEFAULT
    number of messages = DEFAULT
    number of alarms = DEFAULT
    number of pre-allocated extents = DEFAULT
    event buffers per engine = 8000
    cpu accounting flush interval = DEFAULT
    i/o accounting flush interval = DEFAULT
    sql server clock tick length = DEFAULT
```

```
    runnable process search count = 1
    i/o polling process count = DEFAULT
    time slice = DEFAULT
    deadlock retries = DEFAULT
    cpu grace time = DEFAULT
    number of sort buffers = DEFAULT
    sort page count = DEFAULT
    number of extent i/o buffers = DEFAULT
    size of auto identity column = DEFAULT
    identity grab size = DEFAULT
    lock promotion HWM = DEFAULT
    lock promotion LWM = DEFAULT
    lock promotion PCT = DEFAULT
    housekeeper free write percent = DEFAULT
    partition groups = DEFAULT
    partition spinlock ratio = DEFAULT

[User Environment]
    number of user connections = 160
    stack size = DEFAULT
    stack guard size = DEFAULT
    systemwide password expiration = DEFAULT
    permission cache entries = DEFAULT
    user log cache size = DEFAULT
    user log cache spinlock ratio = DEFAULT

[Lock Manager]
    number of locks = 50000
    deadlock checking period = DEFAULT
    freelock transfer block size = 1000
    max engine freelocks = DEFAULT
    address lock spinlock ratio = DEFAULT
    page lock spinlock ratio = DEFAULT
    table lock spinlock ratio = DEFAULT
```

NOTE: During the upgrade process, the *sybinit* utility creates a default configuration file for your SQL Server 11.

In releases prior to SQL Server 11, when SQL Server starts up, it obtains its default parameter settings from the first 2K block of the master device. Because SQL Server hides these values in the master device, they are not accessible to users. In SQL Server 11, these values are readily available in the configuration file.

How the Configuration File Works

When you boot SQL Server 11, it reads in the values from the configuration file. By default, SQL Server 11 looks for a configuration file named *servername*.cfg in the $SYBASE directory.

TIP! SQL Server 11 uses the environmental variable $DSLISTEN for the *servername* portion of the configuration file's name and the $SYBASE variable for the Sybase home directory. So, the default configuration file is *servername*.cfg, where *servername* = $DSLISTEN.

The following example demonstrates how SQL Server 11 finds the default configuration file. Assume that you define the previously mentioned environmental variables as follows:

```
$SYBASE = /home/sybase11
$DSLISTEN = MYSERV
```

This means your default configuration file has the following path and filename:

```
/home/sybase11/MYSERV.cfg
```

If you have a server named MYSERV and your Sybase home directory is */home/sybase11*, when SQL Server 11 starts up, it sets the configuration parameters to the values specified in the file */home/sybase11/MYSERV.cfg*. Figure 5-2 shows SQL Server 11 reading configuration parameters from its default configuration file at bootup time.

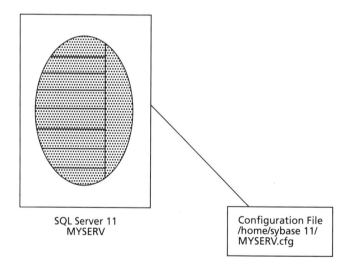

SQL Server 11
MYSERV

Configuration File
/home/sybase 11/
MYSERV.cfg

Figure 5-2: *Reading configuration parameters from the default configuration file*

You can change the name and the path for the default configuration file. If you do this, you must specify the new name and path in SQL Server's *runfile*. You do this by using the new -c command line flag for *dataserver*. (Recall that *dataserver* is the SQL Server executable, which you usually start from the *runfile*.) The -c flag to *dataserver* specifies the path and the name of the configuration file that SQL Server should use at boot time.

TIP!   The -c flag is required only for the default configuration file—that is, the file that you want SQL Server 11 to read when it boots. As detailed later in this chapter, you may have numerous configuration files with different names which you use with *sp_configure's read* and *write* subcommands. Because SQL Server doesn't need to read in these files at boot time, you don't need to point to them with the -c flag.

The following example shows a *runfile* that includes the -c flag:

```
/home/sybase11/bin/dataserver -d/ch_ts2/devices/master.dat
-e/home/sybase11/install/errorlog -c/home/sybase11/MSERV_oltp.cfg
```

If you boot the SQL Server named MYSERV_oltp by using this *runfile*, the SQL Server sets the configuration parameters to the values specified in */home/sybase11/MSERV_oltp.cfg*. If the file you specify with the -c flag is not found at boot time, the SQL Server will not start up.

When SQL Server 11 boots, it creates a file named $SYBASE/*servername*.bak. This file, which contains the boot-up configuration settings, exists solely as a backup in case your configuration file is accidentally overwritten or lost. Note that SQL Server 11 overwrites this backup file each time you start the system, so you always have only one copy of $SYBASE/*servername*.bak. For example, assume that you boot the SQL Server with configuration file A and then bring down the SQL Server. If you then boot the SQL Server with configuration file B, the backup configuration file will contain the values from configuration file A.

In addition to their ease of use, configuration files can help you perform several useful tasks. By using configuration files, you can maintain several sets of parameters for use in different situations. For example, you might maintain a configuration file with settings that optimize SQL Server for use as a server for a decision support system (DSS). A DSS typically performs complex queries, joining several tables together and returning large result sets. For this type of application, you might configure SQL Server 11 to use named caches and large I/O. (Chapter 6, "The Buffer Manager," discusses named caches and large I/O.)

You might maintain another configuration file with settings that optimize SQL Server as the server for an online transaction processing (OLTP) system. An OLTP system typically performs brief updates and inserts on a table. The appropriate configuration for this type of server differs from that of a decision support server. For example, you would not use large I/O for an OLTP system, and you would maintain the update tables in a cache. You might also change the way in which the system flushes the cache buffers.

To summarize, by using configuration files, you can maintain numerous configuration setups. When you need a particular setup, you simply restart SQL Server 11 using the appropriate configuration file.

With configuration files, you can also replicate the settings from one SQL Server to other systems in your environment. After finding the optimal settings on one SQL Server, you can use that setup on the other SQL Servers in your environment by simply copying that configuration file to the other systems and using it to boot the other SQL Servers. Figure 5-3 shows SQL Servers on two host systems, each using a copy of the same configuration file.

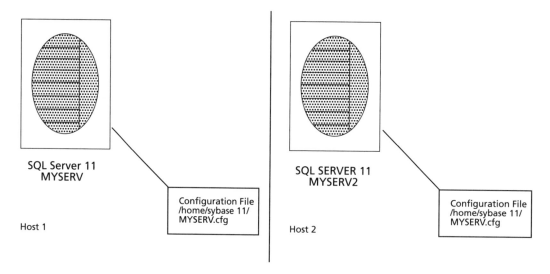

Figure 5-3: *The configuration file mechanism in SQL Server 11 allows you to easily replicate your optimal setup on numerous systems.*

Finding Default Configuration Values

In the default configuration file that's created when you install SQL Server 11, many of the values are set with the word *default* instead of a number. Similarly, the *sysconfigures* table lists zeros in the value fields for those parameters. The zeros mean that SQL Server uses its default values for those parameters. To determine the value SQL Server 11 actually uses for any of those defaults, look up the parameter in the *System Administration Guide*.

Setting Values in the Configuration File

With the introduction of the configuration file in SQL Server 11, you now have two means for configuring your system: using a text editor to change the settings in the configuration file, or using the *sp_configure* command to set a specific parameter. The following sections provide in-depth coverage of these methods.

Setting Values in the Configuration File by Using a Text Editor

You can change configuration parameter settings by editing the configuration file. For example, to add a new named cache, you simply add the appropriate lines to the configuration file. SQL Server 11 processes your changes when it reads the modified configuration file.

TIP!   When you modify the configuration file, you must maintain the correct format; otherwise, the file will fail verification.

The following example shows a section of the configuration file *before* you add a new named cache:

```
[Named Cache:default data cache]
    cache size = DEFAULT
    cache status = default data cache

[4K I/O Buffer Pool]
    pool size = 5.0000M
    wash size = DEFAULT
```

This example shows the same section of the configuration file *after* you add the new named cache *new_cache1*:

```
[Named Cache:default data cache]
    cache size = DEFAULT
    cache status = default data cache

[Named Cache:new_cache1]
    cache size = 1M
    cache status = mixed cache
```

```
[4K I/O Buffer Pool]
    pool size = 5.0000M
    wash size = DEFAULT
```

Setting Values in the Configuration File by Using the *sp_configure* Command

In addition to editing the configuration file with a text editor, you can use any of the four new subcommands to *sp_configure*. In SQL Server 11, the *sp_configure* command includes a new parameter:

```
"configuration file"
```

This parameter—the phrase, *configuration file*, enclosed in quotation marks—allows interaction between SQL Server 11 and a configuration file. By using this parameter with the *sp_configure* command, you can reset SQL Server 11 values to those stored in a specified configuration file or you can write out current SQL Server 11 values to a configuration file. This form of *sp_configure* also allows you to verify or restore the settings in a configuration file.

In SQL Server 11, the *sp_configure* command has the following syntax:

```
sp_configure "configuration file" [,0, "subcommand","filename"]
```

The *sp_configure* command takes the following arguments:

- "configuration file". As mentioned, this new parameter to the *sp_configure* command permits interaction between SQL Server 11 and a specified configuration file. (When using this parameter, you must enclose the phrase *configuration file* in quotation marks.)

- 0. The zero is required for backward compatibility, but SQL Server 11 ignores it.

- "subcommand". You enter a subcommand to specify the action you want SQL Server 11 to perform with the configuration file. The valid subcommands are "read", "write", "verify", and "restore".

- "filename". This argument specifies the name of the configuration file that is being used.

TIP!   You must enclose the subcommand and the filename in quotation marks.

For example, the following command specifies that you want to write the configuration parameters to a file called *config1.cfg*:

```
sp_configure "configuration file",0, "write", "config1.cfg"
go
```

To verify the configuration parameters in a file called *config2.cfg*, you issue the following command:

```
sp_configure "configuration file", 0, "verify", "config2.cfg"
go
```

Reading from the Configuration File

The *read* subcommand reads in parameter values from the specified configuration file. This subcommand performs a validation check on all of the values contained in the specified configuration file and retrieves into SQL Server 11 only those values that pass validation. In other words, SQL Server 11 determines whether each setting in the configuration file contains a valid value for that parameter. The *read* subcommand has the following syntax:

```
sp_configure "configuration file" ,0, "read", "filename"
```

The *read* subcommand works only for dynamic parameter values. If you try to change static parameters with the *read* subcommand, the command fails (unless the configuration file contains the same static parameter settings as SQL Server's current settings of static parameters) and SQL Server 11 prints a message to the errorlog. If you try to change both static and dynamic parameters, the read fails and none of the values are changed. In this case, SQL Server 11 still performs validation on the specified configuration file but the configuration settings remain unchanged.

If some parameters are missing from the configuration file, the currently used values remain in effect. Consequently, you can create several different configuration files that each contain a few specific values. When you need a particular setup, you simply read in the appropriate configuration file to set the necessary parameter values for the task at hand. When you complete that task, you simply reset SQL Server 11 to its original values.

To change the configuration parameters to the values in the file *configA.cfg*, you issue the following command:

```
sp_configure "configuration file", 0, "read" "configA.cfg"
go
```

To change the configuration parameters to the values in the file *configB.cfg*, you issue the following command:

```
sp_configure "configuration file", 0, "read" "configB.cfg"
go
```

Writing to the Configuration File

The *write* subcommand writes out the current SQL Server 11 parameter values to a specified file. The *write* subcommand has the following syntax:

```
sp_configure "configuration file" ,0, "write", "filename"
```

If the specified file ("*filename*") already exists, SQL Server 11 writes an informational message to the errorlog and renames the existing file using the following convention: *filename*.001, *filename*.002, *filename*.003, ... *filename*.999. So, if the files filename.cfg and filename.001 exist when you issue the *write* subcommand, the original filename.cfg is renamed filename.002 and filename.cfg is written as the new file.

As mentioned earlier in this chapter, if you don't specify a directory for the filename, SQL Server writes the file in the $SYBASE directory. The naming convention for the boot-time configuration file is *servername*.cfg. In a standard environment, you should follow this convention, and thus have a *servername*.cfg configuration file, several variants with filenames that follow the *servername*.001, *servername*.002 convention, and several other configuration files with completely different names that you use for specific situations such as the DSS and OLTP scenarios described earlier in this chapter. Don't forget that you also have a backup file named *servername*.bak.

TIP! Each time you change a configuration value by using the *sp_configure* command, SQL Server creates a new configuration file, using the previously described naming convention. For example, assume that your $SYBASE directory contains MYSERV.cfg and MYSERV.001, and you then issue the following command:

```
sp_configure "number of open databases",50
```

Your $SYBASE directory now contains the following files: MYSERV.cfg, MYSERV.001, and MYSERV.002. The file MYSERV.cfg has the *number of open databases* parameter set to 50, and MYSERV.002 contains the values found in the original MYSERV.cfg.

The following listing shows a typical set of configuration files in a $SYBASE directory:

```
-rw-rw-rw-   1 sybase    unixdba    3423 Jul 15 11:32 NYTSRV1.bak
-rw-rw-r—    1 sybase    unixdba    3423 Jul 16 17:08 NYTSRV1.cfg
-rw-rw-r—    1 sybase    unixdba    3291 May 24 15:19 NYTSRV1.001
-rw-rw-rw-   1 sybase    unixdba    3291 Jun  3 10:33 NYTSRV1.002
-rw-rw-r—    1 sybase    unixdba    3285 Jun  3 12:01 NYTSRV1.003
-rw-rw-r—    1 sybase    unixdba    3291 Jun 16 03:51 NYTSRV1.004
-rw-rw-r—    1 sybase    unixdba    3291 Jun 18 12:20 NYTSRV1.005
-rw-rw-r—    1 sybase    unixdba    3285 Jun 19 08:39 NYTSRV1.006
-rw-rw-r—    1 sybase    unixdba     868 Jan 22 18:03 NYTSRV1_daily
-rw-r—r—     1 sybase    unixdba     316 Mar 24 17:37 NYTSRV1_weekly
```

The combination of the *read* and *write* subcommands offers tremendous flexibility for managing SQL Server's configuration. You can maintain many different configuration files and easily use them to suit your various needs. As mentioned, you might have one file that optimizes SQL Server for a DSS environment and another file for an OLTP environment. You can also use a configuration file to replicate the same setup to many different systems.

Verifying the Configuration File

The *verify* subcommand checks the validity of the values in the specified configuration file. The *verify* subcommand has the following syntax:

```
sp_configure "configuration file" ,0, "verify", "filename"
```

Note that this command does not change any parameter settings in SQL Server 11 or the configuration file. You might use this command after changing a configuration file with a text editor, or to check a possibly corrupted file.

The following example validates the contents of the configuration file *configC.cfg*:

```
sp_configure "configuration file", 0, "verify", "configC.cfg"
go
```

If the specified file contains an invalid value, this command reports an error.

Restoring the Configuration File

This section provides in-depth coverage of the *restore* subcommand, because this subcommand tends to cause confusion. The *restore* subcommand has the following syntax:

```
sp_configure "configuration file" ,0, "restore", "filename"
```

Like the *write* subcommand, *restore* creates a configuration file with values from SQL Server 11. The difference between these subcommands involves the source of the values that SQL Server 11 uses for creating the configuration files, which in turn determines the appropriate use for each subcommand.

When you issue the *restore* subcommand, SQL Server 11 writes a configuration file that contains the current *config values*—that is, the values SQL Server lists in the Config Value column of the *sp_configure* output:

```
Parameter Name                    Default  Memory Used  Config Value  Run Value
------------------------------    -------  -----------  ------------  ---------
additional network memory              0            0          1024          0
allow remote access                    1            0             1          1
default network packet size          512            0           512        512
```

The *restore* subcommand obtains these config values from the *sysconfigures* system table. In contrast, the *write* subcommand obtains its values from the *syscurconfigs* table. As listed in Table 5-1, the settings from *sysconfigures* represent current config values; the *syscurconfigs* table contains current *run-time* values.

Table 5-1: *Values Used by the **restore** and **write** Subcommands*

Subcommand	System Table Used	Type of Values
restore	*sysconfigures*	Current config values
write	*syscurconfigs*	Current run-time values

Run-time values are the settings that SQL Server 11 is currently using. Config values are the settings currently configured in SQL Server 11. Note that a config value may differ from a run-time value. For example, if a DBA uses the *sp_configure* command to update several static parameters but has not yet restarted the SQL Server, those static parameters have different config and run-time values. The following example shows how this works.

First, the DBA issues the command to display the current setting for the parameter *number of user connections:*

```
sp_configure "number of user connections"
go
```

SQL Server 11 responds with the following information:

```
Parameter Name                    Default  Memory Used  Config Value  Run Value
------------------------------    -------  -----------  ------------  ---------
number of user connections            25            0           400        400
```

The DBA also issues the command to display the current setting for the parameter *number of open databases*:

```
sp_configure "number of open databases"
go
```

SQL Server 11 displays the following information:

Parameter Name	Default	Memory Used	Config Value	Run Value
number of open databases	12	0	25	25

Then, the DBA updates the settings for these parameters:

```
sp_configure "number of open databases", 40
sp_configure "number of user connections", 500
```

If the DBA were to issue the *restore* subcommand at this point, the configuration file would contain the following values:

- Number of open databases: 40

- Number of user connections: 500

On the other hand, if the DBA issues the *write* subcommand, the configuration file contains the following values:

- Number of open databases: 25

- Number of user connections: 400

You already know when and how to use the *write* subcommand, and you now know how the *write* subcommand differs from the *restore* subcommand. The question remains: When do you use the *restore* subcommand?

In essence, the *restore* subcommand exists for one purpose: creating a new configuration file in the event that all copies of SQL Server 11's configuration file are lost or damaged. You might be wondering why you can't use the *write* subcommand to restore the missing configuration file. Although this may seem logical, this is not a practical solution. If SQL Server 11 cannot find a configuration file when it tries to boot, it uses its default values, which SQL Server 11 permanently stores in a static array. If SQL Server 11 must boot without a configuration file, it sets its run-time values to these factory-installed defaults. Fortunately, these default values do not overwrite the config values in the *sysconfigures* table. If they did, you might lose months of work in fine-tuning your server.

Because SQL Server stores your previous config values in the *sysconfigures* table, you can issue the *restore* subcommand to produce a configuration file with those values. You cannot do this with the *write* subcommand, because that subcommand writes the run-time values. (Recall that SQL Server sets its run-time values to the factory-installed defaults when it boots without a configuration file.)

If all copies of SQL Server 11's configuration file are lost or damaged, you should immediately issue the *restore* subcommand and then reboot SQL Server. Make sure that SQL Server reads the configuration file you just created with the *restore* subcommand. To do this, either name it *servername*.cfg or ensure that the runfile points to that file.

A Case Study

The following common configuration problem demonstrates how SQL Server 11 simplifies configuration management. Assume that you increase the number of user connections from its default value of 25 to 2,000. Because *number of user connections* is a static parameter, you then bring down the SQL Server and try to restart it. You attempt this reconfiguration during the business day (only on your development server, of course), and you are horrified to see that SQL Server will not start.

As your phone starts ringing off the hook with calls from irate developers, you check the errorlog, which includes an error message stating that you don't have enough memory to start SQL Server. You look up the parameter *number of user connections* in the *System Administration Guide* and find that each user connection uses approximately 50K of memory (70K in SQL Server 11). Consequently, your reconfiguration attempted to grab 100 MB of memory from SQL Server. Because you have 80 MB of memory available in your SQL Server, you decide to reset the number of user connections to 1,000.

In releases prior to SQL Server 11, you would have to reset some or all of the configuration parameters to their new or default values by using the buildmaster utility. Once SQL Server came up with the new or default values, you would have to reconfigure the parameters to the desired values and then reboot SQL Server, for the changes to take effect. With SQL Server 11, however, you simply open the configuration file with a text editor and change the *number of user connections* setting to 1,000. When you restart SQL Server 11, it automatically uses the new value and successfully boots up with 1,000 user connections.

You should also note that SQL Server 11 lets you determine the *total memory* value for a server by looking in the configuration file, even if SQL Server 11 is not running. In the preceding example, you need to know how much memory the system allocates to SQL Server, so that you can estimate how many user connections the system can support. Although you might know that number without checking the configuration file, having easy access to this information simplifies configuration management—especially in an environment where you maintain numerous servers.

New Configuration Features in SQL Server 11

In addition to dozens of new configuration parameters, SQL Server 11 introduces three new features to simplify system administration:

- Changes to two of *sp_configure*'s output columns

- The concept of groups

- The concept of display levels

TIP!   In addition to these enhancements, some parameter names have changed.
See Appendix B for a list of these changes.

These changes affect both the look and feel of SQL Server's display and the content of that display. Specifically, these changes help you to focus on only those parameters that you need to examine. They also help SQL Server to provide more detailed and useful information about the parameters. The following sections examine these new features.

New Format for Displaying Configuration Parameters

The columnar output of *sp_configure* has changed somewhat from previous releases. Specifically, two of the five columns of information differ from those displayed by previous releases.

In versions prior to SQL Server 11, the server displays parameter output in the following five columns:

- *name*. The name of the parameter.

- *minimum*. The minimum value allowed.

- *maximum*. The maximum value allowed.

- *config_value*. The new setting for the parameter. For a static parameter, the config value does not take effect until you restart SQL Server.

- *run_value*. The currently used setting for the parameter.

The column for displaying the maximum value doesn't provide particularly useful information because this represents the maximum value accepted by the parameter's data type rather than the maximum practical value for the parameter. For example, the maximum value listed for *recovery interval* is 32,767. This represents the maximum value for a signed, two-byte integer rather than a practical recovery interval value.

The following example shows the system output for the *user connections* parameter, for versions prior to SQL Server 11:

```
name               minimum    maximum     config_value   run_value
----------------   -------    ----------  ------------   ---------
user connections         5    2147483647           400         400
```

Like previous versions, SQL Server 11 displays *sp_configure* output in five columns, but two of the columns differ from those displayed by previous releases. SQL Server 11 replaces the columns *minimum* and *maximum* with two new columns: *Memory Used* and *Default*. SQL Server 11 uses the following columns for displaying the output from the *sp_configure* command:

- *Parameter Name*. The name of the parameter. Although this column provides the same information as in previous releases, note that the column heading has changed from *name* to *Parameter Name*. Also remember that many of the parameter names in SQL Server 11 differ slightly from those in previous versions. See Appendix B for a complete list of parameter name changes.

- *Default*. The out-of-the-box value for each parameter—that is, the value with which SQL Server ships.

- *Memory Used*. The amount of memory (in kilobytes) used by the parameter setting. SQL Server calculates this value based on the current setting for the parameter. Many configuration parameters use system memory resources, and the information in this column simplifies the process of monitoring memory use.

- *Config Value*. The parameter's current setting, which may not be in effect, yet.

- *Run Value*. The currently used value of the parameter.

The following example shows the system output for the *user connections* parameter in SQL Server 11:

```
Parameter Name                   Default  Memory Used  Config Value   Run Value
------------------------------   -------  -----------  ------------   ---------
number of user connections            25            0           400         400
```

Configuration Groups

SQL Server 11 uses hierarchical groups to organize its configuration parameters. Each parameter belongs to a primary group and may also belong to several secondary groups. For example, the parameter *number of remote connections* belongs to the *Network Communications* group as its primary group. However, you also find this parameter in the *SQL Server Administration* group and the *Memory Use* group.

SQL Server 11 recognizes the following configuration groups:

- Backup/Recovery
- Cache Manager
- Disk I/O
- General Information
- Languages
- Lock Manager
- Memory Use
- Network Communication
- Operating System Resources
- Physical Memory
- Processors
- SQL Server Administration
- User Environment

Recall that the new syntax of the *sp_configure* command allows you to specify a group name:

```
sp_configure [parameter [value] | group_name | non_unique_parameter_fragment]
```

By using a group name with the *sp_configure* command, you can display a list of the parameters that belong to that group. For example, you can obtain a listing of the parameters in the *Disk I/O* group by entering the following command:

```
sp_configure "Disk I/O"
go
```

When you execute this command, SQL Server 11 displays the following output:

```
Group: Disk I/O
Parameter Name            Default  Memory Used  Config Value  Run Value
-----------------------   -------  -----------  ------------  -----------
allow sql server async i/o    1         0             1            1
disk i/o structures         256         0           256          256
number of devices            10         0            10           10
page utilization percent     95         0            95           95
```

With this support for groups, the *sp_configure* command allows you to simultaneously view several related parameters. As you work with the various parameters and become familiar with their respective groups, you will soon recognize the benefits of this feature.

Without groups, you could use two methods for isolating several parameters. You could either run the *sp_configure* command several times and write down all of the information or you could create a script that would redirect to a file the output of several *sp_configure* commands. Working with groups provides an efficient alternative to these methods.

TIP! When you enter the *sp_configure* command, you must specify the correct name for any group or parameter. Any mistakes in spelling or case will cause the command to fail. For example, the following commands both produce errors:

  sp_configure "Network communication"
  sp_configure "Network Communications"

In the first command, the first letter in *communication* should be capitalized. In the second command, the correct name for the specified group does not end with the letter *s*.

However, the following command works correctly:

  sp_configure "Net"

The *sp_configure* command parses parameters as "%parameter%", where % is the standard Sybase wildcard character.

Listing the Configuration Groups

In SQL Server 11, you can display a list of all the configuration groups and their respective parameters by running the *sp_configure* command with no parameters:

```
sp_configure
go
```

For each group listed in the resulting output, SQL Server displays a group heading and the parameters that belong to that group. The following excerpt shows the format of this output:

```
Group: Configuration Options

Group: Backup/Recovery

Parameter Name               Default  Memory Used  Config Value  Run Value
-------------------------    -------  -----------  ------------  -----------
allow remote access             1          0            1            1
print recovery information      0          0            0            0
recovery interval in minutes    5          0            1            1
tape retention in days          0          0            0            0

Group: Cache Manager

Parameter Name               Default  Memory Used  Config Value  Run Value
-------------------------    -------  -----------  ------------  -----------
memory alignment boundary     2048         0          2048         2048
number of index trips           0          0            0            0
number of oam trips             0          0            0            0
procedure cache percent        20        9136           5            5
total data cache size           0      167352           0         167352
total memory                 7500      204800        102400       102400
.
.
.
Group: User Environment

Parameter Name               Default  Memory Used  Config Value  Run Value
-------------------------    -------  -----------  ------------  -----------
default network packet size   512       #338          512          512
number of pre-allocated extent  2         0            2            2
number of user connections     25      11948          160          160
permission cache entries       15        #91           15           15
stack guard size             4096       #784         4096         4096
stack size                  34816      #6665        34816        34816
systemwide password expiration  0         0            0            0
user log cache size          2048         0          2048         2048
user log cache spinlock ratio  20         0           20           20
(return status = 0)
```

Appendix C provides a complete listing of all the configuration groups.

TIP!   When you examine the complete list of parameters generated by entering the *sp_configure* command with no parameters, remember that SQL Server lists several parameters more than once (because they belong to more than one group).

Note that the *Physical Resources* group contains the subgroups *Physical Memory* and *Processors*. However, the *Physical Resources* group does not contain any parameters of its own. This group-subgroup relationship can cause confusion because the *sp_configure* output does not indent the information about the *Physical Resources* subgroups:

```
Group: Physical Resources
Group: Physical Memory
Parameter Name                  Default  Memory Used  Config Value  Run Value
-------------------------       -------  -----------  ------------  ----------
additional network memory          0           0            0           0
lock shared memory                 0           0            0           0
shared memory starting address     0           0            0           0
total memory                    7500           0        15000       15000

Group: Processors
Parameter Name                  Default  Memory Used  Config Value  Run Value
-------------------------       -------  -----------  ------------  ----------
max online engines                 1           0            1           1
min online engines                 1           0            1           1
```

You should also note that the *sp_configure* output begins with the following line:

```
Group: Configuration Options
```

This indicates that each group is a subgroup of the *Configuration Options* group.

Working with Configuration Groups

By using groups, you can work with a subset of the parameters that SQL Server 11 supports and thus focus on only those parameters that interest you. As the following scenario demonstrates, SQL Server's configuration groups can also help you identify other parameters that might relate to the task at hand.

Assume that you want to change the network packet size for a client application—perhaps because this application transfers large amounts of data. For example, you might have a PowerBuilder® front-end application that calls a stored procedure in SQL Server. This stored procedure then returns 2,500 rows of information to the front-end application, with each row containing 200 bytes of data. In other words, SQL Server transfers more than 500,000 bytes of information to the client.

TIP!   Note that *more than* 500,000 bytes will pass through the network. In addition to the data, meta-data is sent across the network. *Meta-data* is extra data that the SQL Server uses in its network protocols, to describe the data being sent. You must be aware of this overhead when dealing with network packet issues; otherwise, you might underestimate the amount of information traveling across the network.

The initial value for SQL Server's default network packet size is 512 bytes. Unless a client application specifies otherwise, SQL Server uses this default packet size. You might want to use a larger network packet size for the client application in this example, but a client application can only use packets as large as the value of the *maximum network packet size* parameter. For example, if you increase the maximum network packet size from 512 bytes to 2,048 bytes, the client application can transfer four times more data with each packet. If you look up *maximum network packet size* in the *System Administration Guide*, you see that this parameter belongs to the *Network Communication* group. Now, issue the following command to see all the related parameters of the *Network Communication* group:

```
sp_configure "Network Communication"
go
```

SQL Server 11 responds by displaying the following information:

```
Group: Network Communication

Parameter Name                  Default  Memory Used  Config Value  Run Value
---------------------------     -------  -----------  ------------  -----------
additional network memory          0          0            0            0
allow remote access                1          0            1            1
default network packet size      512          0          512          512
max network packet size          512          0          512          512
number of remote connections      20          0           20           20
number of remote logins           20          0           20           20
number of remote sites            10          0           10           10
remote server pre-read packets     3          0            3            3
(return status = 0)
```

By looking at the *Network Communication* group, you remember that you must consider two other parameters when dealing with network packet sizes. You must check the default network packet size and change the *additional network memory* parameter, to allow the client application to use larger packet sizes. The maximum network packet size must be at least as large as the default packet size. Until you change this setting, SQL Server 11 has the maximum network packet size set to the same value as the default network packet size. The maximum network packet size must be at least as large as the packets that you want the client application to use.

Perhaps less obvious is the fact that you may have to increase the setting for the *additional network memory* parameter. If the maximum network packet size exceeds the default network packet size, you must increase the setting for the *additional network memory* parameter. SQL Server reserves all allocated network memory for users of the default packet size, and an additional memory pool handles any requests for a packet size larger than the default size. The *additional network memory* parameter sets this additional pool. So, any packets larger than the default network packet size are allocated from the *additional network memory* pool and do not affect the memory allocated to the SQL Server.

Display Levels

SQL Server 11 introduces the concept of *display levels*. In SQL Server 11, you can view the output of the *sp_configure* command on three different display levels:

- Basic

- Intermediate

- Comprehensive

Each display level allows you to view a wider range of parameters than the preceding level. Setting display levels does not change the amount of information that you see for a particular parameter; instead, this limits which parameters you see. For example, the intermediate level lets you see more rows of parameters for a given group than you can see with the basic level. And the comprehensive level lets you see more parameters than either the basic level or the intermediate level.

Changing Display Levels

To change a login's display level, you issue the *sp_displaylevel* command:

```
sp_displaylevel [login_name [,level] ]
```

The *sp_displaylevel* command has the following arguments:

- *login_name*. This must be a valid login name. If you have the *sa_role*, you can set the display level for any login name. Otherwise, you can only set your own level.

- *level*. This is one of the three levels: basic, intermediate, or comprehensive.

For example, the following command sets the display level to comprehensive for user *suzy*:

```
sp_displaylevel suzy, comprehensive
go
```

When you issue this command, SQL Server displays the following response:

```
The display level for login 'suzy' has been changed to 'comprehensive'.
```

To see the display level for your own login, enter the following command:

```
sp_displaylevel
go
```

SQL Server responds by displaying a message similar to the following example:

```
The current display level for login 'sa' is 'comprehensive'.
```

The following command lets a user other than *suzy* see the display level for the login *suzy*:

```
sp_displaylevel suzy
go
```

SQL Server responds to this command by displaying the following message:

```
The current display level for login 'suzy' is 'comprehensive'.
```

Working with Display Levels

The following examples show how changes in the display level affect the output from the *sp_configure* command. Specifically, these examples show how the display level controls the number of parameters that you can display by using the *sp_configure* command.

First, change the display level for the login *sa* to comprehensive by issuing the *sp_displaylevel* command:

```
sp_displaylevel sa, comprehensive
go
```

In response, SQL Server displays the following message:

```
The display level for login 'sa' has been changed to 'comprehensive'.
```

The comprehensive display level lets you see all of the parameters in a group. To see a complete list of the parameters in the *Network Communication* group, enter the following command:

```
sp_configure "Network Communication"
go
```

With the display level set to comprehensive, SQL Server displays all 10 parameters in the *Network Communication* group:

```
Group: Network Communication

Parameter Name              Default  Memory Used  Config Value  Run Value
--------------------------  -------  -----------  ------------  ----------
additional network memory      0         0            0             0
allow remote access            1         0            1             1
default network packet size  512         0          512           512
max network packet size      512         0          512           512
max number network listeners  15         0           15            15
number of remote connections  20         0           20            20
number of remote logins       20         0           20            20
number of remote sites        10         0           10            10
remote server pre-read packets 3         0            3             3
tcp no delay                   0         0            0             0
```

Now, change the display level for the login *sa* to intermediate:

```
sp_displaylevel sa, intermediate
go
```

SQL Server confirms this change:

```
The display level for login 'sa' has been changed to intermediate.
```

To see what happens when you change the display level from comprehensive to intermediate, take another look at the *Network Communication* group:

```
sp_configure "Network Communication"
go
```

With the display level set to intermediate, the *sp_configure* command produces output on eight parameters in the *Network Communication* group:

```
Group: Network Communication

Parameter Name            Default  Memory Used  Config Value  Run Value
------------------------- -------  -----------  ------------  -----------
additional network memory       0            0             0            0
allow remote access             1            0             1            1
default network packet size   512            0           512          512
max network packet size       512            0           512          512
number of remote connections   20            0            20           20
number of remote logins         20            0            20           20
number of remote sites          10            0            10           10
remote server pre-read packets   3            0             3            3
```

To complete the example, change the display level to basic:

```
sp_displaylevel sa, basic
go
```

Again, SQL Server confirms the change:

```
The display level for login 'sa' has been changed to basic.
```

To see the effects of this change, display information about the *Network Communication* group, one more time:

```
sp_configure "Network Communication"
go
```

With the display level set to basic, the *sp_configure* command doesn't display any parameters in the specified group:

```
Group: Network Communication
```

To summarize the effects of the display levels for the *Network Communication* group:

- The comprehensive level shows all 10 parameters in the group.

- The intermediate level shows eight of the 10 parameters, omitting the *tcp no delay* parameter and the *max number network listeners* parameter. Intermediate- and basic-level users do not need to deal with either of these advanced-level parameters.

- The basic level does not show any parameters in this group. All 10 of the *Network Communication* group's parameters deal with topics that are beyond the scope of the basic user.

When working with configuration parameters, not all users have the same needs. For example, an application programmer might be interested solely in the sizes of the data and procedure caches or the number of available locks. On the other hand, the lead DBA on a project might need to reconfigure the *tcp no delay* parameter. Depending on your needs, you may find it convenient to work with just a subset of parameters, as determined by your login's display level.

To modify parameters by using *sp_configure*, you must have the *sa_role*. The system security officer (SSO) can also modify some parameters. Although a login with the *sa_role* may have a display level of intermediate, that login can still change comprehensive-level parameters. Display level, as its name implies, affects only what SQL Server displays on the screen.

TIP!   If you are migrating from SQL Server 4.x, you may not be familiar with the concept of roles, a security feature that Sybase introduced in SQL Server 10.x. A user who has the *sa_role* has permission to perform system administration tasks, even though that user is not using the sa login. For more information about roles, see the *SQL Server System Administration Guide*.

Tables 5-2 through 5-14 list all of the configuration groups and the parameters in each group. For each parameter, the tables list the display level and the type—static or dynamic.

Table 5-2: *The General Information Group*

Parameter	Display Level	Type
configuration file	comprehensive	dynamic

Table 5-3: *The Backup/Recovery Group*

Parameter	Display Level	Type
print recovery information	intermediate	static
recovery interval in minutes	basic	dynamic
tape retention in days	intermediate	static

Table 5-4: *The Cache Manager Group*

Parameter	Display Level	Type
memory alignment boundary	comprehensive	static
number of index trips	comprehensive	dynamic
number of oam trips	comprehensive	dynamic
procedure cache percent	comprehensive	static
total data cache size	basic	static

Table 5-5: *The Disk I/O Group*

Parameter	Display Level	Type
allow sql server async i/o	comprehensive	static
disk i/o structures	comprehensive	static
number of devices	basic	static
page utilization percent	comprehensive	dynamic

Table 5-6: *The Languages Group*

Parameter	Display Level	Type
default character set id	intermediate	static
default language id	intermediate	dynamic
default sortorder id	comprehensive	static
number of languages in cache	intermediate	static

Table 5-7: *The Memory Use Group*

Parameter	Display Level	Type
executable code size	basic	static

Table 5-8: *The Network Communication Group*

Parameter	Display Level	Type
allow remote access	intermediate	dynamic
default network packet size	intermediate	static
max network packet size	intermediate	static

(continues)

Table 5-8: *(continued)*

Parameter	Display Level	Type
max number network listeners	comprehensive	static
number of remote connections	intermediate	static
number of remote logins	intermediate	static
number of remote sites	intermediate	static
remote server pre-read packets	intermediate	static
tcp no delay	comprehensive	static

Table 5-9: *The O/S Resources Group*

Parameter	Display Level	Type
max async i/os per engine	comprehensive	static
max async i/os per server	comprehensive	static
o/s asynch i/o enabled	comprehensive	static
o/s file descriptors	comprehensive	static

Table 5-10: *The Physical Memory Group*

Parameter	Display Level	Type
additional network memory	intermediate	static
lock shared memory	comprehensive	static
shared memory starting address	comprehensive	static
total memory	intermediate	static

Table 5-11: *The Processors Group*

Parameter	Display Level	Type
max online engines	intermediate	static
min online engines	intermediate	static

Table 5-12: *The SQL Server Administration Group*

Parameter	Display Level	Type
allow nested triggers	intermediate	static
allow updates to system tables	comprehensive	dynamic
audit queue size	intermediate	static
cpu accounting flush interval	comprehensive	dynamic
cpu grace time	comprehensive	static
deadlock retries	intermediate	dynamic
default database size	intermediate	static
default fill factor percent	intermediate	static
event buffers per engine	comprehensive	static
housekeeper free write percent	intermediate	dynamic
i/o accounting flush interval	comprehensive	dynamic
i/o polling process count	comprehensive	dynamic
identity burning set factor	intermediate	static
identity grab size	intermediate	dynamic
lock promotion HWM	intermediate	dynamic
lock promotion LWM	intermediate	dynamic
lock promotion PCT	intermediate	dynamic
number of alarms	comprehensive	static
number of extent i/o buffers	comprehensive	static
number of mailboxes	comprehensive	static
number of messages	comprehensive	static
number of open databases	basic	static
number of open objects	basic	static
number of pre-allocated extents	comprehensive	static
number of sort buffers	comprehensive	dynamic
partition groups	comprehensive	static
partition spinlock ratio	comprehensive	static
print deadlock information	intermediate	dynamic
runnable process search count	comprehensive	dynamic
size of auto identity column	intermediate	dynamic
sort page count	comprehensive	dynamic

(continues)

Table 5-12: *(continued)*

Parameter	Display Level	Type
sql server clock tick length	comprehensive	static
time slice	comprehensive	static
upgrade version	comprehensive	dynamic

Table 5-13: *The User Environment Group*

Parameter	Display Level	Type
number of user connections	basic	static
permission cache entries	comprehensive	static
stack guard size	comprehensive	static
stack size	basic	static
systemwide password expiration	intermediate	dynamic
user log cache size	intermediate	static
user log cache spinlock ratio	intermediate	static

Table 5-14: *The Lock Manager Group*

Parameter	Display Level	Type
address lock spinlock ratio	comprehensive	static
deadlock checking period	comprehensive	dynamic
freelock transfer block size	comprehensive	dynamic
max engine freelocks	comprehensive	dynamic
number of locks	basic	static
page lock spinlock ratio	comprehensive	static
table lock spinlock ratio	comprehensive	static

The reconfigure *Command*

In releases prior to SQL Server 11, you have to run the *reconfigure* command after changing a parameter with the *sp_configure* command:

```
sp_configure "procedure cache", 25
go
reconfigure
go
```

With SQL Server 11, you do not use the *reconfigure* command:

```
sp_configure "procedure cache percent", 25
go
```

If you have any scripts that run the *sp_configure* command, you should edit them to remove any references to the *reconfigure* command. At the time of this writing, the use of the word *reconfigure* does not produce any errors; it has no effect. However, this will not be the case in future releases of SQL Server, so you should remove all references to the *reconfigure* command at your earliest convenience.

Administration and Management Issues

During your migration to SQL Server 11, you must consider some new administrative issues:

- Backup, security, and purging of the configuration file

- A new command line flag to the *dataserver* executable

As you know, the configuration file is an integral part of your SQL Server 11 environment. Because the configuration file is an operating system file rather than a part of the SQL Server, you must institute a separate maintenance procedure to ensure that your configuration files are routinely backed up. You should integrate this task with the normal file system backup procedures on your host operating system.

You must also ensure that you provide adequate protection for the configuration file. Prevent unauthorized users from altering the configuration file, and ensure that the user who starts the SQL Server (almost always the user *sybase*) has read and write permission on the configuration file.

Recall that each time you change a parameter, SQL Server writes a new version of the configuration file and increases the numeric filename extension of the old configuration file (for example, MYSERV.001, MYSERV.002, MYSERV.003). This naming convention can support 1,000 different versions of the configuration file. To ensure that you don't burden the file system with hundreds of unneeded files, you must regularly purge these outdated configuration files.

Many of these files may differ from one another in only one parameter setting, and many may be the result of experimentation. (While you search for an optimal setting for your SQL Server, each change you make produces another version of the configuration file.) You should check these files frequently and remove any that you do not need. Retaining too many configuration files wastes storage space and may cause confusion.

One last administrative issue to keep in mind involves the -c flag to the *dataserver* executable. If you use this flag in a *runfile* to bring up SQL Server with a specific configuration file, you must remember to maintain the environment specified in that *runfile*. If SQL Server cannot find the specified configuration file, it will not boot up. In other words, if you use the -c flag and SQL Server can't find the specified configuration file, SQL Server will not use the default configuration file. Ensure that the *runfile* points to the correct path and file, and be sure to set the proper read and write permissions for that file.

Summary

This chapter describes the tools you use for configuring SQL Server 11 and explains how this process has changed from previous releases. You use the techniques from this chapter when dealing with the topics covered in many other chapters of this book. For example, Chapter 9, "SQL Server 11 Performance and Tuning," concentrates on setting certain configuration parameters to improve the performance of your server.

The next chapter discusses named caches and large I/O. Your newfound configuration skills come into play as you learn how to configure new data caches and buffer pools.

Migration Checklist

The following list summarizes the key migration tasks covered in this chapter:

- Learn the new form of the *sp_configure* command.

- Become familiar with the new columnar output of the *sp_configure* command.

- Understand the purpose of configuration files.

- Study the default configuration file that the *sybinit* utility created for your SQL Server 11.

- Learn the new names for configuration parameters.

- Become familiar with the new configuration parameters.

- Become familiar with groups and display levels.

- Learn how to use the new *sp_displaylevel* command.

- Maintain directory structures, file permissions, and backup schedules for configuration files.

◆ Learn how to use the *read* and *write* subcommands of *sp_configure*. Use these sub-commands to replicate SQL Server 11 settings to multiple SQL Servers, and to maintain readily available settings for various tasks such as OLTP and decision support.

◆ Remove the *reconfigure* command from any existing scripts.

◆ Learn about the -c flag to the *dataserver* executable.

Command Reference

sp_configure

Syntax

```
sp_configure [parameter [value] | group_name | non_unique_parameter_fragment]
sp_configure "configuration file", 0, {"write" | "read" | "verify" |
"restore"} "file_name"
```

Examples

```
sp_configure "configuration file", 0, "write", "config1.cfg"
sp_configure "configuration file", 0, "verify", "config2.cfg"
sp_configure "configuration file", 0, "read", "configA.cfg"
sp_configure "number of open databases",50
sp_configure "configuration file" ,0, "restore", "configC.cfg"
sp_configure "Disk I/O"
sp_configure "max"
```

sp_displaylevel

Syntax

```
sp_displaylevel [login_name [,level] ]
```

Examples

```
sp_displaylevel suzy, comprehensive
sp_displaylevel
```

6

The Buffer Manager

In This Chapter

◆ Understanding how data caches work

◆ Learning about the enhancements to data caches and the Buffer Manager in SQL Server 11

◆ Finding out how SQL Server 11 uses memory

◆ Understanding how the Buffer Manager reduces contention and enhances scalability

◆ Creating, deleting, and using named caches

◆ Creating, deleting, and using buffer pools and large I/O

◆ Using cache strategy hints

When a user issues a request to the SQL Server, the SQL Server parses the query by reading a SQL language statement, which it then converts into a query execution plan. The SQL Server then uses this plan to access the data. The data resides either in memory—in an area called the *data cache*—or on disk. The Buffer Manager is the SQL Server component that obtains the data and maintains the data cache. Specifically, the Buffer Manager is responsible for maintaining the internal data structures that store data in memory and reading data from disk.

SQL Server 11 includes significant enhancements to the Buffer Manager, with especially important benefits for SMP systems. However, do not write off this chapter if you have a single-processor system. Although the Buffer Manager improvements are intended to significantly increase performance in SMP environments, you can also achieve significant performance gains in single-processor systems. (Chapter 1 discusses SMP and single-processor systems).

Two new features of the Buffer Manager distinguish SQL Server 11 from previous releases:

- Named caches (also known as *user-defined caches*). In addition to the default data cache used by previous versions, SQL Server 11 lets you work with individual, named data caches.

- Large I/O (also known as *prefetch*). SQL Server 11 offers the capability to transfer data in chunks larger than the 2K buffer size supported by previous releases.

This chapter explores the reasons for these changes and introduces the related concepts and commands. Chapter 9, "SQL Server 11 Performance and Tuning," shows you how to improve SQL Server performance by using named caches and large I/O.

Understanding How SQL Server 11 Allocates Memory

As mentioned, the Buffer Manager is the SQL Server component that manages the area of memory known as the *data cache*. To help you understand how the Buffer Manager works, this section describes the allocation of memory in SQL Server 11. The next section in this chapter takes a close look at the data cache itself.

At boot time, SQL Server determines how much memory is available by checking the *total memory* configuration parameter. This parameter specifies the amount of memory that SQL Server grabs from the computer system and thus determines how much memory SQL Server 11 has available to use. For example, if you set *total memory* to 65,536 (you specify this parameter in units of 2K), SQL Server 11 has 128 MB of memory available for its use (assuming, of course, that your host computer has that much memory to spare). As shown in Figure 6-1, most of this total memory is then allocated to the following parts of the SQL Server:

- The SQL Server executable. The amount of memory required for the SQL Server's executable code depends on the platform but generally ranges from 3 MB to 4 MB. You can determine the actual value by using the *sp_configure* command:

```
sp_configure "executable code size"
```

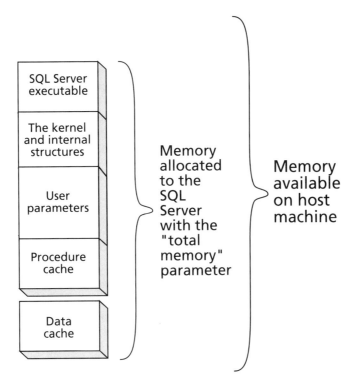

Figure 6-1: SQL Server must allocate available memory to several components.

- The kernel and internal server structures. SQL Server's internal data structures occupy approximately 3 MB of memory.

- Configuration parameters. As you recall from Chapter 5, "Configuring SQL Server 11," each configuration parameter uses some of the SQL Server's memory. Some parameters—for example, *number of user connections*—use large amounts of memory. Of course, the actual memory use depends on the parameter's setting. A setting of 1,000 for the *number of user connections* parameter takes significantly more memory from the SQL Server than does a setting of 50 connections.

- The procedure cache. After allocating memory to the executable, the internal server structures, and the configuration parameters, SQL Server divides the remaining memory between the procedure cache and the data caches. The configuration parameter *procedure cache percent* specifies the percentage of this remaining memory that SQL Server allocates to the procedure cache. The remainder then goes to the data caches. For example, with 30 MB of memory remaining and a *procedure cache percent* setting of 20, the SQL Server allocates 6 MB of memory (20 percent of 30 MB) to the procedure cache and 24 MB (the remaining 80 percent of 30 MB) to the data caches.

• The data caches. Unlike previous releases, SQL Server 11 does not limit you to using just one data cache. Instead, SQL Server 11 can divide the data cache's memory between a single *default data cache* and numerous user-created *named caches*.

Understanding the Data Cache

SQL Server allocates a portion of its available memory to the *data cache*—an area of the SQL Server's memory that contains an in-memory image of database pages as well as the internal structures necessary for managing those pages. Because computer systems can access data much faster from memory than from a disk, it makes sense to minimize disk access as much as possible. Although capacity limitations generally prevent you from storing all or even most of your data in memory, you can store commonly accessed or otherwise important data in memory. SQL Server stores this in-memory data in the data cache, which is maintained by the Buffer Manager.

SQL Server 11 needs to use a disk—rather than keep data solely in memory—simply because memory is not permanent. If SQL Server 11 crashes or memory is corrupted, the database is lost and recovery becomes impossible. Consequently, the SQL Server must frequently write data back out to disk. The topic of *recovery* is complex and beyond the scope of this chapter. It is sufficient to know that the data in cache is written back to disk mostly by the checkpoint process or the *checkpoint* command. The checkpoint process wakes up approximately every minute, checks to see which pages have changed in a database, and writes those changes out to disk. In addition to the checkpoint, SQL Server 11 also writes a buffer out to disk when that buffer reaches the wash marker on the MRU/LRU (most recently used/least recently used) chain.

As shown in Figure 6-2, the data cache comprises a buffer pool and a hash table. A buffer pool is a circular, doubly linked list of the pages of data currently in memory; the hash table is a look-up table that keeps track of this list. Remember that Sybase defines a *page* as a 2K (2,048 bytes) block of data (4K on Stratus machines). The data cache's circular, doubly linked list is actually a list of *buffers*, not pages; however, a buffer is simply a page of data, plus a header. The header is a structure that maintains a small amount of overhead information about the buffer, such as the buffer state and the MRU/LRU chain position. Figure 6-3 shows an MRU/LRU chain of buffers.

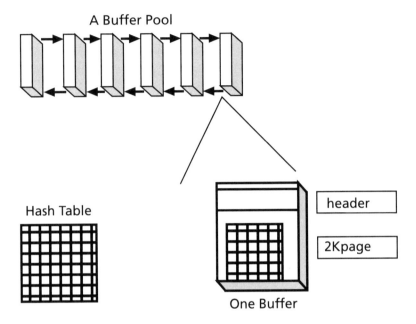

Figure 6-2: *A data cache contains a buffer pool and a hash table. Each buffer in the pool consists of a 2K page and a header.*

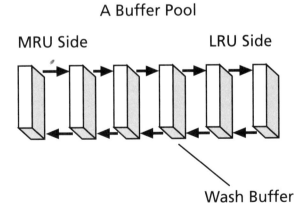

Figure 6-3: *A buffer pool consists of an MRU/LRU chain of buffers.*

To help you understand these terms and concepts, the following list describes the Buffer Manager's components:

- Page. A page is simply a 2K (2,048 bytes) block of data (4K on Stratus machines). When SQL Server needs a page of data from disk, it moves an identical copy of that data from the disk into the data cache in memory.

- Buffer. A buffer is a page of data, plus a header. Because you don't need to know about the header, this book uses the terms *page* and *buffer* interchangeably. So, when you see the term *buffer*, simply think of those 2,048 bytes in memory that contain an exact copy of the data from disk.

- Buffer pool. A buffer pool is a circular, doubly linked list of buffers. The typical user doesn't need to understand the concept of a circular, doubly linked list, so don't feel compelled to dig out your old data structures textbook. Just remember that the buffer pool is a chain of buffers linked together in memory. This MRU/LRU chain is the heart of the data cache.

- Hash table. The hash table is another data structure found in the data cache. This look-up table contains a list of the buffers that the cache currently contains. When the Buffer Manager needs to retrieve some data, it needs to know whether the cache contains this data. If the cache does not contain the required data, the Buffer Manager must perform a disk I/O. Rather than search through each buffer in the buffer pool, the Buffer Manager does a lookup in the hash table. This allows SQL Server to quickly determine whether the data cache contains the required page.

The buffer chain has two sides: the MRU side and the LRU side. The Buffer Manager places the most recently used buffers on the MRU side, with the expectation that these buffers will be used again in the near future. When the Buffer Manager places a new buffer on the MRU side of the chain, all other buffers move down the chain toward the LRU side.

To perform a disk read, the Buffer Manager needs a clean (empty) buffer for the data. The term *clean buffer* refers to a buffer that contains information that SQL Server has already written to disk. In general, the Buffer Manager takes such a buffer from the LRU side of the chain; the LRU side of the chain contains only clean buffers. The Buffer Manager knows that the buffers on the LRU side are clean because each buffer passes through the *wash marker* on its way from the MRU side to the LRU side. The wash marker is simply a point on the buffer chain, between the MRU side and the LRU side, at which dirty buffers are either clean or in the process of being cleaned.

Here's how the MRU/LRU chain works. A buffer pool has a specified number of buffers available to it. As the Buffer Manager reads data from disk into memory, it fills buffers with the data and positions those buffers on the MRU side of the buffer chain. When the Buffer Manager places a buffer at the front of the MRU side, all other buffers make room for that buffer by sliding over toward the LRU side of the chain. When a dirty (full) buffer reaches the wash marker, the Buffer Manager writes that buffer's contents out to disk. In other words, when a buffer reaches the LRU side, the Buffer Manager has written its information to disk and that buffer is available for reuse by the system. Think of this process in the following terms: When a dirty buffer (that is, one filled with data) reaches the wash marker, the Buffer Manager sends it out to be *washed* and it comes back clean—that is, written to disk and hence available for use. (Although this process is somewhat more complicated than the preceding description indicates, the description is sufficient for purposes of this discussion.)

Reducing Contention and Improving Scalability

Significantly improved scalability was an important goal for the engineers who developed SQL Server 11. The term *scalability* refers to a system's capability to take advantage of multiple processors and increase throughput proportionally. This capability continues to gain importance as increasing numbers of corporate consumers purchase multiprocessor machines.

A single-processor machine can perform only one task at a time. Even in a multi-user environment, the single CPU cycles through all the user requests and performs tasks for each user, one at a time. The speed with which the CPU performs these tasks creates the illusion that the system performs multiple tasks simultaneously when, for example, the CPU might actually put your task on hold, process 10 others, and still get back to yours in a fraction of a second. With the advent of *symmetric multiprocessing* (SMP), however, a computer with several CPUs can now process several tasks simultaneously.

Creating software to make use of SMP hardware gives rise to two main difficulties: the efficient delegation of tasks to available CPUs and the contention for system resources. The well-documented *engine 0* problem in previous versions of SQL Server provides an example of these difficulties. In versions prior to SQL Server 11, *engine 0* (the first engine in an SMP system) performs all network I/O. If two tasks run simultaneously on different processors and both tasks need to perform network I/O (a highly likely scenario), both tasks must wait for *engine 0* to process their I/O. Consequently, a bottleneck develops while multiple tasks wait for *engine 0* to handle their respective network I/O. Such scenarios prevent performance scaling—in other words, an increase in the number of processors does not produce a proportional increase in performance.

Sybase designed SQL Server 11 specifically to provide a high degree of scalability. The capability to delegate different tasks to different engines is one of the key mechanisms for achieving this scalability and the resulting performance gains.

You can think of an *engine* as a UNIX process. On an SMP machine, one SQL Server can behave as though it were several SQL Servers, with each server able to communicate with the others. In this way, one SQL Server can provide the processing power of multiple SQL Servers. Of course, this type of performance requires an SMP computer. A single-processor system is less efficient, because each engine competes for the lone CPU.

If your SQL Server 11 runs on a symmetric operating system, SQL Server 11 performs a *network affinity migration*. Network affinity migration allows SQL Server 11 to move the network I/O load from one engine to another. Most SMP systems support this capability. To find out whether your system supports network affinity migration, check the system's installation and configuration guide.

When a user logs-on to SQL Server 11, *engine 0* handles the login connection. Once the logins are completed, *engine 0* delegates this task to another engine (one with a light network load). That engine assumes exclusive responsibility for handling all of that user connection's network I/O. In this way, the system distributes the network I/O load evenly among all of SQL Server 11's engines. Note that this applies only to network I/O and does not imply that this process now runs only on that engine. Any SQL Server task can be run on any free engine; only network I/O is tied to an engine. At any given time, any of SQL Server 11's engines can be running on any of the host machine's CPUs. The UNIX operating system handles this scheduling, at its own discretion.

As mentioned at the beginning of this section, the second difficulty in dealing with SMP hardware involves contention for system resources—for example, the data cache. SQL Server cannot allow two separate processes to access the cache simultaneously. While using the cache, one process must obtain a lock on the cache to prevent another process from changing the contents of the cache and thus corrupting the data. SQL Server uses a lock called a *spinlock* (a type of semaphore) for this purpose.

This spinlock restricts access to the data cache to one task at a time. As shown in Figure 6-4, this can be a point of contention between multiple processes because a process might have to wait until the spinlock becomes available. As detailed in the following sections, SQL Server 11 solves the contention and scalability issues by using *named caches*.

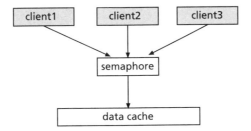

Figure 6-4: *In versions prior to SQL Server 11, if several clients simultaneously try to use the default data cache, a bottleneck develops on the data cache's semaphore.*

What Is a Named Cache?

Named caches, also known as *user-defined caches* are among the most useful features of SQL Server 11. As in previous versions of SQL Server, you always have the default data cache. As shown in Figure 6-5, however, SQL Server 11 lets you create and name any number of additional data caches. You can then use these named caches for many purposes—in particular, to eliminate contention on a single data cache by isolating objects in their own caches.

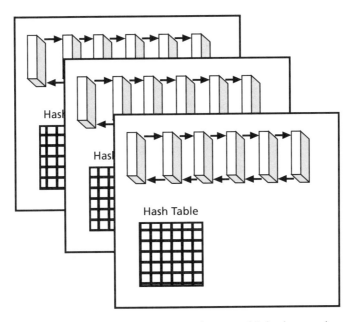

Figure 6-5: *SQL Server 11 can have multiple data caches.*

How Do Named Caches Reduce Contention?

If only one application accesses a particular object—for example, a table or an index—you can create a cache that holds only that object. In this way, you can ensure that the entire object always remains in memory (and thus eliminate any disk I/O) and you can reduce contention on access to that cache by limiting its use. For example, assume that your SQL Server 11 supports 200 users but only a few of those users work with a particular time-critical application. To ensure timely response from that application, you can create a named cache that contains only the objects accessed by that application. You can also set the size of this named cache to ensure that the data always remains available in memory. In this way, you eliminate contention on the objects needed by the users of the time-critical application. You also ensure that queries by users of other applications will not displace your data from the cache.

As shown in Figure 6-6, the use of multiple named caches also helps to alleviate contention on the data cache's spinlock. Rather than force one process to wait until another process releases its lock on the default data cache, SQL Server 11 can maintain multiple named caches, each with its own spinlock. If two users access two different named caches, they do not encounter contention for spinlocks.

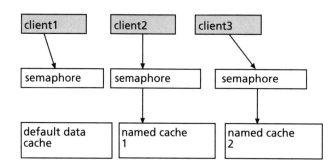

Figure 6-6: *By allowing different clients to access different data caches, the named caches in SQL Server 11 eliminate any contention for the semaphore.*

Only SMP systems can reap the *full* benefits of named caches. To reduce contention on the data cache's spinlock, the system must be able to perform more than one action at the same time. A single-processor system can perform only one task at a time. Regardless of whether your task is waiting for the same semaphore as another task, in a single-processor system, your task can't do anything until the other tasks relinquish control of the SQL Server.

Reducing Disk I/O

The other major improvement Sybase made to the data cache system for SQL Server 11 involves the introduction of large I/O. The term *large I/O* refers to the capability to read larger amounts of data from disk than in previous releases. As you recall from the discussion on pre-SQL Server 11 data caches, a cache contains a pool of buffers, and each buffer can hold 2K bytes of data. When the SQL Server needs information from disk, it reads in this information in 2K pieces and stores each 2K piece of data in a buffer. So, if a query were to return 16K bytes of data from disk, the SQL Server would issue eight separate disk requests.

To improve performance by reducing the number of disk I/Os that SQL Server must perform when accessing large quantities of data, SQL Server 11 introduces the concept of large I/O. SQL Server 11 implements large I/O by allowing each data cache to contain as many as four different buffer pools of different sizes. As shown in Figure 6-7, instead of the single 2K buffer pool available in previous versions, a specific cache may now contain a 2K buffer pool, a 4K buffer pool, an 8K buffer pool, and a 16K buffer pool.

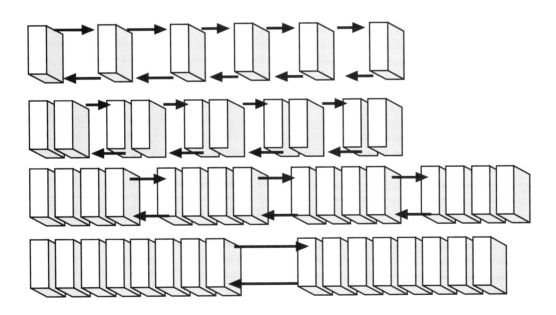

Figure 6-7: *In SQL Server 11, a data cache can have as many as four buffer pools and the sizes of these buffer pools can range from 2K to 16K.*

As shown in Figure 6-8, the availability of larger buffer pools allows you to reduce the amount of disk I/O that SQL Server 11 must perform. For example, if SQL Server 11 needs to read 16K bytes of data from disk and you have a 16K buffer pool allocated for the cache, SQL Server performs just one 16K-byte disk I/O instead of the eight 2K I/Os that a previous version must perform. Large I/O is particularly useful for such tasks as scans or joins on large tables, as well as for *bcp* and *dbcc* operations.

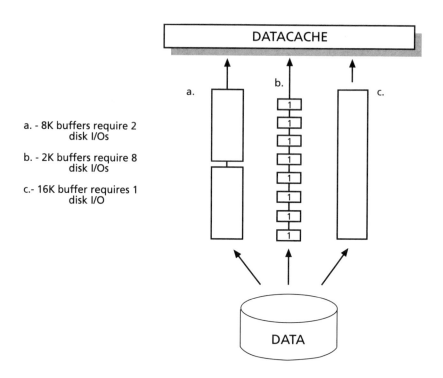

a. - 8K buffers require 2 disk I/Os

b. - 2K buffers require 8 disk I/Os

c.- 16K buffer requires 1 disk I/O

Figure 6-8: *By using larger buffer sizes, you can reduce the number of disk I/Os that SQL Server 11 must perform.*

The following sections delve into the details of data caches. You learn how and when to use named caches, the commands involved, and the most effective way to implement named caches.

Getting Ready for Named Caches

Note that SQL Server does not require the use of named caches; they are optional. Although the potential for significant performance gains will probably lead you to experiment with named caches soon after migrating to SQL Server 11, you can start up your new SQL Server 11 server and never make use of a named cache. After migrating to SQL Server 11, you should take the time to familiarize yourself with the system before you start experimenting with named caches.

Before making any changes that involve named caches, you may also want to benchmark certain queries and processes so that you can measure the performance benefits provided by different caching strategies. Indeed, you might configure your named caches in such a way that you actually degrade system performance. Always benchmark performance and test the results of any system changes. Chapter 8, "Monitoring SQL Server 11," and Chapter 9, "SQL Server 11 Performance and Tuning," provide guidance for determining which named caches you should set up and measuring whether they improve SQL Server's performance.

Managing the Default Data Cache

You do not need any named caches because SQL Server 11 automatically boots up with a default data cache. The default data cache works in exactly the same way as the data cache that previous versions of SQL Server use. If you do not add any named caches to your system, you use the same data cache as you did in your pre-SQL Server 11 server.

Once the upgrade process creates the default data cache, it always remains present in SQL Server 11 and you cannot remove it. SQL Server 11 uses the default data cache whenever you access an object that you have not bound to a named cache.

Like any named caches that you create, the default data cache automatically has a 2K buffer pool. You can add buffer pools of different sizes to this data cache and thus allow the optimizer to choose one of these other sizes. Keep in mind. however, that every buffer pool you add takes memory away from another buffer pool. SQL Server allocates a specific amount of memory to the default data cache, and all of the buffer pools share this memory. For example, if you have a default data cache with 30 MB of memory, SQL Server allocates all of this memory (except for some overhead) to the default 2K buffer pool. If you then create a 10-MB 16K buffer pool in the default data cache, SQL Server reduces the memory allocation for the 2K pool to 20 MB.

You can allocate memory to buffer pools in this way as long as the allocation for the 2K buffer pool never drops below 512K bytes. This is the minimum size for any buffer pool, and SQL Server 11 does not let you change buffer pools if the change will decrease a buffer pool below this amount. (In practice, you never want such a small memory allocation for the 2K buffer pool of the default data cache.) In many circumstances, SQL Server uses the default data cache even though you have several named caches. Similarly, SQL Server 11 may use the default data cache's 2K buffer pool to perform an operation, even though the default data cache contains a 4K buffer pool and a 16K buffer pool that you expect the system to use for that operation. With those points in mind, be sure to allocate sufficient memory to the default data cache and its 2K buffer pool.

You can set a minimum value for the default data cache, and SQL Server 11 will not let you decrease the default data cache below this setting. This can help you avoid accidentally making the default data cache too small when you add several named caches.

You specify a minimum size for the default data cache by using the *sp_cacheconfig* command. For example, the following command sets the minimum size of the default data cache to 25 MB:

```
sp_cacheconfig "default data cache", "25M"
```

For complete details about the *sp_cacheconfig* command, refer to the section, "Working with Named Caches," later in this chapter.

TIP!   To refer to the default data cache in any of the commands that affect data caches, simply use "default data cache" as the name of the cache. Be sure to include the quotation marks.

When working with the default data cache, remember the following points:

- The default data cache is always present; you cannot delete it.

- The default data cache always has a 2K buffer pool, but you may add a pool of another size to it.

- If no named caches are specified for an object, SQL Server uses the default data cache.

- SQL Server uses the default data cache for recovery.

- The default data cache has a minimum size of 512K.

- Each named cache that you create takes memory away from the default data cache.

- To give the default data cache more memory, increase the *total memory* parameter.

Creating Additional Buffer Pools in the Default Data Cache

Once you have SQL Server 11 running, one of the first administrative tasks you may want to perform is to create additional buffer pools in the default data cache. By creating a 16K buffer pool in the default data cache, you allow the optimizer to consider large I/O when accessing data in the default data cache. Remember that the optimizer can only use large I/O if it is using a cache that contains a 16K buffer pool. Otherwise, the optimizer must use a smaller I/O size.

In addition to the 16K pool, you may want to create a 4K buffer pool in the default data cache. The transaction logs of all databases in the default data cache will use this 4K buffer pool (unless, of course, you create a named cache for the exclusive use of the transaction log).

Sybase engineers have determined that the optimal value for log I/O is 4K. In other words, this setting offers the most efficient transfer of data to and from the transaction log. For this reason, SQL Server 11 uses 4K as the default value for log I/O. However, SQL Server 11 cannot use the 4K I/O size unless you bind the transaction log to a cache that contains a 4K buffer pool. If the cache does not have a 4K buffer pool, SQL Server uses the less efficient 2K buffer pool. Until you create a data cache for the transaction log, SQL Server uses the default data cache. Consequently, you should consider creating a 4K buffer pool in the default data cache.

You can see the log I/O size for a database by using the *sp_logiosize* command. This command lets you display or change the log I/O size for the transaction log of a given database. As mentioned, you probably want to keep this at the default value of 4K.

The *sp_logiosize* command has the following syntax:

```
sp_logiosize ["default" | " size " | "all"]
```

This command accepts the following arguments:

- "default". This sets the log I/O size of the current database to the default of 4K. If a 4K buffer pool does not exist, the log I/O uses a value of 2K.

- "*size*". You can specify the size for the log I/O of the current database. Valid values are 2, 4, 8, and 16.

- "all". This displays the log I/O size for all databases.

For example, the following command displays the log I/O size of the current database's transaction log:

```
sp_logiosize
go
```

After experimenting with the log I/O sizes in the *db1* database, you can reset the log I/O size to the default value by issuing the following commands:

```
use db1
go
sp_logiosize "default"
go
```

If you change the log I/O size of a database to any value other than 4K, make sure the named cache contains a buffer pool of the specified size.

Working with Named Caches

After determining that you want to use a named cache, you create it by using system procedure commands to specify a name, the amount of memory that you want to allocate to the named cache, and the cache's status—that is, whether the cache will be used for log only or for both data and log. After you create the cache, you can bind objects to it. A cache is only useful if you bind objects to it. Once you create a named cache, you can create or modify buffer pools of different sizes, for use by the cache.

TIP! Before you can use a named cache, you must bind objects to that cache.

Here are the steps for creating a named cache:

1. Create the cache by using SQL Server 11 system procedures.

2. Bind objects to the cache.

3. Create or modify additional buffer pools for the cache. (This step is optional.)

When working with caches, Remember the following points:

- To use a different I/O size for a particular object such as a table, you must create buffer pools with that I/O size. You create these buffer pools in a cache.
- To use a named cache, you must bind an object such as a table to that cache; otherwise, the object uses the default data cache.
- When you create a named cache, it takes memory away from the default data cache.

The following sections describe the commands you use for creating a named cache. You can create a named cache in one of two ways: by using the *sp_cacheconfig* system procedure or by using the configuration file.

Creating and Modifying Named Caches by Using the *sp_cacheconfig* Command

You use the *sp_cacheconfig* command to create, configure, drop, and obtain information about a named cache. The *sp_cacheconfig* command has the following syntax:

```
sp_cacheconfig [cachename [ , "cache_size[P|K|M|G]" ] [,logonly | mixed ] ]
```

This command accepts the following arguments:

- *cachename*: the unique name you chose for your cache. The name cannot exceed 30 characters.

- *cache_size*: the size of the data cache. In addition to this *cache_size* value, you can specify the desired units: P (for pages), K (for kilobytes), M (for megabytes), or G (for gigabytes). The default unit is K. The minimum cache size is 512K.

- logonly | mixed: the type of cache. A cache can hold log pages only, or it can hold both log pages and data pages.

TIP!   If you create, drop, or change a cache, the command takes effect when you restart the SQL Server. In other words, you cannot bind objects to a cache or configure buffer pools until you restart the SQL Server.

To create the new named cache *my_cache* with 5 MB of memory, issue the following command and then restart SQL Server 11:

```
sp_cacheconfig my_cache, "5M"
```

By default, this cache will be of type *mixed*. In other words, this cache can hold either data or log type pages. Creating this cache takes 5 MB of memory away from the default data cache.

When you create a cache, you can specify the size in different units. For example, the following command creates a cache with 1,024K bytes:

```
sp_cacheconfig my_cache2, "1024K"
```

As with most SQL Server 11 commands, using the *sp_cacheconfig* command without parameters displays information. For example, to see detailed information about the *my_cache* named cache, issue the following command:

```
sp_cacheconfig my_cache
```

SQL Server 11 responds to this command by producing the following output:

```
Cache Name     Status     Type     Config Value    Run Value
----------     ------     -----    ------------    ---------
my_cache       Active     Mixed    5.00 Mb         5.00 Mb
                                   ------------    ---------
                          Total    5.00 Mb         5.00 Mb
==================== Cache: my_cache, Status: Active, Type: Default
Config Size: 5.00 Mb, Run Size: 5.00 Mb
IO Size  Wash Size  Config Size  Run Size
-------  ---------  -----------  --------
2 Kb     2336 Kb    3.00 Mb      3.00 Mb
4 Kb     1024 Kb    2.00 Mb      2.00 Mb
=======================================================
```

This example assumes that you have added a 4K buffer pool to *my_cache*. The Status column displays one of three values: Active, Pend/Act, or Pend/Del. *Active* means that this cache is currently active. *Pend/Act* indicates that this cache is not currently active, but will become active when you restart the SQL Server. *Pend/Del* means that this cache is currently active, but will be deleted when you restart the SQL Server.

Notice that the last section of the output contains information about the buffer pools. The Wash Size column in this section of the output displays the size of the MRU/LRU chain's wash marker.

To delete a named cache, reconfigure its size to zero:

```
sp_cacheconfig my_cache2, "0"
```

When you restart SQL Server 11, this cache will be dropped from the system.

TIP! To create or change a named cache, you must have the *sa_role*.

Creating and Modifying Named Caches by Using the Configuration File

You can also create or modify a cache by using the configuration file. This section of the configuration file has the following syntax:

```
[Named Cache: name of cache]
cache size = size [ P | K | M | G]
cache status = [ default data cache | mixed cache | log only cache ]
```

For example, to create a 10-MB cache named *test_cache_1*, add the following lines to the configuration file:

```
[Named Cache: test_cache_1]
cache size = 10M
cache status = mixed cache
```

The new named cache becomes active when you restart the SQL Server 11 with this configuration file. This method allows you to create new named caches in a configuration file, even when SQL Server 11 is not running. As soon as you start the SQL Server, the named cache is available.

As discussed in Chapter 5, using the configuration file to configure SQL Server 11 boils down to a matter of either preference or functionality. Some users find it more natural and convenient to edit a configuration file, while others prefer to use the system procedure commands. In some cases, however, you will find it more advantageous to configure named caches by using a configuration file. For example, assume that you are a DBA in a mid-sized company that recently upgraded 20 servers to SQL Server 11. Through experimentation and careful study of your business needs, you decide to configure six named caches in each SQL Server 11. If you were to create UNIX scripts to configure these caches in each of your SQL Servers, you would have to perform the following steps:

1. Start up each of the 20 SQL Servers.

2. Run your UNIX script against each of the 20 SQL Servers.

3. Restart each of the 20 SQL Servers. (Remember that the cache configuration does not take effect until you restart the SQL Server.)

At the end of this laborious process, you would have six new named caches in each of your 20 SQL Servers. As an alternative to this tedious process, you can edit a configuration file to add the six named caches, copy the changes to each SQL Server 11's configuration file, and then use this configuration file when starting up the SQL Servers. With this method, you simply edit the configuration files and then start up all of the SQL Servers. When the SQL Servers start up, they each contain the six named caches that you created.

Obtaining Information About a Data Cache

You can find out how much memory SQL Server has allocated to a data cache and its pools by using the *sp_helpcache* command. This command displays information about a data cache, including which objects are bound to that data cache. The *sp_helpcache* command also reports the amount of overhead required for creating a cache of the specified size.

The *sp_helpcache* command has the following syntax:

```
sp_helpcache cache_name | "cache_size [P|K|M|G]"
```

The *sp_helpcache* command accepts the following arguments:

- *cache_name*: the name of a data cache.

- *cache_size*: the size of the cache. You can specify the size in units of P (pages), K (kilobytes), M (megabytes), or G (gigabytes). The default for units is K.

For example, to see information about all of the data caches (before any objects have been bound to them), you issue the following command:

```
sp_helpcache
go
```

SQL Server 11 responds by displaying the following information:

```
Cache Name              Config Size   Run Size   Overhead
--------------------    -----------   --------   --------
default data cache         0.00 Mb    10.73 Mb   0.51 Mb
ncache1                   10.00 Mb    10.00 Mb   0.58 Mb
ncache2                   10.00 Mb    10.00 Mb   0.58 Mb
```

Deleting a Named Cache

SQL Server 11 does not have a *drop* command or a *delete* command for deleting named caches. To delete a named cache, you simply resize it to zero by using the *sp_cacheconfig* command. The following example deletes the *my_cache* named cache:

```
sp_cacheconfig my_cache, "0"
go
```

When you issue this command, the named cache remains active until you restart SQL Server 11. Once you restart SQL Server 11 and the cache is dropped, all objects that were bound to this cache have their bindings marked as invalid, in a message to the errorlog. If you recreate a named cache with the same name as the cache you dropped, SQL Server automatically marks those object bindings as valid again, and those objects use that new named cache.

Binding and Unbinding Objects and Named Caches

You now know how to create and modify named caches. In this section, you learn how to use these caches. Remember that until you bind an object to a cache, the cache does nothing more than take up space. Each cache you create takes memory away from the default data cache. Therefore, you do not want to create caches and then neglect to bind objects to them, because that wastes valuable memory resources.

Once you create named caches, the only way to use them is by binding specific objects to specific caches. Any objects not bound to a cache automatically use the default data cache. You can bind tables, indexes, logs, and even databases to a particular named cache. Although one named cache can contain many objects, you can bind a particular object to only one named cache. However, you can bind an index to one cache and its data to another.

TIP!   To bind and unbind a database, you must be in the *master* database.

You bind an object to a named cache by using the *sp_bindcache* command. This command has the following syntax:

```
sp_bindcache cachename , dbname
        [, [ ownername .] tablename [, indexname | "text only"]]
```

The *sp_bindcache* command accepts the following arguments:

*   *cachename*: the name of an active cache.

*   *dbname*: the name of the database that you want to bind, or the name of the database that contains an object that you want to bind.

*   *ownername*: the table's owner (optional if "dbo" owns the table).

*   *tablename*: the name of the table that you want to bind to the cache, or the name of a table that has an index, a text object, or an image object that you want to bind to a cache.

*   *indexname*: the name of an index that you want to bind to a cache.

- text only: this argument binds text or image objects to a cache.

To unbind an object from a cache, you can use either the *sp_unbindcache* command or the *sp_unbindcache_all* command. The *sp_unbindcache* command has the following syntax:

```
sp_unbindcache dbname [,[ owner. ] tablename
    [, indexname | "text only"]]
```

The *sp_unbindcache_all* command has the following syntax:

```
sp_unbindcache_all cache_name
```

The *sp_unbindcache* command works in exactly the same way as *sp_bindcache*, but with the opposite effect. As its name implies, the *sp_unbindcache_all* command unbinds all of the objects in a given cache. This command is useful when you want to drop a named cache. Before you drop that named cache, you may want to unbind all objects in the cache. If you do not do this, SQL Server marks the bindings as invalid and prints an error message in the errorlog. In this case, however, when you create a new named cache with the same name as the cache that you dropped, the bindings will again become valid. For this reason, you may not want to drop all the bindings before dropping a cache.

The binding and unbinding of objects occurs as soon as you issue the appropriate commands. You do not need to restart SQL Server 11.

Case Studies

Because an important application makes heavy use of a particular table, you might decide to bind the table and its index to a named cache. To accomplish this, you use the *sp_bindcache* command:

```
sp_bindcache "ncache1", "db1", "table1"
go
sp_bindcache "ncache1", "db1", "table1", "table1indx"
go
```

Remember that you can see the bindings of a particular cache by using the *sp_helpcache* command:

```
sp_helpcache ncache1
go
```

After experimenting with this cache-binding setup, you might decide that you do not want to keep it. To drop the bindings, you issue the following commands:

```
sp_unbindcache "ncache1", "db1", "table1"
go
sp_unbindcache "ncache1", "db1", "table1", "table1indx"
go
```

Remember that issuing these commands automatically causes these objects to use the default data cache.

Because many applications make heavy use of the *tempdb* database, you might want to put *tempdb* in its own named cache. If *tempdb* uses the default data cache, the heavy use of *tempdb* may flush other objects' pages out of the cache. By putting *tempdb* in its own named cache, you can isolate its I/O. This technique has the added benefit of spreading I/O evenly among different data caches.

The following example places a 50-MB *tempdb* in its own 75-MB cache. First, you need to determine how much memory overhead such a cache requires:

```
sp_helpcache "75M"
go
```

SQL Server 11 responds with the following information:

```
3.04Mb of overhead memory will be needed to manage a cache of size 75M
```

Next, find out how much memory is available in the default data cache (the overhead for a named cache is taken from the default data cache):

```
sp_helpcache
go
```

SQL Server 11 displays the following information:

```
Cache Name          Config Size  Run Size   Overhead
------------------  -----------  ---------  --------
default data cache  200.00 Mb    200.00 Mb  8.53 Mb
```

You see that the default data cache can easily spare the memory, so you create the named cache:

```
sp_cacheconfig "tempdb_cache", "75M"
go
```

To make the new cache active, you must now reboot SQL Server 11.

Now, you need to bind *tempdb* to the named cache:

```
use master
go
sp_bindcache "tempdb_cache", "tempdb"
go
```

Finally, create a 16K buffer pool, to facilitate large I/O:

```
sp_poolconfig tempdb_cache, "25M", "16K"
go
```

You might also consider creating a named cache and binding the *db1* database's transaction log to that named cache. First, create the new named cache:

```
sp_cacheconfig "log_cache", "5M", logonly
go
```

You don't need a particularly large cache, because you are not trying to cache the entire transaction log. (The *Sybase SQL Server Performance and Tuning Guide* explains how to estimate the appropriate size for this named cache.)

To make this new cache active, reboot the server. To create a 4K buffer pool and then bind the transaction log to the new named cache, issue the following commands:

```
sp_poolconfig log_cache, "4M", "4K"
go
sp_bindcache "log_cache", "db1", "syslogs"
go
```

TIP!   As mentioned at the beginning of this chapter, improper use of named caches can decrease system performance. You should carefully monitor the performance of your named caches, using the techniques described in Chapter 8, "Monitoring SQL Server 11."

Understanding Large I/O

The capability for large I/O provides some of SQL Server 11's greatest performance gains over previous releases. The term *large I/O*—also known as *prefetch*—refers to SQL Server 11's capability to read as many as eight 2K data pages at a time. In previous releases, SQL Server reads data from a disk into the data cache, one page at a time. If the System Administrator configures SQL Server 11 for large I/O, the system can read as much as a full extent of data at a time. (An *extent* is eight pages of data.) In this way, you can experience significant, almost eightfold, performance gains over previous versions of SQL

Server. Whereas previous versions of SQL Server might require eight costly I/O operations for a particular task, SQL Server 11 can accomplish the same task with only one I/O operation.

You will find that people use the terms *large I/O* and *prefetch* interchangeably when referring to SQL Server 11's capability to read more than one page per disk I/O. *Prefetch* refers to the strategy that the optimizer uses when it makes use of these multipage I/Os. One of the optimizer's main goals is to minimize logical and physical I/O. The optimizer knows which named cache a given table is bound to, and it knows what pool sizes are available in that named cache. Using this and other information, the optimizer decides whether it can use a prefetch strategy. Using a prefetch strategy simply means that SQL Server reads in more than one page per I/O. The term *large i/o* is somewhat more intuitive than the term *prefetch* because it clearly indicates that you are using larger I/O sizes—that is, a 4K, 8K, or 16K buffer pool—when reading data.

To use large I/O, you set up buffer pools in a data cache. These pools can be 2K, 4K, 8K, or 16K in size. In previous releases, the data cache simply contains a 2K buffer pool. So, if you configure a cache with just a 2K pool, your system mimics the performance it offered before the upgrade to SQL Server 11.

TIP! When you use buffer pools larger than 2K, keep in mind that SQL Server treats the pages in that pool as a single unit. Consequently, if you change any of those pages, SQL Server writes all of them to disk.

Creating and Modifying Buffer Pools

This section shows you how to create buffer pools and use large I/O. To use large I/O, the System Administrator must first create buffer pools in various data caches. Remember, you can only make use of large I/O by using a data cache that contains large buffer pools. If you use a cache that has buffers of various sizes available, the optimizer determines which buffer pool to use. In other words, once the System Administrator enables large I/O by creating buffer pools, you don't have to take any further action. The optimizer identifies the best prefetch option for a given query and uses the appropriately sized pool. As detailed in the section, "Cache Strategy Hints," however, you can provide *hints* to the SQL Server 11 by requesting that the prefetch strategy be turned on or off. You can provide these hints at the object level, the session level, or the query level.

NOTE: As long as the data cache contains a large buffer pool, the optimizer automatically uses large I/O when it is beneficial.

A user with the System Administrator role can configure buffer pools by using the *sp_poolconfig* command. With this command, you can create a new pool in an existing data cache, delete a buffer pool, get information about buffer pools, or change the size of an existing pool.

The *sp_poolconfig* command has the following syntax:

```
sp_poolconfig cachename [, "memsize[P|K|M|G]","configpool K"
  [, "affected_pool K"]]
```

To change a pool's *wash size*, use the following syntax:

```
sp_poolconfig cachename , "io_size" ,"wash= size [P|K|M|G]"
```

The *sp_poolconfig* command accepts the following parameters:

- *cachename*: the name of an existing data cache.

- *memsize*: the size of the memory pool to be created or the new size for an existing pool. The minimum size of a pool is 512K. Specify the units for pool size with P (pages), K (kilobytes), M (megabytes), or G (gigabytes). The default is K.

- *configpool*: the pool you are creating or changing. Valid values are 2K, 4K, 8K, and 16K.

- *affected_pool*: the pool from which SQL Server takes the memory for the new or modified pool. When you create a new pool or change the size of an existing pool, the memory for that pool must come from another pool. If you do not specify a pool by using this parameter, SQL Server takes the memory from the 2K pool, by default.

- *io_size*: the buffer pool for which the wash size will be reconfigured. Valid values are 2K, 4K, 8K, and 16K. The combination of the cache name and the I/O size uniquely identifies a memory pool.

- wash= *size*: the new wash size. Remember that the wash size defines the size of the wash marker. Make this value large enough so that buffers can be written to disk in the wash marker. Otherwise, a buffer will still be dirty when it reaches the LRU side of the chain and SQL Server 11 will have to wait until the buffer is cleaned before using it. The minimum value for the wash size is 10 buffers and the maximum value is 80 percent of the pool size. The default value is 256, which should be sufficient for most applications. Chapter 8, "Monitoring SQL Server 11," describes techniques for monitoring the wash marker to ensure that it is the right size.

A data cache with a buffer pool of 16K might be useful in a decision support environment, because decision support functions typically return large, contiguous result sets. The following command creates a 16K buffer pool with a total size of 8 MB, in the *dss_cache* data cache (SQL Server takes the 8 MB from the 2K pool):

```
sp_poolconfig dss_cache, "8M", "16K"
go
```

The next example creates a 4K pool in the same cache, but takes the memory from the 16K pool instead of the 2K pool:

```
sp_poolconfig dss_cache, "2M", "4K", "16K"
go
```

Remember that you also use the *sp_poolconfig* command to change the wash size of a buffer pool. After monitoring the buffer pools, you might decide that you need to enlarge the wash size of the 4K buffer pool. To do this, you issue the following command:

```
sp_poolconfig dss_cache, "4K", "wash=512"
go
```

Finally, you can use the *sp_poolconfig* command to display information about all the pools in a cache:

```
sp_poolconfig ncache1
go
```

When you issue this command, SQL Server displays the following information:

```
Cache Name   Status   Type    IO Sz   Wash Sz   Config Value   Run Value
----------   ------   -----   -----   -------   ------------   ---------
ncache1      Active   Mixed   2 Kb    204 Kb    0.00 Mb        1.00 Mb
ncache1      Active   Mixed   4 Kb    204 Kb    1.00 Mb        1.00 Mb
                                                ------------   ---------
                              Total             1.00 Mb        1.00 Mb
```

As with other configurable parameters, you can also configure a buffer pool by using the configuration file. The buffer pool's section in the configuration file appears under that of the corresponding named cache.

The following example shows how you use the configuration file to allocate a 16K buffer pool with a pool size of 4 MB in the *my_cache* named cache:

```
[Named Cache: my_cache]
  cache status= mixed cache
[16K I/O Buffer pool]
  wash size = default
  pool size = 4M
```

Deleting Buffer Pools

In addition to creating and modifying buffer pools, you can delete them. You might want to delete a pool because you don't use it. For example, assume that the named cache *samp_cache* has a 2K buffer pool, a 4K buffer pool, an 8K buffer pool, and a 16K buffer pool. You notice that the 8K pool is never used, so you decide to delete that pool and free up memory for the other pools.

TIP! Every data cache contains a 2K buffer pool. This buffer pool has a minimum size of 512K. You cannot delete the 2K buffer pool in any cache.

There is no command for deleting a pool. You delete a buffer pool by setting its size to zero. For example, the following command deletes the 8K buffer pool from the *samp_cache* named cache:

```
sp_poolconfig samp_cache, "0K", "8K"
go
```

TIP! Remember that you can display information about a buffer pool by using the *sp_poolconfig* command and the *sp_cacheconfig* command.

Cache Strategy Hints

By default, SQL Server 11 enables prefetch. In other words, once you configure buffer pools in a cache, the optimizer can choose whether to use them. The optimizer uses large I/O if it determines that this prefetch strategy will improve performance.

When deciding whether to use prefetch, the optimizer performs a cost-based analysis. During a cost-based analysis, the optimizer considers the various methods it can use for performing your query. For example, the optimizer considers how much logical and physical I/O will result from using a table's various indexes, and it assigns this I/O a relative cost. From all the available alternatives, the optimizer chooses a least-cost plan for accessing the data.

In a cost-based analysis, *cost* represents time. The least-cost access plan is the one that can be completed in the shortest possible time. One of the factors the optimizer considers is whether large I/O will speed up the query. Remember, the optimizer considers the use of large I/O because prefetch is enabled (the default setting). If you disable prefetch, the optimizer does not consider the use of large I/O.

A user can turn prefetch capabilities on or off. You might do this because you need to execute a query that performs differently than those in the current environment. For example, during regular business hours, you might optimize a SQL Server for decision support and therefore have prefetch turned on. Because you perform on-line transaction processing (OLTP) queries at night, you usually reconfigure the SQL Server 11 at the close of business to turn off prefetch. If an emergency arises during the day that requires running some OLTP queries, you must quickly turn off prefetch. You can easily force this change at either the session level or the query level.

You can set the prefetch strategy on three levels:

- The object level. The object level sets the prefetch strategy on a table or an index.

- The session level. The session level sets prefetch on a particular session—for example, an *isql* session or a *db-lib* session.

- The query level. The query level sets prefetch in a *select*, *update*, *insert*, or *delete* command.

Note the hierarchy of these setting levels:

- The object-level setting overrides the session-level setting.

- The session-level setting overrides the query-level setting.

For example, if you turn off the prefetch strategy for the object level and then turn it on for the query level, the object-level setting overrides the query-level setting and SQL Server does not use prefetch. Figure 6-9 shows this hierarchy.

The interplay among the object, session, and query levels can be confusing. You can set prefetch on or off at one level, as long as each higher level also has prefetch turned on. In other words, if prefetch is turned on at the object level, you can turn it off or on at the session level. If prefetch is turned on at the session level, you can turn it off or on at the query level. And if prefetch is turned off at the session level, you cannot turn it on at the query level. However, if prefetch is turned on at the session level, you can turn it off at the query level. Remember that the default for prefetch is on.

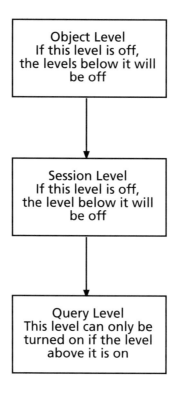

Figure 6-9: *The prefetch settings have a hierarchical relationship.*

Setting Prefetch at the Object Level

You enable or disable prefetch at the object level by using the *sp_cachestrategy* command. You can set prefetch on a table or an index. The *sp_cachestrategy* command has the following syntax:

```
sp_cachestrategy dbname , [ ownername .] tablename
[, indexname | "text only" | "table only" [, prefetch | mru , "on" |
"off"]]
```

The *sp_cachestrategy* command has the following arguments:

- *dbname*: the name of the database that contains your object.

- *ownername*: the table's owner (optional if "dbo" owns the table).

- *tablename*: the name of the table.

- *indexname*: the name of the index.

- prefetch | mru: the setting you want. (For a discussion of mru, see the section "The Fetch-and-Discard Strategy," later in this chapter).

- on | off: the desired setting. Note that "on" or "off" must be enclosed in quotation marks.

TIP!   For details about the other parameters to this command, see the *SQL Server Reference Manual, Volume 2*.

If you issue the *sp_cachestrategy* command without specifying *prefetch*, SQL Server displays the strategy information but doesn't change anything. Any user can issue this command to display the strategy, but only the System Administrator or the owner of the object can change the prefetch strategy setting.

The following example uses the *sp_cachestrategy* command to turn off prefetch for the *titles* table:

```
sp_cachestrategy pubs2, titles, prefetch, "off"
go
```

The following example uses the *sp_cachestrategy* command to display the strategy of the *titleind* index:

```
sp_cachestrategy pubs2, titles, titleind
go
```

Setting Prefetch at the Session Level

You can enable or disable prefetching at the session level—for example, in an *isql* session or a *db-lib* connection—by using the *set prefetch* command. The *set prefetch* command has the following syntax:

```
set prefetch {off | on}
```

For example, you turn off prefetch for a session by issuing the following command:

```
set prefetch off
go
```

Setting Prefetch at the Query Level

Setting prefetch at the query level is complicated and you certainly would not do this on a production system. You may find this method useful for comparing the performance from using different I/O sizes in your test environment. To see the differences in I/O, you use the *set statistics io* command.

You can set prefetch at the query level for *select*, *update*, and *delete* commands. The full syntax for a *select*, *update*, or *delete* command shows that you specify prefetch in the index clause. For example, here's a portion of the syntax for the *select* command:

```
select select_list
   from table_name( index index_name [prefetch size] )
     [,table_name …]
```

In this syntax, valid values for prefetch are 2, 4, 8, and 16. For example, the following query will use a 2K I/O size:

```
select type
from titles(index type_price prefetch 2)
go
```

If the object's cache does not include a pool of the specified size, prefetch cannot use the requested size. In this case, the optimizer chooses the best available size. You can see which size the optimizer chooses by using the *showplan* command. Chapter 9, "SQL Server 11 Performance and Tuning," provides details about the *showplan* command.

Why Disable or Enable Prefetching?

In general, you should not change the default settings for large I/O, because most systems run best with large I/O enabled. This default allows the optimizer to decide whether it should use large I/O for a particular query. If you decide to change the default settings, you should do so only after careful analysis.

At first glance, you may not see any reason for disabling large I/O. After all, enabling large I/O does not mean that the optimizer always chooses large I/O. Enabling large I/O simply means that the optimizer considers whether large I/O can improve performance for a query. SQL Server only uses large I/O if the optimizer determines that it will help performance.

With large I/O enabled, some queries use it and some do not. However, even those queries that do not use large I/O may be affected by its use. The use of large I/O causes pages to move quickly out of the data cache and thus reduces the likelihood that the cache contains a page needed by a particular query.

You should not use large I/O in an OLTP system, because an OLTP system deals with small amounts of data. For example, when a clerk enters a customer order, this transaction might update a record in the database with 200 bytes of data. Clearly, large I/O provides no benefits in this situation. On the other hand, a DSS can benefit greatly from large I/O, because this type of system deals with large amounts of data. For example, a store manager might run a report that returns information on all of the orders from the past year. Queries that return such large amounts of data benefit from the use of large I/O.

Even though you do not want OLTP systems to use large I/O, you can still leave large I/O enabled. Let the optimizer do its job: determining whether to use large I/O in a given situation. If you believe that a specific case warrants forcing a particular strategy, study the output from tools such as *showplan* and the *dbcc* 302 and 310 trace flags. If you are not familiar with the output of these commands, you should not attempt to outsmart the optimizer.

If you decide to set large I/O for a production system, you should consider setting it at only the object level. Use the session and the query levels only for testing in a development system. For example, while using the output of *showplan* and *set statistics io* to observe the performance of your queries, you might experiment by forcing large I/O on a particular query and observing the results. By setting large I/O at the query level, you can quickly and easily perform your tests. However, debugging any queries with a hard-coded prefetch strategy will be confusing and difficult.

The Fetch-and-Discard Strategy

In addition to the prefetch strategy described in the preceding section, the SQL Server 11 optimizer can use another new strategy known as *fetch-and-discard*. The fetch-and-discard strategy—also know as the *MRU* strategy—addresses a caching problem in multi-user systems. This problem is particularly noticeable on SQL Servers that support both OLTP applications and DSSs.

As you know, one of the most effective means for achieving high performance is to ensure that the cache always contains the data you want. In an OLTP system, you constantly write to just a few data pages and those pages can always remain in the cache. If you perform a DSS-type query, however, the OLTP pages may be forced out of the cache. The DSS query reads numerous pages into the cache, and because the cache can contain only so many pages at a time, the DSS pages may replace the OLTP pages in the cache.

This happens on servers that use versions prior to SQL Server 11 because those versions use an LRU strategy rather than an MRU strategy. The names of these strategies refer to the location on the buffer chain at which SQL Server places newly filled buffers. With the LRU strategy, as SQL Server fills buffers with data from the disk, it places those buffers on the MRU side of the chain. With the MRU strategy, SQL Server 11 places those buffers immediately before the wash marker. Figure 6-10 shows these locations on the MRU/LRU buffer chain.

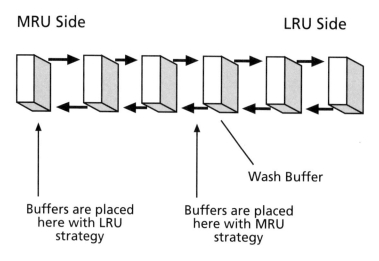

Figure 6-10: *Depending on the strategy that's used, SQL Server places newly filled buffers at different points on the MRU/LRU chain.*

TIP!   The terminology can be confusing. With the LRU strategy, SQL Server places the newly filled buffers on the MRU side of the chain. With the MRU strategy, SQL Server places the buffers closer to the LRU side of the chain (before the wash marker).

The data pages for the OLTP transactions sit on the MRU side of the chain. When the DSS query's pages come in on the MRU side, they push the other data pages past the wash buffer and out of the cache.

SQL Server 11's default behavior is the MRU (fetch-and-discard) strategy. With this new strategy, commonly used data pages remain in the cache, toward the MRU side of the chain. With the MRU strategy enabled, a user performing a select * from a large table will not cause SQL Server to overwrite pages that another user might be updating.

As with the prefetch strategy, the optimizer has the option of deciding whether to use the MRU strategy or the LRU strategy for a query. The *showplan* utility clearly shows which of the two strategies the optimizer uses.

The term *fetch-and-discard* refers to the fact that only the user who fetched a page can then discard that page. Other users cannot cause that page to be discarded from the cache.

The mechanics of the fetch-and-discard strategy are similar to the prefetch strategy. You use the same commands to change both settings and under most circumstances you should stick with the default settings. The only difference between the two strategies is that you cannot set the fetch-and-discard strategy at the session level.

Setting Fetch-and-Discard at the Object Level

You can enable or disable fetch-and-discard at the object level by using the *sp_cachestrategy* command. You can set fetch-and-discard on a table or an index. The *sp_cachestrategy* command has the following syntax:

```
sp_cachestrategy dbname , [ ownername .] tablename
[, indexname | "text only" | "table only" [, prefetch | mru , "on" |
"off"]]
```

The *sp_cachestrategy* command has the following parameters:

- *dbname*: the name of the database that contains your object.

- *ownername*: the table's owner (optional if "dbo" owns the table).

- *tablename*: the name of the table.

- *indexname*: the name of the index.

- prefetch | mru: the setting you want to use. (In other words, you specify either prefetch or mru.)

- on | off: the desired setting. Note that "on" or "off" must be enclosed in quotation marks.

TIP!   For details about the other parameters to the *sp_cachestrategy* command, see the *SQL Server Reference Manual, Volume 2*.

If you issue this command without specifying mru, SQL Server displays the strategy information without changing anything. Any user can use this command to display the strategy, but you must be the System Administrator or the owner of the object to change the strategy.

The following example shows how you use the *sp_cachestrategy* command to turn off MRU for the titles table:

```
sp_cachestrategy pubs2, titles, mru, "off"
go
```

To display the strategy of the *titleind* index, you issue the following command:

```
sp_cachestrategy pubs2, titles, titleind
go
```

Setting Fetch-and-Discard at the Query Level

Setting fetch-and-discard at the query level is complicated, and you certainly should not do this on a production system. You may find this method useful for testing the difference in performance between MRU and LRU strategies in your test environment.

You can set fetch-and-discard at the query level for *select*, *update*, and *delete* commands. The syntax for a *select*, *update*, or *delete* command shows that you specify fetch-and-discard in the index clause. For example, here's a portion of the syntax for the *select* command:

```
select select_list
   from table_name( index index_name [mru | lru] )
      [,table_name …]
```

Within the index clause, the *mru* setting turns on the fetch-and-discard strategy and *lru* turns off the fetch-and-discard strategy. For example, the following query forces the use of the LRU strategy:

```
select type
from titles(index type_price lru)
go
```

The following example shows how to get the pre-SQL Server 11 behavior for a query (in terms of large I/O and MRU/LRU strategies):

```
select * from table1( index table1_indx prefetch 2 lru)
go
```

TIP! You can display the strategies used by the optimizer by using the *showplan* command. Chapter 8, "Monitoring SQL Server 11," shows you how to use this command.

Summary

This chapter describes two important enhancements to SQL Server—named caches and large I/O—and introduces the methods for using them. Named caches and large I/O provide simple but powerful means for improving the performance of your SQL Server 11 system. After analyzing your system's requirements, you can create named caches, configure buffer pools of various sizes in those named caches, and bind various tables and indexes to the caches.

Migration Checklist

The following list summarizes the key migration tasks covered in this chapter:

- With the help of the monitoring and performance and tuning tools described in Chapters 8 and 9, create named caches and buffer pools to increase your SQL Server 11's performance.

- Make sure you have enough memory configured for the default data cache.

- Decide which objects you should bind to their own named caches and which you should bind to the default data cache.

- Consider creating a 16K buffer pool and a 4K buffer pool in your default data cache.

- Decide whether you want to create named caches for database transaction logs.

- Consider creating a named cache for *tempdb*.

- Set the cache strategies for specific objects, as needed.

Command Reference

set prefetch

Syntax

```
set prefetch {off | on}
```

Example

```
set prefetch on
```

sp_bindcache

Syntax

```
sp_bindcache cachename , dbname[, [ ownername .] tablename [, indexname |
"text only"]]
```

Example

```
sp_bindcache "ncache1", "db1", "table1"
```

sp_cacheconfig

Syntax

```
sp_cacheconfig [cachename [ , "cache_size[P|K|M|G]" ] [,logonly | mixed ] ]
```

Example

```
sp_cacheconfig my_cache, "5M"
```

sp_cachestrategy

Syntax

```
sp_cachestrategy dbname , [ ownername .] tablename[, indexname | "text
only" | "table only" [,  prefetch | mru ,  "on" | "off"]]
```

Examples

```
sp_cachestrategy pubs2, titles, prefetch, "off"
sp_cachestrategy pubs2, titles, mru, "off"
```

sp_helpcache

Syntax

```
sp_helpcache cache_name | " cache_size [P|K|M|G]"
```

Examples

```
sp_helpcache ncache1
sp_helpcache "75M"
```

sp_logiosize

Syntax

```
sp_logiosize ["default" | " size " | "all"]
```

Example

```
sp_logiosize "default"
```

sp_poolconfig

Syntax

```
sp_poolconfig cachename [, "memsize[P|K|M|G]","configpool K" [,
"affected_pool K"]]
sp_poolconfig cachename , " io_size " ,"wash= size [P|K|M|G]"
```

Examples

```
sp_poolconfig dss_cache, "2M", "4K", "16K"
sp_poolconfig dss_cache, "4K", "wash=512"
```

sp_unbindcache

Syntax

```
sp_unbindcache dbname [,[ owner. ] tablename[, indexname | "text only"]]
```

Example

```
sp_unbindcache "ncache1", "db1", "table1"
```

sp_unbindcache_all

Syntax

```
sp_unbindcache_all cache_name
```

Example

```
sp_unbindcache_all cache2
```

SQL Server 11 Enhancements

In This Chapter

◆ Understanding SQL Server 11's improvements to the logging system

◆ Finding out how SQL Server 11 eliminates the *begin transaction* problem for front-end applications

◆ Using the new *syslogshold* table and finding the oldest open transaction

◆ Improving performance by using variable log I/O buffer sizes

◆ Understanding SQL Server 11's improvements to the locking system and the Parallel Lock Manager

◆ Configuring the locking system

◆ Using dirty reads

◆ Configuring table lock promotions

◆ Changing a database's online/offline status

◆ Partitioning tables for improved performance

◆ Understanding and using the housekeeper task

This chapter discusses four important new features that Sybase has introduced in SQL Server 11. These easy-to-use features greatly enhance SQL Server's performance:

- The logging system

- The locking system

- Table partitioning

- The housekeeper task

Improvements to the Logging System

In previous releases, the logging system can cause contention and limit scalability. SQL Server 11 includes several important changes that address these issues. In particular, SQL Server 11 uses what is known as a *user log cache* (ULC) and it has a variable log I/O size. Instead of one log cache that everyone shares, each user now has a private ULC. This reduces contention and greatly improves scalability. Variable log I/O size is simply the capability to change the I/O size for the log. In previous versions, the log I/O can be only 2K in size. With SQL Server 11, it can now have values up to 16K.

SQL Server 11 also has a new system table called the *syslogshold* table. This table's main purpose is to keep track of the oldest open transaction.

Transaction Management

A DBMS must guarantee the recoverability of all data modifications. To make this possible, a DBMS must log all data modifications—that is, updates, inserts, and deletes. By logging these actions, SQL Server 11 can recover from system failures and thus provide the integrity necessary for a production environment.

A *transaction* is a single unit of work that consists of one or more Transact-SQL (T-SQL) statements. SQL Server 11 treats these statements as a cohesive unit. In other words, either all the statements succeed or all the statements fail. By using a transaction as the smallest unit of work, SQL Server 11 can either *roll back* or *roll forward* all data manipulations. In this way, SQL Server 11 maintains database integrity.

When SQL Server rolls back a transaction, all of the completed statements for that transaction are undone. If a transaction is rolled forward, SQL Server applies all of the completed statements to the database.

Elimination of Bottlenecks in the Transaction Management System

In versions prior to SQL Server 11, several areas of the logging system can cause system bottlenecks and thus prevent the SQL Server from achieving optimal performance. By introducing the user log cache (ULC) and variable log I/O size, SQL Server 11 virtually eliminates these bottlenecks. (The following sections provide in-depth coverage of the user log cache and variable log I/O size.)

SQL Server 11 also includes two new features to eliminate annoying quirks found in previous versions. With versions prior to SQL Server 11, certain front-end tools issue a *begin transaction* command that can cause the transaction log to fill up. Versions prior to SQL Server 11 also lack capabilities for easily finding the oldest open transaction. The oldest open transaction often causes log overflow situations.

For a detailed explanation of how the ULC helps solve the *begin transaction* problem, see the section, "Front-end Applications and the ULC," later in this chapter. The section, "The New *syslogshold* Table," discusses the oldest open transaction issue.

The User Log Cache

In versions prior to SQL Server 11, when the system performs a transaction, SQL Server writes the information to the last page of the in-memory transaction log. Once the transaction is *committed*, SQL Server flushes the transaction's information from memory onto disk. In this way, versions prior to SQL Server 11 save all transactions to disk in the transaction log, which provides for recovery in the event of a system failure.

Because the in-memory portion of the transaction log is an internal data structure, it must be protected by a *semaphore*—a lock that protects internal data structures from concurrent access. In other words, while one user works with a data structure such as the transaction log, the SQL Server must make sure that a second user does not try to use that data structure. Otherwise, the data could become corrupted.

As shown in Figure 7-1, users of the transaction log system in versions prior to SQL Server 11 must contend with two performance-related issues. First, the semaphore can become a source of serious bottlenecks in SMP systems. Every process must write to the last page of the log. Consequently, several processes might have to wait until another process relinquishes the log semaphore so that they can obtain it and write to the log. Second, because SQL Server transfers each record into the log separately, a transaction may have to go through the semaphore and write to the log several times.

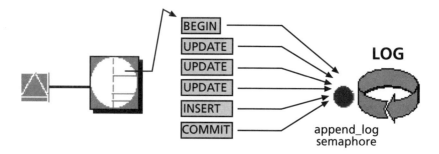

- Each log record is transferred into the log separately
- Each log transfer goes through the a_log semaphore
- Semaphore is *database-wide* ➜ Engines must wait for it

Figure 7-1: *With the pre-SQL Server 11 logging system, SQL Server transfers each record to the log individually, and multiple engines must pass through one semaphore. (Reprinted with permission from Peter Thawley and the Sybase Product Performance Group.)*

Resolving the Logging Bottlenecks

To resolve the transaction logging issues found in previous versions, SQL Server 11 introduces the user log cache (ULC), which is also known as the private log cache, or PLC. In SQL Server 11, each user connection has its own ULC. Rather than write database manipulations to the last page of the log, each user first writes these changes to a private ULC. Because each SQL Server task now has its own log cache, a user does not have to wait for the log semaphore and SQL Server 11 can write transaction records to the log in batches rather than one at a time. Several records can accumulate in the private cache before it flushes to the log.

SQL Server 11's user log cache and multiple log semaphores offer significant performance gains in an SMP system, because SMP systems can perform multiple tasks at the same time (and thus take advantage of multiple log semaphores). Single-processor systems will perform at least as fast as they did with previous versions of SQL Server. Figure 7-2 shows the new logging system with a user log cache. To clearly see the changes to the logging system, compare this figure with Figure 7-1.

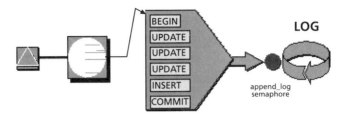

- Records written in batch to the log buffer, reducing log semaphore contention
- Minimizes log truncation issues
    - Buffers errant "Begin Tran" in memory, not on disk
    - New *Virtual* table shows oldest active transaction in each database
- Totally transparent to applications

Figure 7-2: *With the SQL Server 11 logging system, SQL Server can transfer records to the log in batches and multiple engines can use the multiple semaphores of each user log cache. (Reprinted with permission from Peter Thawley and the Sybase Product Performance Group.)*

The graph in Figure 7-3 shows the performance benefits from using the ULC in SMP systems. The graph shows how the addition of engines to the system affects throughput and contention. As shown in Figure 7-3, adding engines to the system increases throughput but does not increase contention.

append_log( ) Performance with PLC

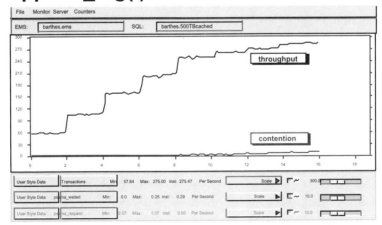

Figure 7-3: *Adding engines to a SQL Server 11 system improves throughput but does not increase contention. (Reprinted with permission from Peter Thawley and the Sybase Product Performance Group.)*

NOTE: The user log cache is available automatically. You do not take any action to enable it and under most circumstances you leave it alone.

With the new logging system, several records can accumulate in the ULC before SQL Server 11 flushes them to the log. The following circumstances cause SQL Server to flush these records:

- SQL Server reaches the end of a transaction.

- A checkpoint occurs.

- The ULC is low on space.

- SQL Server has written to a different database.

Configuring and Maintaining a User Log Cache

As mentioned in the preceding section, the user log cache is available automatically. You do not take any action to enable a ULC and under most circumstances you leave it alone. However, two configuration parameters affect the ULC:

- *user log cache size*

- *user log cache spinlock ratio*

In most cases, you should not change the settings for these parameters because you may cause more harm than good. Setting a ULC too high can waste memory and increase contention on the spinlocks. Setting a ULC too low can increase log contention because the ULC will flush more than once per transaction.

As with all configuration parameters, you change the settings for these parameters by using the *sp_configure* command. Here is the syntax you use for changing the ULC size:

```
sp_configure "user log cache size", ulc_size
```

This command sets all of the user log caches to the size specified by the *ulc_size* parameter. For example, the following command sets the user log cache size to 4,096:

```
sp_configure "user log cache size", 4096
go
```

The default value for the *user log cache size* parameter is 2,048 bytes. That is also the minimum size.

In general, the setting for this parameter should be no larger than the largest transaction that you expect to use; otherwise, you waste valuable memory resources. On the other hand, setting this parameter too low may cause SQL Server to flush the ULC too frequently, which degrades performance by causing increased contention on the log pages.

Use the *sp_sysmon* utility to monitor ULC performance. The information provided by this utility can help you determine the right size for the ULC. For more details about the *sp_sysmon* utility, see Chapter 8, "Monitoring SQL Server 11."

The other ULC-related parameter—*user log cache spinlock ratio*—specifies the ratio of user connections to spinlocks. For example, a spinlock ratio of 20 means that 20 users share a single spinlock. In general, you should not change the setting for this parameter from its default value of 20.

TIP! The *user log cache spinlock ratio* parameter pertains only to multi-engine systems. If the *max on-line engines* parameter is set to one, SQL Server ignores the *user log cache spinlock ratio* setting. In this case, the system has only one spinlock.

Front-end Applications and the ULC

In versions prior to SQL Server 11, users of front-end tools such as PowerBuilder and Gupta SQL Windows® often notice an annoying problem with transactions. Many of these front-end tools automatically issue a *begin transaction* statement when they connect to the SQL Server. This statement explicitly begins a unit of work, and all subsequent statements must wait for an explicit end to the transaction. If a user connects to the SQL Server and then leaves the workstation unattended for the rest of the day, an open transaction remains in the transaction log. This situation may keep the transaction log from being *truncated* past a certain point and the log can prematurely fill up. SQL Server 11 prevents this from happening by writing the *begin transaction* statement to the ULC rather than to the log itself.

The New syslogshold *Table*

SQL Server 11 includes a new table, the *syslogshold* table, which you find only in the *master* database. SQL Server 11 creates this dynamic table only when you query it. The *syslogshold* table exists to help you identify the oldest open transaction and the Replication Server truncation point (if any). As mentioned in the preceding section, a transaction that remains open and active for an extended period of time can prevent you from truncating the transaction log. Consequently, the transaction log can fill up. This scenario has frustrated DBAs using previous versions of SQL Server. With the implementation of the *syslogshold* table in SQL Server 11, you can easily identify the offending transaction and either notify the user or *kill* the transaction's process.

In addition to the oldest open transaction, the *syslogshold* table can inform you of the *truncation point*, if you have Replication Server®. The *truncation point*, which you find in the transaction log of a replicated SQL Server, marks the spot at which replication last took place. That is, everything that precedes the *truncation point* has already been submitted for replication, and everything after it has not yet been replicated. Only the part of the log that precedes the *truncation point* can be *truncated*; the remainder of the log must first be replicated.

For each database in SQL Server 11, the *syslogshold* table has zero, one, or two rows. With no open transactions and no truncation point, the *syslogshold* table has zero rows. If the system has either an open transaction or a replication truncation point, the *syslogshold* table has one row. If the system has both an open transaction and a replication truncation point, the *syslogshold* table has two rows.

Remember that the *syslogshold* table can change every time you view it, because SQL Server creates this table dynamically when you query it. If a problem transaction remains open, however, you will notice it every time you query the *syslogshold* table. Table 7-1 shows the format of the *syslogshold* table.

Table 7-1: *The Table Structure of the* **syslogshold** *Table*

Column	Datatype	Description
dbid	smallint	Database ID
reserved	int	Unused
spid	smallint	Server process ID of the user that owns the oldest active transaction (always 0 for Replication Server)
page	int	Starting page number of the portion in syslogs defined by oldest transaction
xactid	char(6)	ID of the oldest active transaction (always 0x000000 for Replication Server)
masterxactid	char(6)	ID of the transaction's master transaction (always 0x000000 for Replication Server)
starttime	datetime	Date and time the transaction started
name	char(67)	Name of the oldest active transaction

Querying *syslogshold* to Find the Process That's Blocking Log Truncation

To use the *syslogshold* table, you must query it. One query you can issue will find the process ID (*spid*) and the transaction name (*name*) of the process that has the oldest open transaction. If this process is preventing you from truncating the log, you can either kill the process or notify the user.

As shown in the following example, this first query relies on the fact that the object ID of the *syslogs* table is always 8. This query checks that the *syslogshold's spid* is not zero, because a zero *spid* represents the truncation point. The primary purpose of the query is to find the row in which the first page of the log equals the first page of the *syslogshold* table. The following example finds the process with the oldest open transaction in the *db1* database:

```
use db1
go
select sysl.spid, sysl.name
  from master..syslogshold sysl,   sysindexes I
    where sysl.dbid = db_id()
     and
     I.id = 8
       and
     sysl.page = I.first
       and
     sysl.spid != 0
go
```

This query returns the following information:

```
spid    name
----    --------------
54      upd_custs_tran
```

A second query you can issue on the *syslogshold* table finds the host and the application that owns the oldest open transaction. This query joins with the *sysprocesses* table to get the application information:

```
use db1
go
select P.hostname, P.hostprocess, P.program_name, sysl.name, sysl.starttime
   from master..syslogshold sysl,   master..sysprocesses P
    where P.spid = sysl.spid
     and
   sysl.dbid = db_id()
```

```
    and
  sysl.spid != 0
go
```

This query returns the following information:

```
hostname   hostprocess   program_name   name    starttime
--------   -----------   ------------   ------  ------------------
pluto      15826         isql                   updtrn  Sep 6 1995 4:29PM
```

You can come up with your own variations to these queries, as necessary. For example, you can check for the replication truncation point or you can check specific databases by using a parameter to the *db_id()* function. With the advent of the *syslogshold* table, you no longer have to worry about open transaction problems.

Variable Log I/O Buffer Sizes

In previous versions of SQL Server, the in-memory transaction log writes its data to disk in a buffer size of 2K. This buffer size can cause bottlenecks when the system transfers large amounts of information to disk.

To eliminate this problem, SQL Server 11 supports a variable log I/O size. In SQL Server 11, you can set the log I/O buffer size to values ranging from 2K to 16K (that is, 2K, 4K, 8K, and 16K). The log I/O size has a default value of 4K.

SQL Server 11 can only use the log I/O size you choose if you bind the log to a data cache that contains a buffer pool of the chosen size. For this reason, you may want to consider creating a 4K buffer pool in the default data cache. The transaction logs of all databases in the default data cache will use this 4K buffer pool. If you do not create this 4K buffer pool in the default data cache, you should create a named cache for the exclusive use of the transaction log. Until you do so, however, the transaction log uses the default data cache.

TIP! The transaction log can only use the requested log I/O size if a buffer pool of that size is available. Otherwise, the transaction log uses a 2K buffer pool.

Sybase engineers have determined that the optimal value for log I/O is 4K. Because this is the most efficient value for the transaction log to use when transferring data, the log I/O size has a default value of 4K. Keep in mind, however, that SQL Server 11 cannot use the 4K I/O size unless you bind the transaction log to a cache that contains a 4K buffer pool. If the cache does not have a 4K buffer pool, SQL Server uses the less efficient 2K buffer pool. Until you create a data cache for the transaction log, SQL Server uses the default data cache.

You can display the log I/O size for a database by using the *sp_logiosize* command. This command displays or changes the log I/O size for the transaction log of a specified database. As mentioned, you should probably leave this setting at the default value of 4K.

The *sp_logiosize* command has the following syntax:

```
sp_logiosize ["default" | " size " | "all"]
```

The *sp_logiosize* command accepts the following parameters:

- default. This sets the log I/O size of the current database to the default of 4K. If a 4K buffer pool does not exist, the log I/O uses a value of 2K.

- *size*. This value sets the log I/O of the current database to the specified size. Valid values for the *size* argument are 2, 4, 8, and 16.

- all. This displays the log I/O size for all databases.

For example, the following command displays the log I/O size of the current database's transaction log:

```
sp_logiosize
go
```

After experimenting with the log I/O sizes in the *db1* database, you might want to use the default value again. To do this, you issue the following commands:

```
use db1
go
sp_logiosize "default"
go
```

If you change the log I/O size of a database to a value other than 4K, make sure the named cache contains a buffer pool of the size you specify.

TIP! When changing the log I/O size, you may reach a point of diminishing returns. Do not assume that you should set this parameter to the largest possible value. If you want to change the log I/O size from its default value, experiment with different sizes and benchmark the results.

Locking in SQL Server 11

No, SQL Server 11 does not have row-level locking, a feature that many people think they want but almost no one needs. As in previous releases, the SQL Server 11 locking system operates on the *page* level, which Sybase has determined to be the most efficient way of handling locking in the SQL Server. Row-level locking may be offered in future releases simply because of this buzzword's popularity, but you should carefully investigate the need for this feature because it is rarely necessary. Although you can simulate this functionality—for example, by setting the maximum rows per page to one—these techniques waste system resources and you should not use them.

The SQL Server 11 locking system includes several features that improve performance, especially in multi-engine environments. The following sections discuss three features of the SQL Server 11 locking system:

- The Parallel Lock Manager

- Lock configurations

- Dirty reads

Improvements to the Parallel Lock Manager

The Parallel Lock Manager (PLM) enhances SQL Server 11's performance in much the same way as many other SQL Server 11 features: It improves concurrency and scalability by allowing multiple engines to perform without contention.

A *lock* is an internal SQL Server structure. Like any other system resource, a lock must be protected from corruption caused by multiple accesses. When SQL Server 11 needs a lock, it must request this resource. All free locks are stored in a structure known as the *Global Freelock List*. When you set the number of locks available to the system by using the *number of locks* configuration parameter, SQL Server stores these locks in the Global Freelock List.

The Global Freelock List has a *spinlock* semaphore for protection from multiple accesses. If more than one engine wants to obtain a locking structure at the same time, this spinlock can cause a delay. As shown in Figure 7-4, however, SQL Server 11 solves this contention by supporting *multiple freelock caches*. Each engine has a number of locks allocated to its own private freelock cache. Instead of using the Global Freelock List, each engine obtains locks from its cache. This greatly reduces contention because each engine can obtain a lock from its freelock cache without using or waiting for a spinlock semaphore.

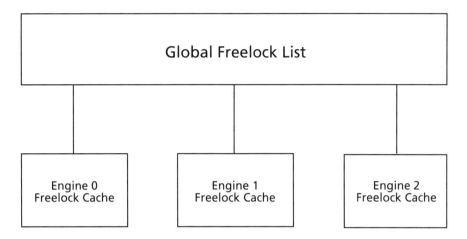

Figure 7-4: *Each engine obtains locks by using a dedicated freelock cache instead of the Global Freelock List.*

Configuring Locking Parameters

You can tune the PLM by using two configurable parameters. The *max engine freelocks* parameter specifies the maximum number of *freelocks* that SQL Server can allocate for each engine. Specifically, this parameter specifies the percentage of the total number of locks (which you set by using the *number of locks* parameter) that you want to divide evenly among all the engines. For example, the *max engine freelocks* parameter's default value of 10 specifies that 10 percent of the total number of locks should be divided equally among all of the engines. So, if you set the *number of locks* parameter to 10,000 and *max engine freelocks* to 10, and you have four engines configured, each freelock cache contains 250 locks: (10,000 * .10)/4.

Be aware that setting the *max engine freelocks* value too high may leave too few locks in the Global Freelock List. If this happens and an engine's freelock cache runs low, SQL Server cannot replenish that freelock cache. Even though the other engines have plenty of locks to spare, SQL Server can only replenish the supply of locks in a freelock cache by using the Global Freelock List. If the Global Freelock List doesn't have enough locks, you may see the 1279 error message:

```
SQL Server has run out of locks on engine %d. Re-run your command when
there are fewer active users, or contact a user with System Administrator
(SA) role to reconfigure max engine freelocks.
```

If this happens, you can either decrease the value of *max engine freelocks* or increase the *number of locks*.

When an engine's freelock cache runs out of locks, it must get more from the Global Freelock List. The *freelock transfer block size* parameter—the other configurable parameter you can use for tuning the PLM—specifies how many locks SQL Server will move from the Global Freelock List to the engine's freelock cache. You should not change this value.

One other configurable parameter also deals with locking: the *deadlock checking period* parameter. When a process requests a lock, the process either gets the lock or waits because some other process already has the lock. While a process waits for a lock, the SQL Server must perform a *deadlock search*, to ensure that this process has not entered a deadlock situation with another process.

A deadlock situation occurs when two processes hold locks and each process is also waiting for the lock that the other process already holds. In this case, both processes never give up their locks because they can never finish their respective transactions. When this happens, SQL Server must choose one of these processes as a deadlock victim, roll back that process's transaction, and thus allow the other process to finish.

Prior to SQL Server 11, the system immediately performs a deadlock search every time a process waits for a lock. SQL Server 11 takes a different approach to these resource-intensive deadlock searches. Instead of immediately performing a deadlock search when a process has to wait for a lock, SQL Server 11 puts the process to sleep. The *deadlock checking period* parameter specifies the amount of time that the process sleeps. When the process wakes up, it tries again to get the lock. If it receives the lock, it can continue without ever performing a deadlock search. If it still cannot obtain the lock, it performs the deadlock search.

You set the *deadlock checking period* by using the *sp_configure* command. This parameter has a default value of 500 milliseconds. If you set this parameter to zero, the system immediately initiates a deadlock search when a process waits for a lock. (This mimics the pre-SQL Server 11 behavior.) If you expect few deadlocks in your applications, you can try setting this value a little higher, to avoid the overhead of deadlock searches. Remember that setting this value higher produces longer delays before SQL Server detects deadlocks.

Using Dirty Reads

The ANSI standard defines four isolation levels for SQL transactions. These isolation levels deal with the accuracy and the consistency of data. SQL Server 11 supports three of these levels:

- Isolation level 0 allows dirty reads. This is a new option in SQL Server 11.

- Isolation level 1 prevents dirty reads. This is the normal SQL Server behavior.

- Isolation level 3 prevents phantom reads.

Dirty reads can provide tremendous performance benefits, if you can accept a potentially significant trade-off in terms of data integrity.

What Is a Dirty Read?

With SQL Server's normal behavior (that is, isolation level 1), when a process needs to modify data, it obtains an exclusive lock on that data's page and thus prevents any other process from reading the data (*select* statements). This exclusive lock is necessary because the data is about to change, and a user who reads it and then immediately re-reads it would see different results. Isolation level 1 ensures accurate results, but significantly reduces system concurrency by forcing one process to wait until another process completes its data manipulation.

With SQL Server 11, you can now choose isolation level 0 and perform a dirty read. When you use dirty reads, you can read the data that another user's process is manipulating. This greatly increases concurrency, but it also adversely affects accuracy.

In other words, you cannot completely trust the data that you obtain by using dirty reads. You should only use this option when data accuracy is not essential. For example, if you run a query to get a rough count of the day's sales, you can perform this query as a dirty read because you probably don't care if you miss the last one or two orders. If you run a query to quote a price to a customer, however, you should not use dirty reads.

Isolation level 0 requires a unique index, because the rows SQL Server reads at isolation level 0 can move during a dirty read. If this happens, the SQL Server must know where it left off reading, which requires the use of a unique index. Although you might successfully complete a dirty read without the index, the read might also fail. For this reason, you should ensure that the data has a unique index.

Setting the Isolation Level

You can set isolation levels at the session level or the query level. To set the isolation level at the session level, use the *set isolation level* command. The *set isolation level* command has the following syntax:

```
set transaction isolation level {0 | 1 | 3 }
```

For example, if you want to use dirty reads in your *isql* session, you issue the following command:

```
set transaction isolation level 0
go
```

To set the isolation level at the query level, you use the *at isolation* clause of the *select* statement. The three choices for this clause are as follows:

- read uncommitted. This specifies isolation level 0.

- read committed. This specifies isolation level 1.

- serializable. This specifies isolation level 3.

For example, to query the *titles* table of the *pubs2* database with a dirty read, use the following syntax:

```
select * from titles at isolation read uncommitted
go
```

TIP! Before using dirty reads, be absolutely sure that you can afford the inaccuracy.

Working with Table Lock Promotions

When a user has locks on only individual pages in a table, other users can continue to access data on different pages in that table. After a user acquires 200 page locks on the same table, however, the SQL Server locks the entire table—that is, it promotes the page locks to a table lock. Once a user has a table lock, no one else can use that table until the user releases the table lock.

SQL Server 11 offers configurable lock promotion instead of a fixed lock promotion value of 200 pages. You can configure the lock promotion value at the server level, the database level, or the table level. If you do not specify the lock promotion value at the table level, SQL Server uses the database level's value. Similarly, if you do not specify a lock promotion value at the database level, SQL Server uses the server level's value.

The lock promotion value has three facets:

- The lock promotion percentage (PCT). This value specifies the percentage of pages in a table to use as a lock promotion value.

- The low-water mark (LWM). This setting specifies the minimum lock promotion value. In other words, if the lock promotion value determined by the PCT setting falls below this minimum value, the LWM overrides that lock promotion value.

- The high-water mark (HWM). This setting specifies the maximum lock promotion value. If the lock promotion value determined by the PCT setting exceeds this maximum value, the HWM overrides that lock promotion value.

You set the PCT as a percentage value between 1 and 100. SQL Server 11 uses that percentage to calculate the lock promotion value for a given table. For example, if you set PCT to 20 and tableA has 100 pages, tableA has a lock promotion value of 20 pages (20 percent of 100). In this scenario, SQL Server promotes 20 page locks to a table lock.

You might note that a value of 20 pages is definitely too small for page lock promotions. The LWM comes into play here. If the lock promotion value falls below the LWM, the LWM takes precedence and becomes the lock promotion value. If you set the LWM to 150 in this example, SQL Server sets the lock promotion value for tableA to 150 instead of 20.

If the lock promotion value exceeds the HWM, the HWM takes precedence. For example, if tableB has 10,000 pages and you set the PCT to 20 and the HWM to 300, SQL Server uses a lock promotion value of 300. The calculated lock promotion value of 2,000 (20 percent of 10,000) exceeds the HWM of 300, so the HWM takes precedence.

Setting the Lock Promotion Value

You can set the lock promotion value by using the *sp_setpglockpromote* command. This command has the following syntax:

```
sp_setpglockpromote "server" | "database" | "table", object, new_lwm,
new_hwm, new_pct
```

The *sp_setpglockpromote* command has the following parameters:

- "server" | "database" | "table": the level at which you want to set the lock promotion value. You can set it at the server level, the database level, or the table level.

- *object*: the name of the database or table for which you are setting the lock promotion value, or NULL if you are setting a server value.

- *new_lwm*: the new LWM value. This value must be greater than 2 and less than *new_hwm*.

- *new_hwm*: the new HWM value. This value must be greater than *new_lwm* and less than 2,147,483,647.

- *new_pct*: the new lock promotion percentage, which must be between 1 and 100.

The following example sets the lock promotion value for the *titles* table to 20 percent, with a low-water mark of 100 and a high-water mark of 200:

```
sp_setpglockpromote "table" , titles, 100, 200, 20
go
```

You can also set promotions on the *server* level by using the *sp_configure* command or the configuration file to set the following parameters:

- *lock promotion HWM*

- *lock promotion LWM*

- *lock promotion PCT*

For example, to set the server-wide LWM to 100, you issue the following command:

```
sp_configure "lock promotion LWM", 100
go
```

Dropping a Lock Promotion

By using the *sp_dropglockpromote* command, you can drop any lock promotions you have set. The *sp_dropglockpromote* command has the following syntax:

```
sp_dropglockpromote "database" | "table", objname
```

The *sp_dropglockpromote* command has the following parameters:

- "database" | "table": the type of object (that is, a database or a table) for which you want to drop the promotion.

- *objname*: the name of the database or the table.

For example, to drop the promotions set in the previous example, you use the following command:

```
sp_dropglockpromote "table", titles
go
```

TIP!   You cannot drop promotions on the server level.

Lock promotion involves a trade-off between concurrency and the use of system resources. The system has a limited number of locks and each allocated lock takes up system memory. If you choose a low lock promotion value, the system quickly promotes page locks to table locks. This causes concurrency problems because the system locks users out of entire tables. On the other hand, a high lock promotion value causes the system to use numerous page locks. This increases the memory that SQL Server 11 dedicates to locks, and it can increase the likelihood that SQL Server will run out of locks.

Turning Databases online and offline

SQL Server 11 includes a new mechanism that's used with database loads and dumps. A database can now be either *online* or *offline*. When SQL Server 11 takes a database offline, no one can use that database. SQL Server 11 uses this capability during database loads to prevent users from making any changes to the database.

When you start a database load, SQL Server 11 automatically sets that database to offline. Therefore, you no longer have to set the *no chkpt on recovery*, *dbo use only*, and *read only* options with the *sp_dboption* command.

When you finish with the database and transaction loads, you must explicitly issue the *online database* command. This command makes the database available to the public. If you forget to issue this command, the database remains inaccessible.

To summarize, the loading of a database involves the following sequence of events:

1. Loading the database (this automatically sets the database to offline).

2. Loading one or more transactions.

3. Issuing the *online database* command. (To make the database accessible, you must explicitly run this command.)

Users who are new to SQL Server 11 often forget to set a database to online. If you experience problems in accessing a database, make sure that the database is set to online. You can see a database's online/offline status by using the *sp_helpdb* command.

TIP!   The *load database* command automatically takes a database offline. You must explicitly bring a database online by issuing the *online database* command. SQL Server 11 does not have an *offline database* command.

The *online database* command has the following syntax:

```
online database database_name
```

The *database_name* parameter represents the name of the database that you want to turn online.

The following example checks the online/offline status of the *pubs2* database and then sets it to online:

```
sp_helpdb pubs2
go
online database pubs2
go
```

The *online database* command has one other function: upgrading a SQL Server 10.x database dump to a SQL Server 11 dump. Remember that SQL Server 11 can read a SQL Server 10.x database dump. It does this by upgrading the dump to a SQL Server 11 dump. The *online database* command enables this functionality. When you upgrade a database, you must then dump the database to create a dump at the current release level. When you then issue the *online database* command, you convert the dump to the SQL Server 11 level.

TIP!   If you have scripts to perform your database loads, make sure you add the *online database* command to those scripts.

Partitioning Tables for Improved Performance

By partitioning tables, you can improve performance when inserting rows into a heap table. A *heap table* is any table that does not have a clustered index. In such a table, any inserts automatically occur on the last page of the table. Consequently, tremendous contention can occur on this last page. If multiple users perform multiple inserts on this table, each user must wait until the previous process releases its exclusive lock on the last page. Waiting for these locks slows down system performance. Partitioning a table creates multiple last pages for a table. SQL Server randomly distributes table inserts among these last pages, and thus eliminates the contention for the last page. If one process has a lock on one last page, another process can still obtain a lock on a different last page.

You may be wondering how a table can have more than one last page. Figure 7-5 illustrates how previous versions of SQL Server store and insert data. The system stores the data in a chain of pages, and each page contains a pointer to the previous and next pages. When you insert a new row, SQL Server places it in the last page of the chain.

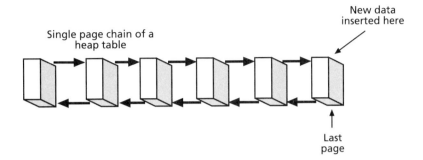

Figure 7-5: *In versions prior to SQL Server 11, the system adds new rows to the last page in a heap table's single page chain.*

In SQL Server 11, a heap table can have multiple page chains instead of a single page chain. When you partition a table, you create multiple page chains and each of these page chains has its own last page. Figure 7-6 illustrates SQL Server 11's multiple page chains.

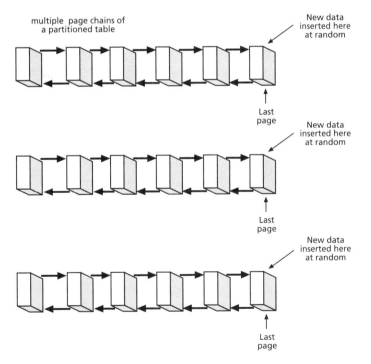

Figure 7-6: *SQL Server 11 adds new rows at random to the last page of any of a heap table's multiple page chains.*

You can modify a table so that it has any number of page chains. For example, if you modify a table to have 200 partitions, SQL Server 11 has 200 separate places to randomly insert new rows. By properly using table partitioning, you can improve the performance of table inserts to match that of inserts on separate tables.

You partition a table by using the *alter table* command. You cannot create a table as partitioned, you must first create the table and then alter it. In addition, you cannot create partitions on a table with a clustered index. Remember, the table must be a heap table. When used for partitioning, the *alter table* command has the following syntax:

```
alter table table_name partition num_partitions
```

This syntax includes the following parameters:

- *table_name*: the name of the table that you want to partition.

- *num_partitions*: the number of partitions that you want to create.

To unpartition a table, you use the unpartition form of the *alter table* command. You cannot truncate or drop a partitioned table. You must first unpartition such a table, then you can truncate or drop it. Similarly, if you want to change the number of partitions in a table, you must unpartition the table and then repartition it. To unpartition a table, you use the following syntax:

```
alter table table_name unpartition
```

The *table_name* parameter specifies the name of the table that you want to unpartition.

You can obtain information about table partitions by using the *sp_helpartition* command or the *sp_help* command. The *sp_helpartition* command has the following syntax:

```
sp_helpartition table_name
```

The *table_name* parameter represents the name of the partitioned table in the current database.

The following example alters the *sales* table so that it has four partitions and then displays information about these four partitions:

```
alter table sales partition 4
go
sp_helpartition sales
go
```

SQL Server responds by displaying the following information:

```
partitionid  firstpage    controlpage
-----------  ---------    -----------
1            145          146
2            312          313
3            384          385
4            392          393
```

The next set of commands repartitions the *sales* table to 100 partitions:

```
alter table sales unpartition
go
alter table sales partition 100
go
```

You can use table partitioning to improve the performance of a large *bcp*. When you copy large amounts of data, you already drop any clustered indexes to improve performance of the *bcp*. By partitioning the table, you can try using multiple instances of *bcp* at the same time on the same table. The partitions allow the multiple inserts to avoid interfering with each other. To do this in the most efficient way, divide your data into different files. Partition the table and start up multiple instances of *bcp*. The performance should be significantly better than that of a single *bcp*. Chapter 9, "SQL Server 11 Performance and Tuning," provides in-depth coverage of this technique.

The Housekeeper Task

SQL Server 11 includes a new task—the housekeeper—that can significantly improve performance and requires almost no user administration. The housekeeper task deals with data cache page chains and the Buffer Manager system. (For in-depth coverage of these topics, refer to Chapter 6, "The Buffer Manager.") In most cases, you simply ignore the housekeeper and let it perform its tasks. As detailed in the section, "Configuring and Tuning the Housekeeper," later in this chapter, you may encounter one or two advanced situations in which you might want to configure the housekeeper.

What Is the Housekeeper?

The housekeeper task runs in the background of the SQL Server. Whenever SQL Server 11 has idle time, the housekeeper starts writing data pages from cache onto disk (buffer washing). The housekeeper improves CPU utilization by taking advantage of idle SQL

Server cycles. It is important to note that the housekeeper does not interfere with normal server functions. It runs only when SQL Server 11 is idle. If another task needs the SQL Server's resources, the housekeeper relinquishes its control. The housekeeper can relinquish control because it runs at the lowest priority available to SQL Server threads.

> **TIP!**   Prior to SQL Server 11, buffer washing could occur during a transaction and thus cause a delay in that transaction.

How does the housekeeper task benefit SQL Server 11? Physical I/O is a costly operation for SQL Server 11. In fact, physical I/O is one of the most time-consuming tasks that SQL Server 11 performs. By performing physical I/O while SQL Server 11 is otherwise idle, the housekeeper avoids contention with user processes.

> **TIP!**   The housekeeper task does not perform buffer washing in caches of type *logonly*.

You will notice the housekeeper task when you run an *sp_who* command:

```
sp_who
go
```

Other internal SQL Server 11 threads such as *checkpoint* show up in the *sp_who* output, so you should not be surprised that you also see the housekeeper task in this output:

spid	status	loginame	hostname	blk	dbname	cmd
1	running	sa	mars	0	master	SELECT
2	sleeping	NULL		0	master	NETWORK HANDLER
3	sleeping	NULL		0	master	MIRROR HANDLER
4	*sleeping*	*NULL*		*0*	*master*	*HOUSEKEEPER*
5	sleeping	NULL		0	master	CHECKPOINT SLEEP

How Does the Housekeeper Work?

The housekeeper waits for idle cycles in SQL Server 11. When SQL Server 11 is idle, the housekeeper starts washing dirty buffers on the MRU/LRU buffer chain. It starts at the wash marker and works its way toward the MRU side of the chain. If the housekeeper reaches the MRU side of the chain, it wakes up the checkpoint process, which then checkpoints all the databases. This is known as a *free checkpoint* because the checkpoint occurs as a result of the housekeeper's work during free time. These free writes may reduce database recovery time. With more frequent checkpoints, SQL Server may have less data to recover.

TIP! Although free checkpoints may reduce recovery time, they do not affect the *recovery interval* configuration parameter. This parameter still sets the *maximum* recovery time.

To summarize, the housekeeper task may provide the following benefits:

- Improved CPU utilization

- Decreased need for buffer washing during transactions

- Faster checkpoints

- Shorter recovery time

Potential Disadvantages of the Housekeeper

Under one possible scenario, the housekeeper can cause additional overhead for SQL Server 11. If the same database page is updated repeatedly, the housekeeper may write that page to disk many more times than are necessary. If SQL Server 11 has idle cycles and the housekeeper sees that this page has been updated, it writes the page to disk. In this way, the housekeeper may do more work than necessary simply because it has nothing else to do. Although these writes occur during idle time, they still put a workload on the disks. On a system with heavy disk use, this extra overhead may degrade performance.

You can solve this problem by limiting the number of these *free writes* that the housekeeper can perform. To accomplish this, you modify the *housekeeper free write percent* configuration parameter. This parameter specifies the maximum percentage by which the housekeeper can increase database writes over normal activity. For example, if you set the *housekeeper free write percent* to 25, the housekeeper stops working when it has performed 25 percent more writes than normal. To solve the *repeated update* problem, you can choose a smaller percentage value for this parameter or you can disable the housekeeper task altogether. (The next section of this chapter, "Configuring and Tuning the Housekeeper," details the syntax you use for setting the *housekeeper free write percent*.)

You may want to modify the *housekeeper free write percent* configuration parameter if you have the following situations:

- Idle SQL Server 11 cycles

- One page that is repeatedly updated

- Disks that are constantly busy

Configuring and Tuning the Housekeeper

You can only interact with the housekeeper by using the *sp_configure* command to set the *housekeeper free write percent* parameter. As mentioned, you use this parameter to specify the maximum percentage by which the housekeeper can increase database writes over normal activity. You can also use this parameter to disable the housekeeper.

As explained in the preceding section, you use this setting in only a few cases. If you need to use this setting, do so carefully. If you set this value too high, the housekeeper becomes very aggressive and may interfere with other threads. If you set it too low, the housekeeper may cease to be effective. By using the monitoring tools discussed in Chapter 8, "Monitoring SQL Server 11," you can see how the housekeeper is working and you can decide how to configure the *housekeeper free write percent* value. In particular, you should monitor information about idle times and free checkpoints.

You use the following syntax for configuring the *housekeeper free write percent*:

```
sp_configure "housekeeper free write percent", value
```

The *value* must be between 0 and 100; this represents the maximum percentage by which the housekeeper can increase database writes over normal activity.

TIP!   Setting this parameter to 0 disables the housekeeper task. Setting this parameter to 100 allows the housekeeper to work continuously.

The following example sets the *housekeeper free write percent* to 20:

```
sp_configure "housekeeper free write percent", 20
go
```

As with all other configuration parameters, you can specify the *housekeeper free write percent* in the configuration file:

```
[SQL Server Administration]
    lock promotion LWM = DEFAULT
    lock promotion PCT = DEFAULT
    housekeeper free write percent = 25
```

Disabling the Housekeeper

As mentioned in the previous section, you can disable the housekeeper. For example, you may want to disable the housekeeper when you try to establish baseline settings for performance monitoring. Because the housekeeper uses SQL Server 11's idle cycles, it can complicate your efforts to analyze system performance under some circumstances. To disable the housekeeper, simply set the *housekeeper free write percent* to zero:

```
sp_configure "housekeeper free write percent", 0
go
```

Summary

This chapter describes major improvements to two of SQL Server's main systems. The logging and locking systems have undergone complete overhauls to increase scalability and decrease contention. This chapter also discusses two of SQL Server 11's major new features: the housekeeper task, which runs in the background to help utilize idle time, and table partitioning, which greatly improves the performance of insert statements.

The following chapter shows you how to monitor SQL Server 11. By using the techniques that chapter describes, you can monitor the features you covered in this chapter. You can use the monitoring information to make decisions about tuning these features, and to benchmark the performance benefits these features provide.

Migration Checklist

The following list summarizes the key migration tasks covered in this chapter:

- Learn about the user log cache.
- Learn how to query the *syslogshold* table.
- Learn about variable log I/O sizes.
- Configure a 4K pool for log I/O.
- Learn how to configure the locking system.
- Learn when to use dirty reads.
- Learn about database online/offline.
- Change load scripts to turn on a database after loads.
- Learn how to use table partitioning.
- Become familiar with the housekeeper task.
- Find out how to see the housekeeper task when running the *sp_who* command.

◆ If you notice performance problems, monitor the housekeeper task as a potential cause of overhead in rare situations.

◆ Find out how to configure the *housekeeper free write percent* parameter by using the *sp_configure* command or the configuration file (for those rare occasions when this becomes necessary).

Command Reference

alter table partition

Syntax
```
alter table table_name partition num_partitions
```

Example
```
alter table sales partition 4
```

alter table unpartition

Syntax
```
alter table table_name unpartition
```

Example
```
alter table sales unpartition
```

set transaction isolation level

Syntax
```
set transaction isolation level {0 | 1 | 3 }
```

Example
```
set transaction isolation level 0
```

sp_configure

Syntax

```
sp_configure "housekeeper free write percent", value
sp_configure "user log cache size", ulc_size
```

Examples

```
sp_configure "housekeeper free write percent", 20
sp_configure "user log cache size", 4096
```

sp_dropglockpromote

Syntax

```
sp_dropglockpromote "database" | "table", objname
```

Example

```
sp_droplockpromote "table", titles
```

sp_helpartition

Syntax

```
sp_helpartition table_name
```

Example

```
sp_helpartition sales
```

sp_logiosize

Syntax

```
sp_logiosize ["default" | " size " | "all"]
```

Example

```
sp_logiosize "default"
```

sp_setpglockpromote

Syntax

```
sp_setpglockpromote "server" | "database" | "table", object, new_lwm,
new_hwm, new_pct
```

Example

```
sp_setpglockpromote "table" , titles, 100, 200, 20
```

8

Monitoring SQL Server 11

In This Chapter

- Timing SQL statements and procedures

- Using Sybase SQL Server Monitor

- Using *showplan* and interpreting its output

- Using the *statistics i/o* and *statistics time* commands

- Using the *dbcc traceon 302* and *310* commands and interpreting their output

- Using the *sp_sysmon* command and understanding its output

To establish and maintain a high-performance system, you must monitor SQL Server 11. This chapter covers the various methods you can use for monitoring SQL Server 11. By using the techniques described in this chapter, as well as the performance and tuning guidelines that Chapter 9 details, you can tune SQL Server 11 for high performance.

Timing SQL Statements

You often need to determine how long SQL Server 11 takes to complete a stored procedure or a SQL query. You can easily add this capability to your queries by inserting code that uses the *getdate* command and the *datediff* command. Simply use the *getdate* command to obtain the time before and after the query or procedure, and then use the *datediff* function to display the difference between the two times. The *datediff* command can display this information in units of milliseconds. (For detailed information about the *getdate* command and the *datediff* command, refer to the *SQL Server Reference Manual, Volume 1.*)

For example, you can time the stored procedure *proc1* by issuing the following SQL commands:

```
declare @time1 datetime
declare @time2 datetime
select @time1=getdate()
exec proc1
select @time2=getdate()
select "TIME",datediff( ms, @time1,@time2)
go
```

The first two lines in this code declare variables for storing the time data. The third and fifth lines get the time before and after execution of the stored procedure. The last line uses the *datediff* command to display the difference between the start and end times (in milliseconds). Here's the output from this code:

```
(1 row affected)
----  ----------
TIME         13
```

NOTE: This method displays elapsed time, not CPU time. SQL Server displays the elapsed time in units of milliseconds.

Using Sybase SQL Server Monitor

The Sybase SQL Server Monitor product offers a graphical means for maintaining and troubleshooting SQL Server 11. You must purchase this product separately, but it is well worth the investment.

Each window displayed by Sybase SQL Server Monitor provides information about a particular aspect of SQL Server 11's performance. For example, the Data Cache window clearly displays the logical and physical reads for each data cache, as well as the data cache hit ratio, and thus allows you to easily determine whether your data caches are being properly used.

Sybase SQL Server Monitor has two main components: the Sybase SQL Server Monitor server, and the Sybase SQL Server Monitor client. These two separate processes communicate with each other, to provide the information you need for monitoring SQL Server's performance. The Sybase SQL Server Monitor server connects to the shared memory of a running SQL Server, and the client connects to the Sybase SQL Server Monitor server. The client provides the graphical user interface with which you use the information that the server contains. When you start the Sybase SQL Server Monitor client, remember that you connect it to the Sybase SQL Server Monitor server, not the SQL Server. Figure 8-1 shows the main menu for the Sybase SQL Server Monitor client. To display a particular Sybase SQL Server Monitor window, simply click on that window's name in the client's main menu.

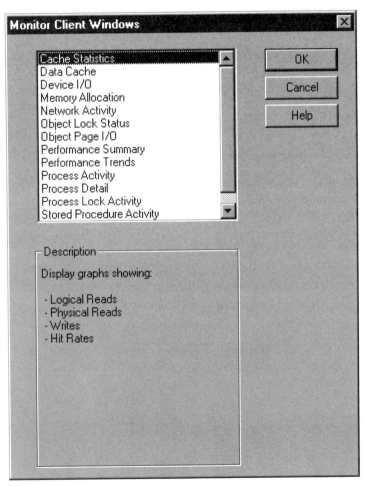

Figure 8-1: *The Sybase SQL Server Monitor client's main menu*

As an alternative to the Sybase SQL Server Monitor, you can obtain most of the same information by using the *sp_sysmon* stored procedure. (For a complete discussion of this stored procedure, refer to the section, "Monitoring SQL Server 11 by Using *sp_sysmon*," later in this chapter.) Sybase SQL Server Monitor's main advantage rests with its graphical display. However, Sybase SQL Server Monitor does provide two categories of useful information that you cannot easily obtain by other means. First, Sybase SQL Server Monitor can display stored procedure run times for all procedures running on SQL Server 11. Sybase SQL Server Monitor tracks and displays average run times and the number of executions, as each stored procedure is used. Figure 8-2 shows the format of this Stored Procedure Activity window.

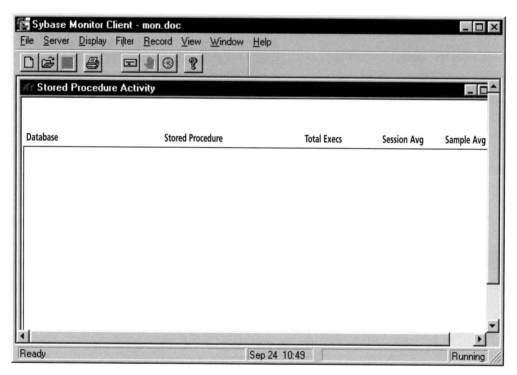

Figure 8-2: *The Sybase SQL Server Monitor client's Stored Procedure Activity window*

The Object Lock Status window shows detailed information about locks, as they occur. Again, this window provides useful information that you cannot easily obtain from other sources. For example, this window shows a page lock on a particular table and identifies the page on which the lock occurs. This can be invaluable for alleviating deadlock and other locking-related performance problems. Figure 8-3 shows the layout of this window.

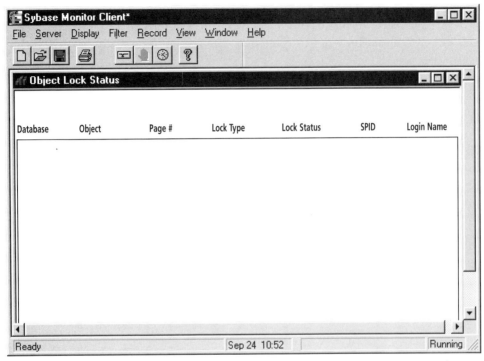

***Figure 8-3:** The Sybase SQL Server Monitor client's Object Lock Status window*

To purchase Sybase SQL Server Monitor, contact Sybase, Inc. You can also consider other, third-party monitoring products.

Monitoring SQL Server 11 by Using showplan

Showplan is perhaps the most important tool that Sybase includes with SQL Server 11. It is essential that you learn how to use *showplan* and interpret its results. By showing you how the optimizer executes your queries, *showplan* provides you with an inside look at what happens when you submit a query.

Showplan shows you the query plan that the optimizer decides to use for processing your query. A *query plan* defines the steps the optimizer uses to perform a query—in other words, it determines the access path to the data. When you submit a query, the optimizer makes various decisions—for example, which index to use and in what order tables should be joined. Based on these decisions, the optimizer formulates a plan that defines the most efficient method for performing the query.

The output from SQL Server 11's version of *showplan* differs dramatically from that of previous versions. Specifically, it is much less cryptic and provides greater detail. For complete information about how to interpret all of *showplan*'s output, refer to the *Sybase SQL Server Performance and Tuning Guide*.

You turn on *showplan* by issuing the *set showplan on* command. You turn it off by using the *set showplan off* command. In many cases—in particular, when your query will return large amounts of data—you use *showplan* with the *set noexec on* command. The *set noexec on* command prevents the SQL Server from executing your query. In this way, you can see the *showplan* output, but not the query output.

TIP!   If you need to use the *set showplan on* command with the *set noexec on* command, make sure you issue the *showplan* command first. Once you issue the *set noexec on* command, the SQL Server does not recognize any commands except the *set noexec off* command.

The following example prepares the SQL Server 11 to use the *showplan* command with *noexec* turned on, and then runs a query:

```
set showplan on
set noexec on
go
select au_id from authors
go
```

These commands produce the following output:

```
QUERY PLAN FOR STATEMENT 1 (at line 1).
    STEP 1
        The type of query is SELECT.

        FROM TABLE
            authors
        Nested iteration.
        Table Scan.
        Ascending scan.
        Positioning at start of table.
        Using I/O Size 2 Kbytes.
        With LRU Buffer Replacement Strategy.
```

Once you become familiar with *showplan*'s terminology, you can easily determine what the optimizer is doing. By using this information, you can find ways to minimize or eliminate any performance problems in a query. In the preceding example, you see that the optimizer performs a table scan on the *authors* table. At first glance, you might wonder why the optimizer doesn't use the index. If you study the *authors* table, however, you might find that it contains only 23 rows. In this case, it is more efficient for the optimizer to perform a small table scan.

The *showplan* output for this example also shows that the optimizer decided to use 2K I/O (instead of large I/O) and the LRU replacement strategy. Because this query will return only 23 rows of one small column, the optimizer determines that large I/O would not be useful.

To gain additional insight into the *showplan* output, consider the following example query:

```
set showplan on
set noexec on
go
select stor_id from salesdetail where stor_id = "5023"
go
```

This produces the following output:

```
QUERY PLAN FOR STATEMENT 1 (at line 1).
   STEP 1
     The type of query is SELECT.
     FROM TABLE
         salesdetail
     Nested iteration.
     Index : salesdetailind
     Ascending scan.
     Positioning by key.
     Index contains all needed columns. Base table will not be read.
     Keys are:
         stor_id
     Using I/O Size 2 Kbytes.
     With LRU Buffer Replacement Strategy.
```

The *showplan* output shows that this query uses the *salesdetailind* nonclustered index. *Showplan* shows you that the index for the *salesdetail* table contains the information this query requires—in other words, this is a covered query. Consequently, SQL Server can respond to the query without reading the *salesdetail* table.

You use *showplan* primarily to ensure that your queries use the indexes and the I/O sizes that you expected. Use *showplan* as one of the first steps in analyzing queries that do not achieve the expected performance levels.

Using Statistics IO *and* Statistics Time

Along with *showplan*, the *set statistics io* and *set statistics time* commands provide simple, useful information for monitoring your queries. The *set statistics io* command provides information about the number of logical and physical reads and writes that SQL Server must perform in response to your queries. You need this information for finding and correcting performance problems. For example, if a query performs physical I/O, you know to change the caches being used. If a query requires many more logical reads than seem necessary, you know that you have a problem in either the query itself or the indexes the query uses. The *set statistics io* command helps you isolate the cause of the problem.

To turn on statistics i/o, you issue the *set statistics io on* command. You turn off statistics i/o by issuing the *set statistics io off* command. Do not use *set noexec on* with *set statistics io on*, because this prevents display of the statistics i/o output.

The following example shows how you use the *set statistics io on* command. First, turn on statistics i/o by issuing the following command:

```
set statistics io on
go
```

Next, issue a query:

```
select stor_id from salesdetail where stor_id = "5023"
go
```

Because you turned on statistics i/o, SQL Server responds with both the query results and the statistics for this query:

```
stor_id
-------
5023
5023
5023
5023

Table: salesdetail   scan count 1,   logical reads: 3,   physical reads: 0
Total writes for this command: 0
```

The output clearly shows how many logical and physical reads result from this query.

The *set statistics time* command displays the amount of time (measured in milliseconds) that SQL Server takes to execute each line of a query, as well as the time it takes to parse and compile the query. To help you gauge the performance of your queries, this command shows the elapsed time and the CPU time for a query. The *elapsed time* measures the amount of time that passes during execution of the query. In other words, the period of time covered by this measure begins when you issue the query and ends when SQL Server returns the query results. The *CPU time* indicates the amount of time the query runs on an engine. Remember that SQL Server 11 gives each task a time slice, and then moves on to process another task or disk or network I/O. The CPU time value represents the amount of time in which a SQL Server 11 engine actually processes the query.

The *set statistics time* command also reports the parse and compile time and the execution time. The *set statistics time* command reports these values in units of timeticks, which are machine dependent. To convert timeticks to milliseconds, you need to know the clock rate for your SQL Server 11. You find this value in the *sql server clock tick length* parameter. To see this value, use *sp_configure*. To convert timeticks to milliseconds, multiply the number of timeticks by this clock rate, and divide the result by 1,000.

You turn on statistics time by issuing the *set statistics time on* command, and you turn it off with the *set statistics time off* command. Do not use *set noexec on* with the *set statistics time on* command, because this prevents display of the *statistics time* output.

The following example demonstrates the use of *set statistics time on* with a simple query. First, turn on statistics time:

```
set statistics time on
go
```

Next, issue a query:

```
select stor_id from salesdetail where stor_id = "5023"
go
```

Because you turned on statistics time, SQL Server responds with both the query results and the statistics for this query:

```
Parse and Compile Time 1.
SQL Server cpu time: 100 ms.
stor_id
-------
5023
5023
5023
Execution Time 0.
SQL Server cpu time: 0 ms.   SQL Server elapsed time: 23 ms.
```

The output shows that this query has a parse and compile time of 1. To convert this value to milliseconds, you first find the clock rate:

```
sp_configure "sql server clock tick length"
go
```

This command returns the following information:

```
100000
```

To express the parse and compile time in milliseconds, you multiply this clock rate by the number of time ticks and then divide the result by 1,000:

```
(100,000 * 1)/1,000 =   100 milliseconds
```

TIP!   The *set statistics io* and *set statistics time* commands have not changed from previous releases.

Monitoring SQL Server 11 by Using dbcc 302 and dbcc 310

If you continue to have performance problems after using the other methods that this chapter describes, you need to use more sophisticated methods, such as the *dbcc 302* and *dbcc 310* trace commands. These SQL Server 11 monitoring tools provide detailed, advanced information about SQL Server 11's optimizer. The *dbcc 302* trace command provides information about the optimizer's index selection, and the *dbcc 310* trace command provides information about the costs of all permutations for a join.

Before using either of these commands, you must issue the *dbcc traceon 3604* command. This command redirects the trace output to the client instead of the errorlog. If you forget to use this command, all output from the trace commands goes to the errorlog. You can combine the *dbcc 3604* command with the *dbcc 302* command and the *dbcc 310* command, or you can use it separately. Remember that you must have the system administrator (sa) role to use these commands.

The *dbcc 3604* command has the following syntax:

```
dbcc traceon (3604)
go
```

As mentioned, you can also combine the commands:

```
dbcc traceon (3604,302,310)
go
```

Using the *dbcc traceon 302* Command

As mentioned earlier in this chapter, the *showplan* command shows you the query plan that the optimizer has chosen as the most efficient means for accessing the required data. The *dbcc 302* command shows you *all* of the query plans considered by the optimizer and the relative cost of each plan.

By studying the output from the *dbcc 302* command, you can follow the logic the optimizer used to choose a query plan. This information can help you determine why your query does not perform as expected. You might have done something wrong in the query or its underlying tables to prevent SQL Server 11 from making the best decisions, or the optimizer may not choose the best path because it makes invalid assumptions. In either case, once you find the underlying problem, you have a starting point for improving the query's performance.

The *dbcc 302* command has the following syntax:

```
dbcc traceon (302)
go
```

TIP!   Be sure to use the *dbcc 3604* command first, and make sure you have system administrator privileges.

The following example shows the output of the *dbcc 302* command along with the *showplan* output for a simple query. The next section in this chapter interprets the results from these commands:

```
use pubs2
go
set showplan on
go
dbcc traceon(3604,302)
go
select stor_id from salesdetail where stor_id = "5023" and
title_id="TC3218"
go
```

SQL Server 11 responds to these commands by displaying the following information:

```
QUERY PLAN FOR STATEMENT 1 (at line 1).
    STEP 1
        The type of query is DBCC.
DBCC execution completed. If DBCC printed error messages, contact a user
with System Administrator (SA) role.
******************************
```

```
Entering q_score_index() for table 'salesdetail' (objectid 144003544,
varno = 0).
The table has 116 rows and 3 pages.
Scoring the SEARCH CLAUSE:
   title_id EQ
   stor_id EQ
Base cost: indid: 0 rows: 116 pages: 3 prefetch: N
   I/O size: 2 cacheid: 0 replace: LRU
Relop bits are: 4
No statistics page-use magicSC
Estimate: indid 2, selectivity 0.100000, rows 12 pages 13
Relop bits are: 5
No statistics page-use magicSC
Estimate: indid 3, selectivity 0.100000, rows 12 pages 13
Cheapest index is index 2, costing 13 pages and
   generating 1 rows per scan, using no data prefetch (size 2)
   on dcacheid 0 with LRU replacement
Search argument selectivity is 0.010000.
*******************************
QUERY PLAN FOR STATEMENT 1 (at line 1).
    STEP 1
         The type of query is SELECT.
         FROM TABLE
              salesdetail
         Nested iteration.
         Table Scan.
         Ascending scan.
         Positioning at start of table.
         Using I/O Size 2 Kbytes.
         With LRU Buffer Replacement Strategy.
  stor_id
  --------
  5023
(1 row affected)
```

Interpreting the *dbcc 302* Output

The first section of the *dbcc 302* output contains a line with a *q_score_index()* for each table involved in the query. The simple example presented in the preceding section uses only one table. For a given table and *where* clauses, the *q_score_index* function determines the best index to use. As shown in the following excerpt from the sample output, this function specifies the table name and the table id:

```
Entering q_score_index() for table 'salesdetail' (objectid 144003544,
varno = 0).
```

It then gives the size of the table in rows and pages:

```
The table has 116 rows and 3 pages.
```

The system obtains this information from the table's OAM (Object Allocation Map) page.

Next, the output evaluates the *where* clause. A *where* clause can be either a search clause or a join clause. This example uses a search clause; the query does not include a join:

```
Scoring the SEARCH CLAUSE:
  title_id EQ
  stor_id EQ
```

You already need to check several items in the output, to evaluate the query. First, make sure that the optimizer has the correct size for the table. If the optimizer uses an incorrect table size, it may make poor choices in the query plan—for example, choosing a table scan. Second, make sure that this section of the *dbcc 302* output mentions all the *where* clauses. A missing clause in this section of the output may indicate a problem. For example, you might expect the optimizer to use an index for a particular clause, only to find that the optimizer does not even consider that clause. This might result from datatype mismatches or a clause that does not qualify as a *SARG*—for example, a clause with a function used on the column. (For more information about the reasons why the optimizer might not use a clause, refer to the section on *SARGs* in the *Sybase SQL Server Performance and Tuning Guide.*)

The next lines in the *dbcc 302* output calculate the base cost the optimizer uses for comparing other costs:

```
Base cost: indid: 0 rows: 116 pages: 3
Relop bits are: 4
```

Remember that *cost* represents the optimizer's estimate of the time required for using a method. A lower cost estimate identifies a more efficient access path. Because the index id in this example is 0, the base cost is the cost of a table scan. For this example, the optimizer estimates that it requires three pages to perform a table scan on this table.

If the base cost seems unreasonable based on your knowledge of the table size, you should investigate further. Try to figure out why the optimizer is using an incorrect size. You may want to run *update statistics*, *dbcc checktable*, or *dbcc checkdb*.

You can ignore the next line in the output, which involves relop bits.

Next, the optimizer determines the costs for each index that it can use. It uses these costs to determine the best index for the query. The next lines of the example output are as follows:

```
No statistics page—use magicSC
Estimate: indid 2, selectivity 0.100000, rows 12 pages 13
```

This analysis of index id 2 shows that the optimizer requires 13 pages to use this index. Although 13 pages may immediately strike you as wrong, note that the preceding line in this excerpt indicates that no statistics page is available for this query.

Whenever you create an index on a table containing data, SQL Server creates a distribution page to store statistics about the index. The optimizer needs these statistics during its decision process. You update this distribution page whenever you run the *update statistics* command. As shown in Figure 8-4, the distribution page has two types of statistics: a distribution of index key values, which it stores in the distribution table, and a proportion of duplicate keys (density), which it stores in the density table.

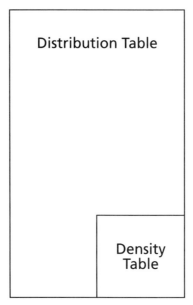

Figure 8-4: *The index distribution page*

The distribution table stores a list of key values, called *steps*. Each step represents a part of the index. By using the distribution table, the optimizer can estimate the number of rows necessary for satisfying the clause. Table 8-1 shows a distribution table with several steps listed.

Table 8-1: *A Distribution Table with Several Steps and Key Values*

Step	Index Value
0	M10100
1	M10123
2	M10137
…	…
90	M101203

The optimizer checks for a value in the distribution table. Any value the optimizer finds falls into one of the following categories:

- The value falls between two consecutive rows in the table.

- The value equals one row in the middle of the table.

- The value equals the first row or the last row in the table.

- The value equals more than one row in the middle of the table.

- The value equals more than one row, including the first row or the last row in the table.

- The value is less than the first row, or greater than the last row in the table.

The *dbcc 302* output displays this information. For example, if the value equals the value in the first or last step of the distribution page, you see the following message in the *dbcc 302* output:

```
equal to a single row (1st or last) — use endsingleSC
```

The density table contains the other type of statistics used by the optimizer. This table contains the average proportion of duplicate keys in the index (density). The density ranges from 0 to 100 percent. In a completely unique table with N rows, the density is 1/N. If the table consists entirely of duplicates, the density is 100 percent.

The optimizer uses the density to help determine the number of rows a query will return. This is especially important when the optimizer does not know the value of a search parameter at compile time—for example, when you use variables in a query. In such cases, the optimizer does not know which value you want when it creates the query plan. Consequently, using different parameters with the same query can return tremendously different results. For example, the following query might return one row if the value of @a is $100, or it might return thousands of rows if @a is $1:

```
select title from titles where price > @a
```

The statistics in the density table help the optimizer to analyze the number of rows returned. It is important to note that if these density statistics are not available, SQL Server 11 uses certain default density statistics, known as *magic numbers*. If these defaults do not fit your particular situation, the optimizer might create a very poor query plan. The following table lists the default densities for three conditions, as well as an example of each condition:

Condition	Default	Example
Equality	10%	col = x
Closed interval	25%	col > x and col < y
Open end range	33%	col > x

According to this table, if the query has an equality clause, the optimizer assumes that 10 percent of the table will be returned. If the query will actually return 50 percent of the table, the optimizer will not create an efficient query plan. As this example shows, you must be very careful if no density statistics are available. In such cases, try running the *update statistics* command.

If *dbcc 302* finds a match on the distribution table for the search value, the *dbcc 302* output includes the following line:

```
Match found on statistics page statistics page information
```

The following output indicates that *dbcc 302* did not find a match:

```
No steps for search value — qualpage for LT search value finds
```

This means the optimizer is looking for the first step value that is less than the search value. The output then displays one of the following three lines, depending on whether the search value is smaller than the first entry on the distribution page, larger than the last entry on the distribution page, or between two steps on the distribution page:

- value < first step — use outsideSC
- value between step K, K+1, K=*step number* — use betweenSC
- value > last step — use outsideSC

With no statistics page at all, you see the following output:

```
No statistics page — use magicSC
```

This is the case in the example output. With no statistics page to use, the optimizer uses the magic numbers. In this example, the optimizer assumes that 10 percent of the table (the magic number for equality clauses) will match the clause. Because the *salesdetail* table has 116 rows, the optimizer assumes that the query will return 11 rows.

Next, the *dbcc 302* output shows the selectivity for the clause. *Selectivity* specifies the fraction of rows in the table that optimizer expects to qualify for the clause. A selective clause returns relatively few rows. The selectivity in this example is .10:

```
Estimate: indid 2, selectivity 0.100000, rows 12 pages 13
```

The last piece of information provided in the *dbcc 302* output is the optimizer's decision of the cheapest index:

```
Cheapest index is index 2, costing 13 pages and
    generating 1 rows per scan
```

However, the base cost of the table scan in this example uses only three pages. For this reason, the optimizer uses a table scan to access the data. (You can see this by using *showplan*.)

The preceding example highlights the need for running *update statistics* on the *salesdetail* table. In the preceding example, the optimizer could not find any statistics to use in its decisions. The following example demonstrates the effect of running the *update statistics* command. Again, the following example shows the output of the *dbcc 302* command along with the *showplan* output for a simple query:

```
use pubs2
go
set showplan on
dbcc traceon(3604,302)
go
select stor_id from salesdetail where stor_id = "5023" and
title_id="TC3218"
go
```

The following listing shows the output of *dbcc 302* after running the *update statistics* command:

```
QUERY PLAN FOR STATEMENT 1 (at line 1).
    STEP 1
        The type of query is DBCC.
```

```
DBCC execution completed. If DBCC printed error messages, contact a user
with System Administrator (SA) role.
*******************************
Entering q_score_index() for table 'salesdetail' (objectid 144003544,
varno = 0).
The table has 116 rows and 3 pages.
Scoring the SEARCH CLAUSE:
  title_id EQ
  stor_id EQ
Base cost: indid: 0 rows: 116 pages: 3 prefetch: N
  I/O size: 2 cacheid: 0 replace: LRU
Relop bits are: 4
Qualifying stat page; pgno: 428 steps: 115
Search value: TC3218
Match found on statistics page
equal to several rows in middle of page-use midseveralSC
Estimate: indid 2, selectivity 0.043478, rows 5 pages 7
Relop bits are: 5
Qualifying stat page; pgno: 612 steps: 115
Search value: 5023
Match found on statistics page
equal to several rows including 1st or last-use endseveralSC
Estimate: indid 3, selectivity 0.430435, rows 50 pages 51
Cheapest index is index 2, costing 7 pages and
  generating 2 rows per scan, using no data prefetch (size 2)
  on dcacheid 0 with LRU replacement
Search argument selectivity is 0.018715.
*******************************
QUERY PLAN FOR STATEMENT 1 (at line 1).
    STEP 1
        The type of query is SELECT.
        FROM TABLE
            salesdetail
        Nested iteration.
        Table Scan.
        Ascending scan.
        Positioning at start of table.
        Using I/O Size 2 Kbytes.
        With LRU Buffer Replacement Strategy.
stor_id
-------
5023
(1 row affected)
```

You can see that the optimizer now finds and uses statistical information, and this makes the estimates more realistic. In this example, the optimizer still chooses a table scan, because the entire *salesdetail* table is so small. With a larger table, however, the optimizer might decide to use an index instead of a table scan—and thus greatly improve performance.

TIP!   If the distribution table does not contain a search value, or no are statistics
available, run the *update statistics* command.

Notice two points about the new *dbcc 302* output. First, because the optimizer found
a statistics page for the search value, the page estimate for index id 2 drops from 13 pages
to seven pages. Second, the optimizer now considers using index id 3 for the query. In the
previous example, the optimizer did not even consider this index.

Using the *dbcc traceon 310* Command

The *dbcc traceon 310* command shows you the costs of all the permutations for a join. Like
the *dbcc 302* command, it shows you what happens "under the hood" of the optimizer. You
see all the possibilities that the optimizer considers for processing the join, as well as the
reasons why the optimizer picked a particular method as the best one. You use the output
of the *dbcc 310* command in much the same way as that of the *dbcc 302* command, to
ensure that the optimizer does what you expect. The *dbcc 310* command has the following syntax:

```
dbcc traceon (310)
go
```

As with the *dbcc 302* command, make sure you first redirect the trace output away
from the errorlog by using the *dbcc traceon (3604)* command. The following example
shows the output generated by the *dbcc 310* command and the *showplan* command, for a
simple join. First, turn on *showplan* and then issue the *dbcc* commands:

```
set showplan on
go
dbcc traceon(3604,310)
go
use pubs2
go
select a.pub_name from ntitles a, npublishers b where a.pub_name =
b.pub_name
go
```

SQL Server 11 responds with the following output:

```
STEP 1
The type of query is DBCC.
DBCC execution completed. If DBCC printed error messages, contact a user
with System Administrator (SA) role.
```

```
STEP 1
The type of query is USE DATABASE.
Finishing q_score_index() for table 'npublishers' (objectid 688005482).
Cheapest index is index 2, costing 10 pages and
  generating 1155 rows per scan, using  data prefetch (size 16)
  on icacheid 0 with LRU replacement
Index covers query.
Search argument selectivity is 1.000000.

******************************
******************************
Entering q_score_index() for table 'ntitles' (objectid 656005368, varno =
0).
The table has 1614 rows and 31 pages.
Scoring the JOIN CLAUSE:
  pub_name EQ pub_name

Base cost: indid: 0 rows: 1614 pages: 31 prefetch: S
  I/O size: 16 cacheid: 0 replace: LRU
Relop bits are: 5
Estimate: indid 1, selectivity 0.000620, rows 1 pages 2

Cheapest index is index 1, costing 2 pages and
  generating 1 rows per scan, using no data prefetch (size 2)
  on dcacheid 0 with LRU replacement
Join selectivity is 1614.000000.

******************************
******************************
Entering q_score_index() for table 'npublishers' (objectid 688005482,
varno = 1).
The table has 1155 rows and 5 pages.
Scoring the JOIN CLAUSE:
  pub_name EQ pub_name

Base cost: indid: 0 rows: 1155 pages: 5 prefetch: S
  I/O size: 16 cacheid: 0 replace: LRU
Relop bits are: 4
Estimate: indid 2, selectivity 0.249989, rows 289 pages 4

Cheapest index is index 2, costing 4 pages and
  generating 289 rows per scan, using  data prefetch (size 16)
  on icacheid 0 with LRU replacement
Index covers query.
Join selectivity is 4.000183.

******************************

QUERY IS CONNECTED

 0 - 1 -
```

```
NEW PLAN (total cost = 32457):

varno=0 (ntitles) indexid=0 ()
path=0xea81a928 pathtype=sclause method=NESTED ITERATION
outerrows=1 rows=1614 joinsel=1.000000 cpages=31 prefetch=S iosize=16
replace=LRU lp=31 pp=31 corder=11

varno=1 (npublishers) indexid=2 (c1)
path=0xea81ab88 pathtype=sclause method=NESTED ITERATION
outerrows=1614 rows=466021 joinsel=4.000183 cpages=10 prefetch=I iosize=16
replace=LRU lp=16140 pp=10 corder=2

NEW PLAN (total cost = 16303):

varno=0 (ntitles) indexid=0 ()
path=0xea81a928 pathtype=sclause method=NESTED ITERATION
outerrows=1 rows=1614 joinsel=1.000000 cpages=31 prefetch=S iosize=16
replace=LRU lp=31 pp=31 corder=11

varno=1 (npublishers) indexid=0 ()
path=0xea81ab88 pathtype=sclause method=NESTED ITERATION
outerrows=1614 rows=466021 joinsel=4.000183 cpages=5 prefetch=S iosize=16
replace=LRU lp=8070 pp=5 corder=0

NEW PLAN (total cost = 13151):

varno=0 (ntitles) indexid=0 ()
path=0xea81a928 pathtype=sclause method=NESTED ITERATION
outerrows=1 rows=1614 joinsel=1.000000 cpages=31 prefetch=S iosize=16
replace=LRU lp=31 pp=31 corder=11

varno=1 (npublishers) indexid=2 (c1)
path=0xea819288 pathtype=join method=NESTED ITERATION
outerrows=1614 rows=466021 joinsel=4.000183 cpages=4 prefetch=I iosize=16
replace=LRU lp=6456 pp=5 corder=2
jnvar=0 refcost=17715 refpages=7 reftotpages=23 ordercol[0]=2  order-
col[1]=11

 1 - 0 -
NEW PLAN (total cost = 4755):

varno=1 (npublishers) indexid=2 (c1)
path=0xea81ab88 pathtype=sclause method=NESTED ITERATION
outerrows=1 rows=1155 joinsel=1.000000 cpages=10 prefetch=I iosize=16
replace=LRU lp=10 pp=10 corder=2

varno=0 (ntitles) indexid=1 (c1)
path=0xea8190f0 pathtype=join method=NESTED ITERATION
outerrows=1155 rows=1155 joinsel=1614.000000 cpages=2 prefetch=S iosize=16
replace=LRU lp=2310 pp=31 corder=11
jnvar=1 refcost=0 refpages=0 reftotpages=0 ordercol[0]=11  ordercol[1]=2
```

```
NEW PLAN (total cost = 4731):

varno=1 (npublishers) indexid=0 ()
path=0xea81ab88 pathtype=sclause method=NESTED ITERATION
outerrows=1 rows=1155 joinsel=1.000000 cpages=5 prefetch=S iosize=16
replace=LRU lp=5 pp=5 corder=0

varno=0 (ntitles) indexid=1 (c1)
path=0xea8190f0 pathtype=join method=NESTED ITERATION
outerrows=1155 rows=1155 joinsel=1614.000000 cpages=2 prefetch=S iosize=16
replace=LRU lp=2310 pp=31 corder=11
jnvar=1 refcost=0 refpages=0 reftotpages=0 ordercol[0]=11  ordercol[1]=2

TOTAL # PERMUTATIONS: 2

TOTAL # PLANS CONSIDERED: 8

CACHE USED BY THIS PLAN:

  CacheID = 0:    (2K) 0    (4K) 0    (8K) 0    (16K) 36

FINAL PLAN (total cost = 4731):

varno=1 (npublishers) indexid=0 ()
path=0xea81ab88 pathtype=sclause method=NESTED ITERATION
outerrows=1 rows=1155 joinsel=1.000000 cpages=5 prefetch=S iosize=16
replace=LRU lp=5 pp=5 corder=0
varno=0 (ntitles) indexid=1 (c1)
path=0xea8190f0 pathtype=join method=NESTED ITERATION
outerrows=1155 rows=1155 joinsel=1614.000000 cpages=2 prefetch=S iosize=16
replace=LRU lp=2310 pp=31 corder=11
jnvar=1 refcost=0 refpages=0 reftotpages=0 ordercol[0]=11  ordercol[1]=2
QUERY PLAN FOR STATEMENT 1 (at line 1).
    STEP 1
        The type of query is SELECT.
        FROM TABLE
            npublishers
        Nested iteration.
        Table Scan.
        Ascending scan.
        Positioning at start of table.
        Using I/O Size 16 Kbytes.
        With LRU Buffer Replacement Strategy.

        FROM TABLE
            ntitles
        Nested iteration.
        Using Clustered Index.
        Index : c1
        Ascending scan.
```

```
        Positioning by key.
        Keys are:
            pub_name
        Using I/O Size 16 Kbytes.
        With LRU Buffer Replacement Strategy.

pub_name
- - - - - - - - - - - - -
New Age Books
```

You already know how to interpret the first part of this output; it provides the same information as the first part of the output from the *dbcc 302* command. You analyze this part of the output in the same way as you do for a query with the *dbcc 302* command. To make sure that the optimizer has considered all of your join clauses, check for lines that resemble the following example:

```
Scoring the JOIN CLAUSE:
   pub_name EQ pub_name
```

If the optimizer fails to consider a join clause, the query may have a problem such as a datatype mismatch.

Next, you should look for the following line:

```
QUERY IS CONNECTED
```

This indicates that the join is legal and can be performed.

The next section of the output shows the optimizer costing all the possible table combinations for the join. The optimizer figures the costs of performing the join in all the possible combinations and thus determines the best join order. The output lists tables in order of their appearance in the join, with the first table listed as 0. For example, the following lines show you the total cost for the permutation in which table 0 and table 1 appear in the join, in that order:

```
0 - 1 -
NEW PLAN (total cost = 32457):
```

The total cost value lists the optimizer's estimate for this combination. The optimizer assumes that this combination takes 2ms per logical read (lp) and 18ms per physical read (pp). It is important to note that SQL Server assigns these values, they do not represent the actual times required for performing these reads.

In the next lines of the output, *varno* simply represents the table that the optimizer is considering—for example, varno 0 is the first table after the *from* clause, and varno 1 is the second. The indexid value identifies the index being considered: 0 is a table scan, 1 is the clustered index, and 2 through 250 represent any nonclustered indexes. The cpages value identifies the number of pages that must be read to satisfy the join using this join order. The lp value gives the estimated number of logical page reads, and pp identifies the number of physical page reads:

```
varno=0 (ntitles) indexid=0 ()
path=0xea81a928 pathtype=sclause method=NESTED ITERATION
outerrows=1 rows=1614 joinsel=1.000000 cpages=31 prefetch=S iosize=16
replace=LRU lp=31 pp=31 corder=11
```

This goes on for all possible permutations of the join. Of course, multitable joins can result in a large amount of output.

The following line identifies the least-cost query plan:

```
FINAL PLAN (total cost = 4731):
```

The sample output shows that the optimizer decided to use the second table (*npublishers*) first, use a table scan on that table, and then use the *ntitles* table with its index:

```
varno=1 (npublishers) indexid=0 ()
path=0xea81ab88 pathtype=sclause method=NESTED ITERATION
outerrows=1 rows=1155 joinsel=1.000000 cpages=5 prefetch=S iosize=16
replace=LRU lp=5 pp=5 corder=0
varno=0 (ntitles) indexid=1 (c1)
path=0xea8190f0 pathtype=join method=NESTED ITERATION
outerrows=1155 rows=1155 joinsel=1614.000000 cpages=2 prefetch=S iosize=16
replace=LRU lp=2310 pp=31 corder=11
jnvar=1 refcost=0 refpages=0 reftotpages=0 ordercol[0]=11  ordercol[1]=2
```

The *showplan* output verifies this usage.

You analyze the *dbcc 310* output primarily to determine whether the optimizer has used the indexes for the join in the way you expected. It is important to note lines that might be missing as well as lines that are present. For example, if the optimizer does not analyze a join clause for a clause in which you intended to have a join, the query clearly has a problem.

When using the *dbcc 302* and *dbcc 310* commands to analyze poorly performing queries after you migrate to SQL Server 11, be especially conscious of datatype mismatches on join columns. Even a mismatch between char and varchar datatypes or between null and not null columns can prevent the optimizer from using an index. If you notice this when analyzing the *dbcc 310* output, change the datatypes of the offending columns or, as a last resort, ask Sybase technical support for any patches that deal with datatype mismatches.

Monitoring SQL Server 11 by Using sp_sysmon

With the release of SQL Server 11, DBAs have a new best friend: *sp_sysmon*. This large, sophisticated system stored procedure provides extremely useful and detailed information on almost every aspect of SQL Server 11. By using the internal SQL Server 11 monitor counters, *sp_sysmon* produces a report of system performance. By analyzing this report, you can study all aspects of your system, find problem areas, and benchmark parameter changes.

TIP!	Because *sp_sysmon* uses monitor counters and Sybase has added or changed many of these counters for SQL Server 11, *sp_sysmon* does not produce correct results on a pre-SQL Server 11 system.

Peter Thawley wrote *sp_sysmon*, and this system stored procedure was tested and refined by several of Sybase's top technical people. Peter is well-known throughout the Sybase community as a leading source of technical information, and if possible, you should attend one of his presentations on SQL Server performance and tuning.

This chapter cannot cover every line of *sp_sysmon* output, but you can turn to several other sources for more detailed information. You can attend one of the performance and tuning seminars given by Peter Thawley and the Sybase Product Performance Group (for dates and information, contact Sybase, Inc. at 1-800-8Sybase), or you can read the technical paper, "Monitoring SQL Server Performance with *sp_sysmon*," written by Karen Paulsell and Tanya Knoop. This paper is available on the Answerbase CD or from Sybase Customer Fulfillment at 1-800-685-8225.

Using *sp_sysmon*

When you start *sp_sysmon*, it zeroes out all the SQL Server 11 internal monitor counters. It waits a specified period of time, reads all the counters, and then generates a detailed report that lists the information gleaned from the counters.

TIP!	Because *sp_sysmon* zeroes out the counters when it starts, its use interferes with Sybase SQL Server Monitor if you run both tools simultaneously. In a similar manner, running a second instance of *sp_sysmon* before a first instance is complete produces erroneous results for the first instance.

You can run *sp_sysmon* by using an *isql* session. This command has the following syntax:

```
sp_sysmon time
go
```

The value you enter for the *time* parameter can range from 1 to 10 minutes. This value specifies how long *sp_sysmon* will run.

Because this command produces a large amount of output that you need to study, you should use the methods described in Chapter 1 to redirect *sp_sysmon's* output to a file. The following example runs a UNIX command in the background to use the *sp_sysmon* command. It produces a file called *sysmon.out.*

The file *sysmon* contains the following lines:

```
sp_sysmon 5
go
```

Issue the following command from a UNIX prompt:

```
isql -Uuser -Ppassword -Sserver_name -isysmon -osysmon.out &
```

This command completes execution in five minutes, and the file sysmon.out will contain the *sp_sysmon* report.

Interpreting the Output from *sp_sysmon*

This section of the chapter describes how to interpret certain key areas of the *sp_sysmon* output. Keep in mind that *sp_sysmon* adds approximately five percent overhead to the system, and thus slightly skews the performance data.

The *sp_sysmon* system stored procedure first displays a header with the report's date and time. You must know the time period covered in a report, because this is your only means for associating certain applications or queries to specific SQL Server 11 responses. If SQL Server 11 remains idle during part of the period you monitor, you may not get useful information. The following example shows the format of the header:

```
===========================================================
Sybase SQL Server 11 System Performance Monitor
===========================================================
Run Date Dec 06, 1995
Statistics Cleared at 17:05:40
Statistics Sampled at 17:10:40
```

Sample Interval 5 min.

Most categories in the *sp_sysmon* output display four columns of information: a count per second, a count per transaction, a total count (for the sampling period), and a percentage. All four columns do not always make sense for a category. For example, the following example displays an excerpt for the number of connections opened:

```
Task Management       per sec  per xact  count   % of total
------------------    -------  --------  -----   ----------
Connections Opened      2.0      2.0       2      n/a
```

For a given category, you can decide which counts provide significant information.

If you have an SMP system, *sp_sysmon* provides information on a per-engine basis. For example, the following section shows a report on context switches:

```
Task Context Switches by Engine
                      per sec  per xact  count   % of total
                      -------  --------  -----   ----------
Engine 0                94.8      0.8     5730     24.5 %
Engine 1                94.6      0.8     5719     24.4 %
Engine 2                92.8      0.8     5609     24.0 %
Engine 3               105.0      0.9     6349     27.1 %
                      -------  --------  -----
Total Task Switches:   387.2      3.7    23407
```

Notice that in cases like this, *sp_sysmon* provides a summary row that lists the total values.

Monitoring Task Management

The *sp_sysmon* output for task management provides the following information:

```
Task Management       per sec  per xact  count   % of total
------------------    -------  --------  -----   ----------
Connections Opened      2.0      2.0       2      n/a
Task Context Switches by Engine
                      per sec  per xact  count   % of total
                      -------  --------  -----   ----------
Engine 0                94.8      0.8     5730     24.5 %
Engine 1                94.6      0.8     5719     24.4 %
Engine 2                92.8      0.8     5609     24.0 %
Engine 3               105.0      0.9     6349     27.1 %
Total Task Switches:   387.2      3.7    23407

Task Context Switches Due To:
```

```
Voluntary Yields              69.1    0.6    4179     7.7 %
Cache Search Misses           56.7    0.5    3428     6.3 %
System Disk Writes             1.0    0.0      62     0.1 %
I/O Pacing                    11.5    0.1     695     1.3 %
Logical Lock Contention        3.7    0.0     224     0.4 %
Address Lock Contention        0.0    0.0       0     0.0 %
Log Semaphore Contention      51.0    0.4    3084     5.7 %
Group Commit Sleeps           82.2    0.7    4971     9.2 %
Last Log Page Writes          69.0    0.6    4172     7.7 %
Modify Conflicts              83.7    0.7    5058     9.3 %
I/O Device Contention          6.4    0.1     388     0.7 %
Network Packet Received      120.0    1.0    7257    13.4 %
Network Packet Sent          120.1    1.0    7259    13.4 %
SYSINDEXES Lookup              0.0    0.0       0     0.0 %
Other Causes                 221.6    1.8   13395    24.7 %
```

This section gives you detailed information about context switches. A context switch occurs when SQL Server switches a task off an engine. Each task runs on an engine for the length of time specified by the *timeslice* parameter (default 100 ms), and then SQL Server 11 switches to the next task. For a number of reasons, however, a task may not get its full time slice. For example, if SQL Server must perform disk I/O on behalf of a task, the system puts that task to sleep while it waits for completion of the I/O. This constitutes a context switch, and places the task on SQL Server 11's sleep queue. By issuing the *sp_who* command and looking at the status column, you can see whether SQL Server has a task on the sleep queue or the run queue. By studying the underlying reasons for context switches, you may be able to find ways to minimize the delays they cause.

The first section of the *sp_sysmon* output for task management shows total context switches and context switches per engine. This information can help you determine whether you can reduce context switching by adding memory or changing caches. By monitoring these values before and after such changes, you can easily identify any improvements.

The next section of this output shows the percentage of context switches caused by various circumstances:

- Voluntary Yields. The task yielded because it used up its allotted time slice. This is the best reason for a context switch; it means there was no contention.

- Cache Search Misses. The task yielded because SQL Server 11 had to perform physical I/O. When SQL Server cannot find a page in a cache, it must read in that page from disk. If this causes numerous context switches, increase the memory for data caches, or reconfigure your named caches.

- System Disk Writes. The task yielded because SQL Server had to perform a disk write. Note that SQL Server performs most writes asynchronously, except for page splits, recovery, and OAM page writes. If you see a high percentage of this type of context switch, check for excessive page split activity.

- Logical Lock Contention. The task yielded because of locking issues such as a page lock or a table lock. If you see a high percentage of this type of context switch, try to reduce lock contention. Chapter 9, "Performance and Tuning," describes methods for reducing lock contention. For additional details, see the *Sybase SQL Server Performance and Tuning Guide.*

- Log Semaphore Contention. The task yielded because of contention for the transaction log semaphore. This occurs only in SMP environments, where more than one task at a time can compete for internal resources. If you see a high percentage of this type of context switch, the user log cache may be too small, or you may want to change applications to perform fewer log writes.

- I/O Device Contention. The task yielded because of contention for a device's semaphore. If you see a high percentage of this type of context switch, distribute tables across multiple devices, or add devices for storing tables and indexes.

- Network Packet Received/Network Packet Sent. The task yielded because it was receiving or sending network packets. If you see a high percentage of this type of context switch, consider increasing the network packet size.

By analyzing the most frequent causes of context switches, you may be able to identify opportunities for greatly reducing context switching problems.

Monitoring the User Log Cache

The *sp_sysmon* output for the user log cache provides the following information:

```
ULC Flushes to Xact Log    per sec   per xact  count   % of total
-------------------------   -------   --------  -----   ----------
by Full ULC                    0.0       0.0        0      0.0 %
by End Transaction           120.1       1.0     7261     99.7 %
by Change of Database          0.0       0.0        0      0.0 %
by System Log Record           0.4       0.0       25      0.3 %
by Other                       0.0       0.0        0      0.0 %
-------------------------   -------   --------  -----   ----------
Total ULC Flushes            120.5       1.0     7286
ULC Log Records              727.5       6.1    43981              n/a
Max ULC Size                   n/a       n/a      532              n/a
```

```
ULC Semaphore Requests
Granted                    1452.3      12.1     87799         100.0 %
Waited                        0.0       0.0         0           0.0 %
-----------------------    -------   --------    -----    ----------
Total ULC Semaphore Req    1452.3      12.1     87799
Log Semaphore Requests
Granted                      69.5       0.6      4202          57.7 %
Waited                       51.0       0.4      3084          42.3 %
-----------------------    -------   --------    -----    ----------
Total Log Semaphore Req     120.5       1.0      7286
Transaction Log Writes       80.5       0.7      4867           n/a
Transaction Log Alloc        22.9       0.2      1385           n/a
Avg # Writes per Log Page     n/a       n/a   3.51408           n/a
```

Recall that the ULC exists to reduce contention on the append log semaphore. To achieve the best possible performance, you need to size the ULC correctly. If you make the ULC too large, you waste memory; if you make it too small, you do not reduce the contention.

The ULC should flush to the transaction log because of an *end* transaction. Make sure that this column in the *sp_sysmon* output has the highest percentage. If the output shows a high percentage of flushes due to a full ULC (greater than 20 percent), you should increase the size of the ULC.

Check the Log Semaphore Requests section of the output, to see the percentage of requests that were granted or waited. Most requests should be granted, because the ULC was created specifically to eliminate the contention resulting from semaphore requests.

Monitoring Data Cache Management

The *sp_sysmon* output for data cache management provides the following information:

```
Data Cache Management
-----------------------------
Cache Statistics Summary (All Caches)
-----------------------    -------   --------    -----    ----------
                           per sec   per xact   count    % of total
Cache Search Summary
Total Cache Hits           1653.2      13.8     99945          95.8 %
Total Cache Misses           73.0       0.6      4416           4.2 %
-----------------------    -------   --------    -----    ----------
Total Cache Searches       1726.2      14.4    104361
Cache Turnover
Buffers Grabbed              56.7       0.5      3428           n/a
Buffers Grabbed Dirty         0.0       0.0         0           0.0 %
Cache Strategy Summary
Cached (LRU) Buffers       2155.8      17.9    130333         100.0 %
Discarded (MRU) Buffers       0.0       0.0         0           0.0 %
```

```
Large I/O Usage
Large I/Os Performed         20.0        0.2    1211         87.4 %
Large I/Os Denied             2.9        0.0     174         12.6 %
------------------------   -------    --------  -----     ----------
Total Large I/O Requests     22.9        0.2    1385
Large I/O Effectiveness
Pages by Lrg I/O Cached       0.0        0.0       0          n/a


named_cache1
                           per sec    per xact  count   % of total
------------------------   -------    --------  -----   ----------
Spinlock Contention          n/a         n/a     n/a         1.3 %
Utilization                  n/a         n/a     n/a        20.9 %
Cache Searches
Cache Hits                 360.3        3.0    21783      100.0 %
Found in Wash                0.0        0.0        0        0.0 %
Cache Misses                 0.0        0.0        0        0.0 %
------------------------   -------    --------  -----
Total Cache Searches       360.3        3.0    21783
```

The *sp_sysmon* output for data cache management presents summary information about all data caches and then provides details for each named cache. The most important information in this section of the *sp_sysmon* output is the cache hit ratio. You want to make sure that all cache searches are found in a cache. If the cache misses rate exceeds a few percentage points, you must make some changes in your caches because a cache miss translates into an expensive disk read. By studying each named cache, you can check its performance.

You should also check the buffers grabbed dirty section. If grabbed dirty is not zero, you must immediately increase the wash size, because this can seriously impede system performance. If a buffer is grabbed dirty, SQL Server 11 must stop its current task and wash that buffer, while every other task waits for SQL Server to complete this procedure.

Compare the large I/Os performed and large I/Os denied ratios. If SQL Server denies a high percentage of large I/Os, you should try to find the cause. Study the buffer pool usage and size allocations for the cache in question.

If you find high spinlock contention on a named cache, try creating additional named caches. This can decrease spinlock contention in an SMP environment.

Use the utilization information to decide whether you have sized various caches correctly. The utilization information shows the percentage of searches that used a particular cache. This information can help you determine whether a cache is over- or underutilized.

The found in wash section indicates that SQL Server found a needed page in the wash section of the cache. A high value for this statistic may indicate that the wash section is too large.

The data cache management section of this output includes information about the buffer pools:

```
Pool Turnover
2 Kb Pool
   LRU Buffer Grab        118.2     3.2     7223      86.1 %
   Grabbed Dirty            0.0     0.0        0       0.0 %
16 Kb Pool
   LRU Buffer Grab         19.1     0.5     1168      13.9 %
   Grabbed Dirty            0.0     0.0        0       0.0 %
----------------------  -------  ------   -----   --------
Total Cache Turnover     137.3     3.8     8391
```

The buffer grab section provides an indication of a pool's usage. Pools with a higher usage should generally have the most memory. A high buffer grab value may indicate that the pool should be larger. In this example, the 2K pool is used more than 85 percent of the time. Therefore, most of the memory should be assigned to the 2K pool.

Monitoring Device Activity

The *sp_sysmon* output for device activity provides the following information:

```
Device Activity Detail

/dev/rdsk/c1t3d0s6
bench_log                 per sec   per xact  count  % of total
----------------------    -------   --------  -----  ----------
Reads                         0.1       0.0      5       0.1 %
Writes                       80.6       0.7   4873      99.9 %
----------------------    -------   --------  -----  ----------
Total I/Os                   80.7       0.7   4878      40.0 %
Device Semaphore Granted     80.7       0.7   4878     100.0 %
Device Semaphore Waited       0.0       0.0      0       0.0 %
----------------------    -------   --------  -----  ----------
d_master master           per sec   per xact  count  % of total
----------------------    -------   --------  -----  ----------
Reads                        56.6       0.5   3423      46.9 %
Writes                       64.2       0.5   3879      53.1 %
----------------------    -------   --------  -----  ----------
Total I/Os                  120.8       1.0   7302      60.0 %
Device Semaphore Granted    116.7       1.0   7056      94.8 %
Device Semaphore Waited       6.4       0.1    388       5.2 %
```

This section gives you detailed information about each device. The total I/O section contains the most important information in this part of the *sp_sysmon* output. By looking at the *percent of total* for each device, you can see how SQL Server has distributed I/O among all the devices. Use this information to balance loads evenly among all the devices.

By comparing the *total i/o per second* value with the hardware capabilities and limitations of your devices, you can determine whether you are maximizing the device, or even reaching hardware's limits. For example, if your hardware device is rated at 60 I/Os per second and you see 60 I/Os per second in the *sp_sysmon* output, you know that you can't get any better performance from this device.

You can use several other entries in the *sp_sysmon* output to analyze your system. Many of them—for example, network packet sizes and number of deadlocks—are self-explanatory. Carefully monitor your system before making any changes, and again after making changes. In this way, you can see how the changes affected SQL Server 11.

Summary

This chapter describes several methods for monitoring your SQL Server, including basic tools such as *showplan* and *statistics i/o*, and advanced tools such as the *dbcc 302* and *dbcc 310* trace flags. With the release of SQL Server 11, some monitoring tools (such as *showplan*) have changed and some (for example, *sp_sysmon*) are new to SQL Server. For maintenance and performance tuning, you should regularly monitor your system.

In the next chapter, you learn how to use the monitoring information to tune SQL Server 11.

Migration Checklist

The following list summarizes the key migration tasks covered in this chapter:

- After you have your new SQL Server 11 up and running, fully monitor the system by using the techniques described in this chapter.

- Benchmark performance before and after you make any tuning changes.

- Monitor poorly performing queries and procedures by using techniques such as *showplan* and *dbcc traceon (302)*.

Command Reference

dbcc traceon 302

Syntax

```
dbcc traceon (302)
```

Example

```
dbcc traceon (3604)
dbcc traceon (302)
```

dbcc traceon 310

Syntax

```
dbcc traceon (310)
```

Example

```
dbcc traceon (3604)
dbcc traceon (310)
```

dbcc traceon 3604

Syntax

```
dbcc traceon (3604)
```

Example

```
dbcc traceon (3604)
```

set showplan on/off

Syntax

```
set showplan {on | off}
```

Example

```
set showplan on
```

set statistics io on/off

Syntax

```
set statistics io {on | off}
```

Example

```
set statistics io on
```

set statistics time on/off

Syntax

```
set statistics time {on | off}
```

Example

```
set statistics time on
```

sp_sysmon

Syntax

```
sp_sysmon time
```

Example

```
sp_sysmon 5
```

9

SQL Server 11 Performance and Tuning

In This Chapter

- Using monitoring information to tune SQL Server 11
- Improving performance by adding memory
- Tuning SQL Server 11 for SMP systems
- Choosing named caches and buffer pools to increase SQL Server 11's performance
- Improving performance by using larger TDS packet sizes
- Improving performance by using *tcp no delay*
- Improving performance by partitioning tables
- Using partitions to run multiple instances of *bcp*

In this chapter, you learn various techniques and tricks for tuning SQL Server 11. This chapter builds on the previous chapters by showing you how to use the techniques described in those chapters (for example, setting configuration parameters and creating named caches) to achieve the best possible performance with SQL Server 11. For example, Chapter 8, "Monitoring SQL Server 11," shows you how to interpret *sp_sysmon's* output, and this chapter explains how you can put *sp_sysmon's* information to practical use.

Achieving optimal system performance involves many factors in addition to tuning SQL Server—for example, the quality of your SQL code, database design, and application design. Keep in mind that although SQL Server tuning can be very beneficial, these other issues also affect SQL Server's performance.

Improving SQL Server's Performance by Adding Memory

Almost any system can benefit from added memory. If you add memory to your system, make sure you increase the amount SQL Server 11 gets by increasing the *total memory* configuration parameter. (For in-depth coverage of SQL Server 11's memory requirements, refer to Chapter 2, "The Migration Process.")

You must be careful to avoid setting the *total memory* parameter to a value larger than the amount of memory available on the machine. Such a setting causes a page fault, which completely stops the entire SQL Server 11 process until the page fault finishes. In terms of performance, this is the worst thing you can do to SQL Server 11.

To find out whether additional memory will significantly improve performance, you can look at the cache hit rates. Relatively low cache hit rates may indicate that the caches do not have enough memory. However, the only way you can really determine whether additional memory helps is by adding the memory and reanalyzing SQL Server's performance. After you add memory, recheck cache hit ratios and context switches due to cache search misses, as well as stored procedure times. If you see improvements, you know the additional memory helped.

TIP!   Remember to leave plenty of memory for the default data cache and any named caches you create.

Taking Advantage of SMP Systems

SQL Server 11's scalability—that is, its capability to take full advantage of SMP architecture—provides some of the system's greatest performance increases over previous versions. *Scalability* means that SQL Server 11's performance improves in direct proportion to the number of engines you add. Many customers have seen performance improve by several hundred percent after moving to an SMP machine and SQL Server 11. Figures 9-1 and 9-2 graphically depict the dramatic improvements in throughput and response time made possible by adding engines. These figures show the results of tests conducted by the Sybase Product Performance Group, with 200 users and 16 engines on a Sun SparcCenter 2000 running Solaris 2.4. As shown in Figure 9-2, increasing the TDS packet size can also help performance.

Multiple Network Engines Performance

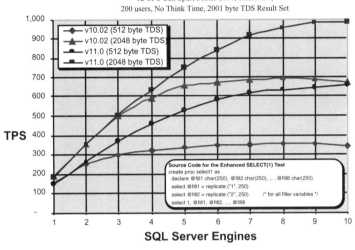

Figure 9-1: You can improve throughput on SQL Server 11 by increasing the number of available engines. (Reprinted with permission from Peter Thawley and the Sybase Product Performance Group.)

Multiple Network Engines Performance

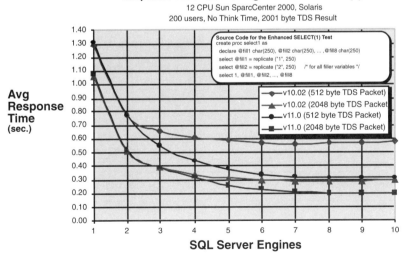

Figure 9-2: Query response times decrease on SQL Server 11, as the number of engines increases. (Reprinted with permission from Peter Thawley and the Sybase Product Performance Group.)

You cannot accurately estimate how many engines will prove useful to your particular environment. By benchmarking performance as you increase the number of engines, however, you can determine the correct number of engines for your needs. If your company has a productive working relationship with a hardware vendor, you may be able to test on a borrowed SMP machine before purchasing one. As you increase engines by changing the *max online engines* parameter, monitor the system by using *sp_sysmon*. To determine how busy each engine is, analyze such fields as *engine busy utilization*, *disk i/os per engine*, and *network i/os per engine*. For example, if you have six engines and three of them are busy only 20 percent of the time, you have more than enough engines. If all six engines are 90 percent busy, however, you can probably benefit from additional engines. Most SMP systems evenly distribute I/O among all the engines. To verify that this happens on your system, check the *i/o per engines* fields.

Be sure to check for any contention that multiple engines may add to the system. Remember that in SMP systems different engines can request internal (lock-protected) structures at the same time. To analyze the contention, check such fields as the *ULC semaphore requests* and *data cache spinlock contentions*.

Remember that the number of engines you assign to SQL Server 11 cannot exceed the number of CPUs on the machine. And if you have other processes running on the machine, you may want to reserve one CPU for those processes.

Choosing Named Caches and Buffer Pools

With SQL Server 11 up and running, you should have a default data cache with a 4K pool for log I/O and a 16K pool for large I/O. You now need to decide how to configure additional named caches and their buffer pools. Carefully consider these decisions, because improperly configured caches and pools can actually degrade performance.

First, you need to benchmark the performance of your key procedures while they use the default data cache. By doing this, you can ensure that any changes you make improve performance. You also need to carefully benchmark procedure times, and study *sp_sysmon* output before and after every cache change you make.

TIP!   Remember that unused caches and pools simply waste valuable memory.

Choosing named caches and buffer pools involves three decisions:

1. Choosing several tables, indexes, or databases that can benefit from having their own cache.

2. Determining how large each cache should be.

3. Choosing the buffer pools for each cache, and deciding how to distribute memory among the pools.

Binding *Hot* Tables and Indexes

If you have one or two frequently used tables or indexes, consider binding them to their own caches. This ensures that they have a high cache hit ratio and reduces cache contention. Remember that high performance in an SMP system requires reducing contention for named caches. You want to eliminate any waits for internal semaphores.

In most environments, you cannot simply obtain enough memory to place all tables completely in cache. Consequently, you must estimate how much I/O various tables are involved in, and thus identify each *hot* table and choose an appropriate size for its cache. To create caches for your hot tables, you complete the following steps:

1. Using Sybase SQL Monitor (as well as your knowledge of your applications), determine the number of I/Os per object.

2. Identify the tables and indexes with the highest number of I/Os. You will create caches for these *hot* objects.

3. Using the I/O information, estimate the required sizes for these caches.

Unless you are very familiar with the workings of all the applications on your SQL Server 11, the only way you can identify hot tables is by using a tool such as Sybase SQL Monitor to analyze *i/os per object*. You can also use this information to estimate the sizes of the new caches. Once you determine the amount of I/O for a table, create a named cache that has at least enough room to maintain the table's I/O in the cache. The cache should also have plenty of room for overhead and growth. This approach works well for small and medium-size tables, but for very large tables, this process requires lots of memory.

Choosing Memory Allocations for Buffer Pools

Next, you need to allocate the buffer pools in the cache. In general, you do not want more than two pools in a cache, and those two pools should be 2K and 16K pools. By having a 2K pool and a 16K pool, the cache can use either normal or large I/O. If you know that the application will never use large I/O, you might not need to create the 16K pool.

Finally, you need to distribute the cache's memory between the two pools. Unless you have some concrete facts about the applications that will use the cache, you should start by allocating 25 percent to 30 percent for the 16K pool and the rest for the 2K pool. If you know that a large number of queries use table scans or *order by* clauses that will make use of large I/O, you may want to start out with 50 percent to 60 percent allocated to the 16K pool.

Once you have your starting points for the named cache size and bindings and the buffer pool distributions, you must benchmark the queries and use *sp_sysmon* to analyze the cache's performance (as well as how this named cache affects other data caches). Carefully check the cache hits and misses, the cache utilization, and the cache spinlock contention values. Specifically, make sure your new cache is used, spinlock contention is reduced, and cache hit values have increased. Then check the pool turnover for the 2K and 16K buffer pools. Determine which pool SQL Server uses most often, and make sure the cache's memory allocation is proportional to its use.

The following example shows the *sp_sysmon* output before any named caches are added to the system:

```
Data Cache Management
---------------------
Cache Statistics Summary (All Caches)
-------------------------------------
Cache Search Summary
Total Cache Hits      1487.8  12.5  89950  85.8 %
Total Cache Misses      66.4   0.4   4012  14.2 %
--------------------  ------- ----- -----  ------
Total Cache Searches  1554.2  12.9  93962
```

Compare this with the following output, which *sp_sysmon* generates after the *hot_cache* named cache is added:

```
Data Cache Management
---------------------
Cache Statistics Summary (All Caches)
-------------------------------------
Cache Search Summary
Total Cache Hits      1653.2  13.8  99945  95.8 %
Total Cache Misses      73.0   0.6   4416   4.2 %
--------------------  ------- ----- -----  -------
Total Cache Searches  1726.2  14.4 104361

hot_cache
                      per sec  per xact  count    % of total
-------------------   -------  --------  -----    ----------
Spinlock Contention     n/a      n/a     n/a         1.3 %
Utilization             n/a      n/a     n/a        20.9 %
Cache Searches
```

```
Cache Hits               360.3        3.0      21783      100.0 %
Found in Wash              0.0        0.0          0        0.0 %
Cache Misses               0.0        0.0          0        0.0 %
-----------------        -------    --------    -----     ----------
Total Cache Searches     360.3        3.0      21783
```

Notice that the cache hit increases and the spinlock contention decreases, proving that this cache is very useful.

Assume that you originally allocated 65 percent of the *hot_cache* named cache to the 16K buffer pool. The following listing shows the *sp_sysmon* output for *hot_cache*'s pools:

```
Pool Turnover
2 Kb Pool
   LRU Buffer Grab        118.2        3.2       7223       86.1 %
   Grabbed Dirty            0.0        0.0          0        0.0 %
16 Kb Pool
   LRU Buffer Grab         19.1        0.5       1168       13.9 %
   Grabbed Dirty            0.0        0.0          0        0.0 %
-------------------      -------     ----       -----      -------
Total Cache Turnover     137.3        3.8       8391
```

The output shows that the 16K pool is unused for 15 percent of the time. After analyzing this data, you may want to reduce the 16K pool's memory allocation to 20 percent.

Another useful technique for a hot table is to separate the table and its index to different caches. This reduces concurrency problems between the data and its index.

Binding *tempdb* to its own Cache

In addition to tables and indexes, you can bind an entire database to a named cache. One special database you may want to consider binding is *tempdb*. If your applications make heavy use of *tempdb* with temporary tables, joins, and sorts, you may want to isolate *tempdb* in its own cache. This prevents the constant use of *tempdb* from interfering with other processes.

Remember that the entire *tempdb* table doesn't have to fit into a cache; you simply need a cache that can hold the *tempdb* pages that your applications use. To get an idea of the size of any temporary tables that your applications use, you can use tools such as *statistics i/o*. Get a feel for the size of result sets as well as how many concurrent users will make use of *tempdb*. This information gives you a rough starting point, which you can then refine by monitoring the cache.

Creating Separate Caches for DSSs and OLTP Systems

If your system simultaneously runs DSS and OLTP applications, you should configure a separate named cache for each type of processing. Remember that DSS applications generally make good use of large I/O, while OLTP systems do not. Also remember that the key conflict between these two types of systems rests in the fact that DSS queries can quickly flush OLTP tables out of the cache. For this reason, these types of applications should use separate caches. (For more details about this topic, refer to Chapter 6, "The Buffer Manager.")

Create a cache with 16K buffer pools for the DSS applications, and a cache with just the 2K pool (or an additional very small 16K pool) for the OLTP applications. Use the techniques mentioned in the previous sections of this chapter, to analyze and resize both the caches and their pools, based on the system's performance.

Increasing Packet Sizes

Whenever SQL Server 11 performs I/O, it transfers the data by using its internal TDS protocol. By default, this protocol transfers the data in packets of 512 bytes. If you need to transfer large amounts of data at a time, however, you may want to increase the packet size and send fewer, but larger, packets.

In the network I/O section of *sp_sysmon*, check the average number of bytes sent and received. If these values are close to the packet size (default of 512 bytes), you should consider increasing the network packet size. By increasing the packet size, you allow SQL Server 11 to send more information at a time, and thus decrease the number of reads and writes necessary for sending this information. If after increasing the packet size you see an increase in the average number of bytes sent and received, this change has proved beneficial. You should also see improved performance in the procedures and transactions that use the larger packets.

TIP!   Remember that these packet sizes refer to the SQL Server TDS packets, and
         not regular network packets.

Rather than increase the default packet size, you probably want to increase the maximum packet size. This allows most applications to use the default size, while some applications can decide to request larger packets. You typically increase the maximum network packet size to 2,048 or 4,096. Make sure the underlying network can handle those values. (For example, a setting of 4,096 will not help performance if the network maximum is 2,048.)

Remember to increase the *additional network memory* value before increasing the *maximum network packet* size. When a user requests packets larger than the default packet size, the memory for those packets comes from a special memory pool called additional network memory. This parameter has a default value of 0, and you cannot allocate any large packets until you increase this value. Chapter 5, "Configuring SQL Server 11," discusses the procedure for changing this value. As shown in Figure 9-2, increasing the packet size can improve performance, especially when you do this in conjunction with adding engines.

Remember that SQL Server uses the larger packets only when a client requests them. By using the -A flag, you can set standard clients such as *isql* and *bcp* to use the larger packets. For example, to start an *isql* session with a 2,048 packet size, issue the following command:

```
isql -Uuser -Ppassword -Sserver -A2048
go
```

As shown in the following example, you request a larger packet size in an open client *ct-lib* program by using the *ct_con_props* call:

```
ct_con_props(connection, CS_SET, CS_PACKETSIZE, &pktsz, sizeof(pktsz), NULL );
```

Increasing Performance by Setting tcp no Delay

In addition to the packet size, you can set a parameter called *tcp no delay*. In previous releases, this parameter is a flag you set when you bring up the SQL Server. In SQL Server 11, you set this configuration parameter by using the *sp_configure* command.

Normally (that is, without *tcp no delay*), SQL Server waits until a TDS packet is full before sending it out. Although this works fine in most cases, if your application sends or receives small TDS packets (smaller than the default packet size), you may experience delays. By turning on the *tcp no delay* parameter, you tell SQL Server to send each packet as soon as it is ready, rather than waiting until the packet is full. For a limited group of applications, setting this flag can significantly increase performance. Simple trial and error offers the most effective means for determining whether *tcp no delay* can improve the performance of your applications. Set the parameter and benchmark application performance.

Remember that setting *tcp no delay* increases your network traffic because SQL Server will send more packets. To make sure your network can handle the increased traffic, consult with the network administrators or, if necessary, use a network sniffer.

You turn on *tcp no delay* by issuing the following command:

```
sp_configure "tcp no delay", 1
go
```

After changing this parameter, you must restart the server.

Partitioning Tables to Improve Insert Performance

Transactions that perform numerous table inserts may benefit substantially from table partitioning. If transactions or stored procedures that perform inserts do not perform satisfactorily, or if *sp_sysmon* indicates last page lock contention, you may want to partition a table.

Recall that with heap tables (tables with no clustered index), SQL Server places any inserts on the last page of the table. Recall also that table partitioning creates multiple last pages for a table. Any circumstances that perform concurrent inserts to the same heap table cause performance problems, because only one transaction at a time can obtain the exclusive page lock on the table's last page. All other transactions remained blocked while they wait for the first transaction to release the lock. Figure 9-3 illustrates this problem. Because every transaction must insert to the same last page, each transaction must wait for the previous one to relinquish its lock.

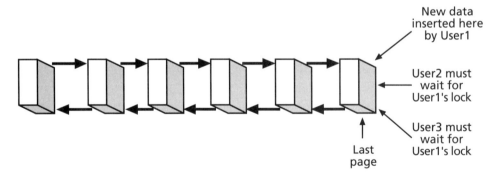

Figure 9.3: *Contention occurs when three users try to insert to the same last page of an unpartitioned table.*

Check the *sp_sysmon* output, to determine whether numerous inserts occur on heap tables. If so, check the *last page locks on heap tables* values in the *Lock Detail* section of the *sp_sysmon* output. By analyzing these numbers, you can see any contention from heap table inserts. A tool such as Sybase SQL Monitor can help you identify which heap tables are experiencing the contention.

The *sp_sysmon* output in the following example shows that SQL Server is performing 120 heap table inserts per second, and these make up 100 percent of all the inserts performed. The output also shows that almost half of those inserts had to wait for a lock before they could be performed. This obviously indicates a serious performance bottleneck:

```
Transaction Profile
-------------------
Transaction Summary     per sec   per xact   count   % of total
-------------------     -------   --------   -----   ----------
Committed Xacts          120.1      n/a       7261      n/a
Transaction Detail      per sec   per xact   count   % of total
------------------      -------   --------   -----   ----------

Inserts
Heap Table               120.1      1.0       7260     100.0 %
Clustered Table            0.0      0.0          0       0.0 %
-------------------      -------   --------   -----   ----------
Total Rows Inserted      120.1      1.0       7260      25.0 %

Lock Management
---------------
Lock Summary            per sec   per xact   count   % of total
-----------             -------   --------   -----   ----------
Last Page Locks on Heaps
Granted                   60.1      1.0       3629      51.4 %
Waited                    50.0      1.0       3431      48.6 %
-------------------      -------   --------   -----   ----------
Total Last Pg Locks      110.1      1.0       7060       4.7 %
```

Using Sybase SQL Monitor (as well as your knowledge of the application), you determine that the heap tables in question are the *auto_parts* table and the *auto_prices* table. You have two options for eliminating the bottleneck. You can add a clustered index to the tables that will randomize the inserts, or you can partition the table. In many cases, you cannot add a clustered index, because it is already used for another purpose or it will not randomize the inserts. Consequently, you need to partition the table. Start with a value such as 30 or 50, and monitor the changes by using *sp_sysmon*. In this way, you can determine whether you need to increase or decrease the number of partitions. Continue monitoring the system while you increase the partitions, until you eliminate the performance bottleneck.

The following example partitions the two tables in question and then shows the change in page locks, as reported by *sp_sysmon*:

```
alter table auto_parts partition 100
go
alter table auto_prices partition 50
go
```

The output from *sp_sysmon* shows that these changes have eliminated the performance bottleneck:

```
Lock Summary                 per sec   per xact   count    % of total
-------------------          -------   --------   -----    ----------
Last Page Locks on Heaps
Granted                        120.1        1.0    7024       100.0 %
Waited                           0.0        0.0       0         0.0 %
```

Using Partitions to Improve bcp Performance

A *bcp* session performs one insert after another, often for very large amounts of data, and so clearly lends itself to table partitioning. You might wonder how partitioning can help, because the *bcp* can perform only one insert at a time. However, you can run multiple occurrences of *bcp* at the same time. As shown in Figure 9-4, effective use of table partitioning can significantly improve *bcp* performance.

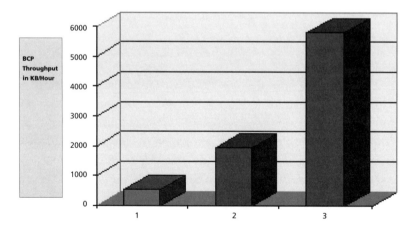

1. SQL Server 10.0.2 performing one bcp
2. SQL Server 11.0 performing one bcp, using large I/O
3. SQL Server 11.0 performing eight bcps on a table with eight partitions

Figure 9-4: Table partitioning can have a positive effect on **bcp** performance.

With this method, you break down the data into several files and use a different *bcp* script to deal with each file. You may be tempted to use the *bcp* with the -F and -L flags, to set the first and last rows to copy and to keep all the data in one file. Although this may work for small files, you will have to wait a long time before the *bcp* even starts if you try this with larger files. For example, if you set the first row to copy as row number 1,000,000 in a 100-MB file, *bcp* must go through each row as it counts up to 1,000,000. For this reason, you should divide the data into separate files.

Partition the target table before you start the *bcp*s. Finding the optimal number of partitions requires experimentation, but you may want to start with a large number, such as 100. You can monitor the inserts by using *sp_sysmon*. Once you have partitioned the table, you can start all the *bcp* scripts. The following example partitions the *tab2* table and uses three *bcp*s to insert data from three data files called *data1*, *data2*, and *data3*:

```
alter table tab2 partition 100
go
bcp db1..tab2 in data1 -m1000 -Udavid -Pmeemoo -Sdev01
bcp db1..tab2 in data2 -m1000 -Udavid -Pmeemoo -Sdev01
bcp db1..tab2 in data3 -m1000 -Udavid -Pmeemoo -Sdev01
```

If you have trouble running multiple instances of *bcp*, you may need to switch to a later version of *bcp*. You can use the *bcp* -v flag to see which version you are running. If you are running a SQL Server 10.x version of *bcp*, try a SQL Server 11.x version. The SQL Server 11.x release of *bcp* uses the open client *ct-lib* libraries instead of the *db-lib* libraries. It performs faster than its predecessor and is more stable when you run multiple *bcp*s. Your copy of SQL Server 11 should include all the version 11.x open client products and libraries.

Summary

This chapter introduces several techniques for fine-tuning SQL Server 11 to achieve optimal performance. Tuning SQL Server 11 is as much an art as it is a science, and developing the necessary skills requires time and effort. Once you have SQL Server 11 up and running, you should spend some time experimenting with the techniques this chapter describes. Although you might not need to try all of these techniques, you will likely find at least a few (properly implemented, of course) to be helpful for tuning your system.

Migration Checklist

The following list summarizes the key migration tasks covered in this chapter:

- Use *sp_sysmon* to monitor SQL Server 11's performance.

- If necessary, add memory to the system.

- If necessary, configure additional engines.

- Create named caches and buffer pools.

- Increase the maximum network packet size.

- Determine whether you can improve performance by setting *tcp no delay*.

- Partition heap tables, to improve insert performance.

- Use multiple *bcp* sessions, whenever possible.

Sample Benchmark Results

S QL Server 11 provides significant performance increases over previous releases. The following graphs provide examples of these performance gains. Most of these benchmarks are measured in transactions per second.

Windows NT benchmark

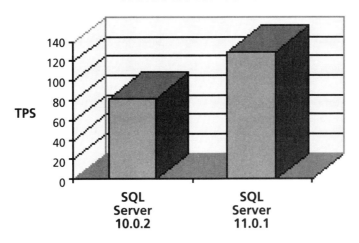

Platform:	Windows NT
SQL Server 10.0.2:	82.3 TPS
SQL Server 11.0.1:	130.6 TPS
Improvement:	59%

Windows NT benchmark

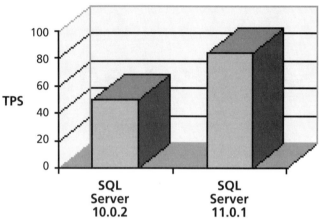

Platform: Windows NT
SQL Server 10.0.2:   50 TPS
SQL Server 11.0.1:   84 TPS
Improvement: 68%

Windows NT benchmark

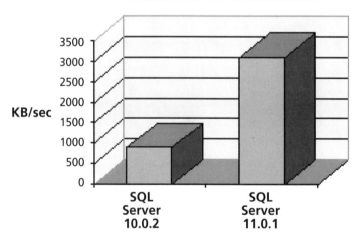

Platform: Windows NT
SQL Server 10.0.2:   883 KBytes/sec
SQL Server 11.0.1:   3,088 KBytes/sec
Improvement: 350%

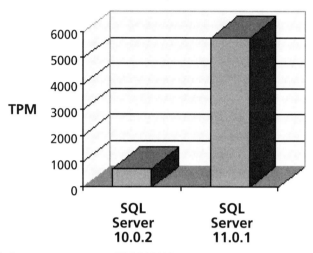

IBM RS6000, AIX 4.1.4 benchmark

TPM

6000	
5000	
4000	
3000	
2000	
1000	
0	

SQL Server 10.0.2   SQL Server 11.0.1

Platform:	IBM RS6000, AIX 4.1.4
SQL Server 10.0.2:	735.27 TPM (Note: one CPU)
SQL Server 11.0.1:	5,774.07 TPM (Note: eight CPUs)
Improvement:	785%

New Reserved Words, System Tables, and System Stored Procedures

New Reserved Words in SQL Server 11

```
max_rows_per_page
online
partition
unpartition
```

New Reserved Words in SQL Server 10.x

```
arith_overflow
at
authorization
cascade
check
close
constraint
current
cursor
deallocate
double
endtran
escape
fetch
foreign
identity
identity_insert
isolation
key
level
mirror
national
```

```
noholdlock
numeric_truncation
of
only
open
option
precision
primary
privileges
read
references
replace
role
rows
schema
shared
some
stripe
syb_identity
syb_restree
user
user_option
varying
work
```

New System Tables in SQL Server 11

sysattributes
syslogshold
syspartitions

New System Tables in SQL Server 10.x

In all Databases

sysconstraints
sysreferences
sysroles
systhresholds

In the Master Database

syslisteners
sysloginroles
syssrvroles

New System Stored Procedures in SQL Server 11

```
sp_bindcache
sp_cacheconfig
sp_cachestrategy
sp_chgattribute
sp_configure
sp_displaylevel
sp_dropglockpromote
sp_helpartition
sp_helpcache
sp_logiosize
sp_poolconfig
sp_procqmode
sp_setpglockpromote
sp_unbindcache
sp_unbindcache_all
```

New System Stored Procedures in SQL Server 10.x

```
sp_addauditrecord
sp_addthreshold
sp_auditdatabase
sp_auditlogin
sp_auditobject
sp_auditoption
sp_auditsproc
sp_bindmsg
sp_checkreswords
sp_configurelogin
sp_cursorinfo
sp_dbremap
sp_displaylogin
sp_dropthreshold
sp_estspace
sp_helpconstraint
sp_helpthreshold
sp_locklogin
sp_modifylogin
sp_modifythreshold
sp_procxmode
sp_remap
sp_role
sp_thresholdaction
sp_unbindmsg
sp_volchanged
```

APPENDIX C

Configuration Groups

To simplify configuration management, SQL Server 11 organizes its configuration parameters into hierarchical groups. This appendix provides a complete listing of these groups. To display this listing in SQL Server 11, enter the *sp_configure* command with no parameters:

```
sp_configure
go
```

TIP! When you examine the complete list of parameters generated by entering the *sp_configure* command with no parameters, remember that SQL Server lists several parameters more than once (because they belong to more than one group).

Group: Configuration Options

Group: Backup/Recovery

Parameter Name	Default	Memory Used	Config Value	Run Value
allow remote access	1	0	1	1
print recovery information	0	0	0	0
recovery interval in minutes	5	0	1	1
tape retention in days	0	0	0	0

NOTE: A hash mark (#) preceding a value in the Memory Used column indicates that the parameter depends on other parameters.

Group: Cache Manager

Parameter Name	Default	Memory Used	Config Value	Run Value
memory alignment boundary	2048	0	2048	2048
number of index trips	0	0	0	0
number of oam trips	0	0	0	0
procedure cache percent	20	9136	5	5
total data cache size	0	167352	0	167352
total memory	7500	204800	102400	102400

Group: Disk I/O

Parameter Name	Default	Memory Used	Config Value	Run Value
allow sql server async i/o	1	0	1	1
disk i/o structures	256	15	200	200
number of devices	10	#30	80	80
page utilization percent	95	0	95	95

Group: General Information

Parameter Name	Default	Memory Used	Config Value	Run Value
configuration file	0	0	0	/var/syb/sy

Group: Languages

Parameter Name	Default	Memory Used	Config Value	Run Value
default character set id	1	0	1	1
default language id	0	0	0	0
default sortorder id	50	0	50	50
disable character set conversi	0	0	0	0
number of languages in cache	3	4	3	3

Group: Lock Manager

Parameter Name	Default	Memory Used	Config Value	Run Value
address lock spinlock ratio	100	0	100	100
deadlock checking period	500	0	500	500
freelock transfer block size	30	0	1000	1000
max engine freelocks	10	0	10	10
number of locks	5000	4688	50000	50000
page lock spinlock ratio	100	0	100	100
table lock spinlock ratio	20	0	20	20

Group: Memory Use

Parameter Name	Default	Memory Used	Config Value	Run Value
additional network memory	0	0	0	0
audit queue size	100	42	100	100
default network packet size	512	#338	512	512
disk i/o structures	256	15	200	200
event buffers per engine	100	#782	8000	4000
executable codesize + overhead	0	5118	0	5118
max number network listeners	15	1124	15	15
max online engines	1	1056	2	2
number of alarms	40	1	40	40
number of devices	10	#30	80	80
number of extent i/o buffers	0	0	0	0
number of languages in cache	3	4	3	3
number of locks	5000	4688	50000	50000
number of mailboxes	30	1	30	30
number of messages	64	1	64	64
number of open databases	12	1650	50	50
number of open objects	500	1895	2000	2000
number of remote connections	20	33	20	20
number of remote logins	20	22	20	20
number of remote sites	10	749	10	10
number of user connections	25	11948	160	160
partition groups	1024	21	1024	1024
permission cache entries	15	#91	15	15
procedure cache percent	20	9136	5	5
remote server pre-read packets	3	#32	3	3
stack guard size	4096	#784	4096	4096
stack size	34816	#6665	34816	34816
total data cache size	0	167352	0	167352
total memory	7500	204800	102400	102400

Group: Network Communication

Parameter Name	Default	Memory Used	Config Value	Run Value
additional network memory	0	0	0	0
allow remote access	1	0	1	1
allow sendmsg	0	0	0	0
default network packet size	512	#338	512	512
max network packet size	512	0	512	512
max number network listeners	15	1124	15	15
number of remote connections	20	33	20	20
number of remote logins	20	22	20	20
number of remote sites	10	749	10	10
remote server pre-read packets	3	#32	3	3
syb_sendmsg port number	0	0	0	0
tcp no delay	0	0	0	0

Group: O/S Resources

Parameter Name	Default	Memory Used	Config Value	Run Value
max async i/os per engine	2147483647	0	200	200
max async i/os per server	2147483647	0	2147483647	2147483647
o/s asynch i/o enabled	0	0	0	0
o/s file descriptors	0	0	0	1024
tcp no delay	0	0	0	0

Group: Physical Resources

Group: Physical Memory

Parameter Name	Default	Memory Used	Config Value	Run Value
additional network memory	0	0	0	0
lock shared memory	0	0	0	0
shared memory starting address	0	0	0	0
total memory	7500	204800	102400	102400

Group: Processors

Parameter Name	Default	Memory Used	Config Value	Run Value
max online engines	1	1056	2	2
min online engines	1	0	1	1

Group: SQL Server Administration

Parameter Name	Default	Memory Used	Config Value	Run Value
allow nested triggers	1	0	1	1
allow updates to system tables	0	0	0	0
audit queue size	100	42	100	100
cpu accounting flush interval	200	0	200	200
cpu grace time	500	0	500	500
deadlock retries	5	0	5	5
default database size	2	0	2	2
default fill factor percent	0	0	0	0
event buffers per engine	100	#782	8000	4000
housekeeper free write percent	1	0	1	1
i/o accounting flush interval	1000	0	1000	1000
i/o polling process count	10	0	10	10
identity burning set factor	5000	0	500	500
identity grab size	1	0	1	1
lock promotion HWM	200	0	200	200
lock promotion LWM	200	0	200	200
lock promotion PCT	100	0	100	100
number of alarms	40	1	40	40
number of extent i/o buffers	0	0	0	0
number of mailboxes	30	1	30	30

```
number of messages               64        1        64        64
number of open databases         12     1650        50        50
number of open objects          500     1895      2000      2000
number of pre-allocated extent    2        0         2         2
number of sort buffers            0        0         0         0
partition groups               1024       21      1024      1024
partition spinlock ratio         10        0        10        10
print deadlock information        0        0         1         1
runnable process search count  2000        0         1         1
size of auto identity column     10        0        10        10
sort page count                   0        0         0         0
sql server clock tick length 100000       0    100000    100000
time slice                      100        0       100       100
upgrade version                1100        0      1101      1101
```

Group: User Environment

Parameter Name	Default	Memory Used	Config Value	Run Value
default network packet size	512	#338	512	512
number of pre-allocated extent	2	0	2	2
number of user connections	25	11948	160	160
permission cache entries	15	#91	15	15
stack guard size	4096	#784	4096	4096
stack size	34816	#6665	34816	34816
systemwide password expiration	0	0	0	0
user log cache size	2048	0	2048	2048
user log cache spinlock ratio	20	0	20	20

Command Reference

alter table partition

Syntax

```
alter table table_name partition num_partitions
```

Example

```
alter table sales partition 4
```

alter table unpartition

Syntax

```
alter table table_name unpartition
```

Example

```
alter table sales unpartition
```

dbcc traceon 3604

Syntax

```
dbcc traceon (3604)
```

Example

```
dbcc traceon (3604)
```

dbcc traceon 302

Syntax

```
dbcc traceon (302)
```

Example

```
dbcc traceon (3604)
dbcc traceon (302)
```

dbcc traceon 310

Syntax

```
dbcc traceon (310)
```

Example

```
dbcc traceon (3604)
dbcc traceon (310)
```

set prefetch on/off

Syntax

```
set prefetch {off | on}
```

Example

```
set prefetch on
```

set showplan on/off

Syntax

```
set showplan {on | off}
```

Example

```
set showplan on
```

set statistics io on/off

Syntax

```
set statistics io {on | off}
```

Example

```
set statistics io on
```

set statistics time on/off

Syntax

```
set statistics time {on | off}
```

Example

```
set statistics time on
```

set transaction isolation level

Syntax

```
set transaction isolation level {0 | 1 | 3}
```

Example

```
set transaction isolation level 0
```

sp_addlogin

Syntax

```
sp_addlogin loginame, passwd, [,defdb [, deflang [, fullname]]]
```

Example

```
sp_addlogin david, davidpw, db1
```

sp_adduser

Syntax

```
sp_adduser loginame [, name_in_db [, groupname]]
```

Example
```
sp_adduser lucyd, lucy, grp1
```

sp_bindcache
Syntax
```
sp_bindcache cachename, dbname [, [ ownername .] tablename [, indexname |
"text only"]]
```

Example
```
sp_bindcache "ncache1", "db1", "table1"
```

sp_cacheconfig
Syntax
```
sp_cacheconfig [cachename [ , "cache_size[P|K|M|G]" ] [,logonly | mixed]]
```

Example
```
sp_cacheconfig my_cache, "5M"
```

sp_cachestrategy
Syntax
```
sp_cachestrategy dbname , [ ownername .] tablename [, indexname | "text
only" | "table only" [, prefetch | mru , "on" | "off"]]
```

Examples
```
sp_cachestrategy pubs2, titles, prefetch, "off"

sp_cachestrategy pubs2, titles, mru, "off"
```

sp_checkreswords
Syntax
```
sp_checkreswords [username]
```

Example

```
use db1
sp_checkreswords
```

sp_configure

Syntax

```
sp_configure [parameter [value] | group_name |
non_unique_parameter_fragment]

sp_configure "configuration file", 0, {"write" | "read" | "verify" |
"restore"} "file_name"
```

Examples

```
sp_configure "configuration file", 0, "write", "config1.cfg"
sp_configure "configuration file", 0, "verify","config2.cfg"
sp_configure "configuration file", 0, "read", "configA.cfg"
sp_configure "configuration file" ,0, "restore", "configC.cfg"
sp_configure "number of open databases",50
sp_configure "housekeeper free write percent", 20
sp_configure "user log cache size", 4096
sp_configure "Disk I/O"
sp_configure "max"
```

sp_dboption

Syntax

```
sp_dboption [dbname, optname, {true | false}]
```

Example

```
use master
sp_dboption pubs2, "select into", true
use pubs2
checkpoint
```

sp_depends

Syntax

```
sp_depends objname
```

Example

```
sp_depends title
```

sp_displaylevel

Syntax

```
sp_displaylevel [login_name [,level]]
```

Examples

```
sp_displaylevel suzy, comprehensive
```

```
sp_displaylevel
```

sp_dropglockpromote

Syntax

```
sp_dropglockpromote "database" | "table", objname
```

Example

```
sp_droplockpromote "table", titles
```

sp_droplogin

Syntax

```
sp_droplogin loginame
```

Example

```
sp_droplogin mitchell
```

sp_dropuser

Syntax

```
sp_dropuser name_in_db
```

Example

```
sp_dropuser david
```

sp_helpcache

Syntax

```
sp_helpcache cache_name | " cache_size [P|K|M|G]"
```

Examples

```
sp_helpcache ncache1
```

```
sp_helpcache "75M"
```

sp_helpdb

Syntax

```
sp_helpdb [dbname]
```

Example

```
sp_helpdb db1
```

sp_helppartition

Syntax

```
sp_helppartition table_name
```

Example

```
sp_helppartition sales
```

sp_helprotect

Syntax

```
sp_helprotect [name [,username [,"grant"]]]
```

Example

```
sp_helprotect titles
```

sp_logiosize

Syntax

```
sp_logiosize ["default" | " size " | "all"]
```

Example

```
sp_logiosize "default"
```

sp_password

Syntax

```
sp_password old_password, new_password
```

Example

```
sp_password 123456, aj5Gh1
```

sp_ poolconfig

Syntax

```
sp_poolconfig cachename [, "memsize[P|K|M|G]","configpool K" [,
"affected_pool K"]]

sp_poolconfig cachename , " io_size " ,"wash= size [P|K|M|G]"
```

Examples

```
sp_poolconfig dss_cache, "2M", "4K", "16K"

sp_poolconfig dss_cache, "4K", "wash=512"
```

sp_procqmode

Syntax

```
sp_procqmode [objname [,detail]]
```

Example

```
sp_procqmode null, detail
```

sp_rename

Syntax

```
sp_rename objname, newname
```

Example

```
sp_rename "books.title", newbkname
```

sp_renamedb

Syntax

```
sp_renamedb dbname, newname
```

Example

```
sp_renamedb db1, newdbname
```

sp_setpglockpromote

Syntax

```
sp_setpglockpromote "server" | "database" | "table", object, new_lwm,
new_hwm, new_pct
```

Example

```
sp_setpglockpromote "table" , titles, 100, 200, 20
```

sp_sysmon

Syntax

```
sp_sysmon time
```

Example

```
sp_sysmon 5
```

sp_unbindcache

Syntax

```
sp_unbindcache dbname [,[ owner. ] tablename[, indexname | "text only"]]
```

Example

```
sp_unbindcache "ncache1", "db1", "table1"
```

sp_unbindcache_all

Syntax

```
sp_unbindcache_all cache_name
```

Example

```
sp_unbindcache_all cache2
```

sybinit

Syntax

```
sybinit -r resource_file_name [-option] [parameter]
```

Example

```
sybinit -r resource.dmp -T IGNORE_WARNING
```

Appendix E

SyBooks
Installation Guide

Welcome to SyBooks, the Sybase online documentation facility. This CD-ROM includes the following collections:

Sybase SQL Server
Release 11.0.x

Replication Server
Release 11.0.x

System Management
Release 11.0.x

Open Client/Server
Release 10.0.3

Open Client/Server Supplements (for UNIX, PC, Macintosh)
Release 10.0.3

Online viewing is now the standard means of presenting Sybase documentation. SyBooks' advantages include:

- Distributed access to documentation. Once SyBooks is installed in a network environment, Sybase users can access any book and no longer have to depend on a single set of documentation.

- Instant access to information. Links within and between individual books and comprehensive search capabilities enable instant access to related information.

- Decreased reliance upon paper products. Online documentation does not use paper and, therefore, helps preserve the earth's resources.

SyBooks uses the Electronic Book Technologies, Inc. (EBT) DynaText Browser to display documentation online. The *Dyna*Text Browser provides a flexible graphical environment, including search, annotation, and print capabilities throughout the SyBooks online documentation.

Using This Guide

This guide:

- Details the procedures associated with installing SyBooks on UNIX, Windows 3.1, and Macintosh systems

- Introduces both SyBooks and EBT's *Dyna*Text Browser to new users

This booklet is neither a comprehensive guide nor a tutorial for the SyBooks environment. For a thorough guide to the Browser's functionality, we recommend that you access the DynaText online help, *Reader Guide*, available through the *Dyna*Text Browser's Help facility. The online book *SyBooks Frequently Asked Questions* is also available.

SyBooks Features

With the help *of Dyna*Text's flexible environment, SyBooks users can locate information anywhere in the Sybase documentation quickly and efficiently. SyBooks features include:

- **Search capabilities**. Users can search through individual or multiple books for occurrences of words or phrases. Search query instances are highlighted in the current book's text, and the number of query instances in each of the book's sections is displayed in the table of contents view. Boolean, proximity, and wildcard character search capabilities are supported.

- **Annotation capabilities**. Users can create publicly or privately accessible annotations within books, including margin notes, bookmarks (placeholders accessible via hypertext links), and hypertext links (links between specified locations in the book).

- **Printing capabilities**. Users can print an entire book or selected sections of a book, including the table of contents, using a PostScript printer.

*   **SKILS integration**. SyBooks is integrated within the SKILS (Sybase Knowledge Through Interactive Learning Systems) environment, providing users with instant access to Sybase documentation from the Sybase online education facility.

Supported Platforms

For platform requirements and dependencies, refer to the SyBooks *Release Bulletin*.

For More Information

Other documents that you may find useful include:

*   The SyBooks *Release Bulletin*, which includes special installation instructions and other platform-specific information

*   *SyBooks Frequently Asked Questions*, an online document that includes useful information about SyBooks

*   The *DynaText Reader Guide*, an online guide to the DynaText browser

Installing SyBooks on the Macintosh

Before installing SyBooks, be aware of the following:

*   You can run SyBooks from the CD-ROM drive, but you will not be able to use annotations or modify the collections on the CD. If performance is a concern, install SyBooks on a hard disk.

*   During the installation process, you can:

    *   Install new collections
    *   Install new books in existing collections, if the book and the collection have the same release number
    *   Delete an entire installation
    *   Update the *Dyna*Text Browser version and environment

*   The SyBooks installation program must be copied to and run from a hard disk. If you are running System 7.0 or 7.1, you must run the installation program from the hard disk onto which SyBooks will be installed.

*   You must have *both* AppleScript 1.1 and the Scripting Additions folder installed to run the installation program. If you do not have AppleScript and the Scripting

Additions folder installed, you may install the versions provided on the SyBooks CD. (See the next section.)

- The system requirements are:

  - A CD-ROM drive.
  - 4MB of RAM.
  - Free space on your hard disk. The amount varies with each installation configuration. The installation program will state how much space is needed.

- The supported operating system is: MacOS System 7.x running AppleScript 1.1 and Applescript Scripting Additions.

To install AppleScript and the Scripting Additions folder:

1. Insert the SyBooks CD into the CD-ROM drive.

2. Open the SYBOOKS CD.

3. Open the *sybooks* folder.

4. Open the *mac* folder.

5. If AppleScript 1.1 is not installed on your system, copy AppleScript to the *Extensions* folder, located in the *Systems folder.*

6. Copy the Scripting Additions folder to the *Extensions* folder, located in the *Systems folder.*

7. Restart the computer.

Installing SyBooks

You may choose from three installation configurations:

- *Compact* installs only the *Dyna*Text browser and allows you to read books from the CD.

- *Custom* allows you to specify the books and collections that you would like to install onto your hard disk.

- *Full* installs the *Dyna*Text browser and all collections and books contained on the CD.

- The *Deinstall* option deinstalls any installation, whether partially or completely installed.

To install SyBooks:

1. If you do not have a previously installed version of SyBooks, create a folder by choosing New Folder from the File menu. You may choose any name for the folder; *SyBooks* is the default. Later, you will specify this folder as the Destination Folder when running the installation program.

2. Insert the SyBooks CD into the CD-ROM drive.

3. Open the SYBOOKS CD.

4. Open the *Sybooks* folder.

5. Open the *mac* folder.

6. Copy the *install.me* file to a hard disk. If you are running System 7.0 or 7.1, you must run the installation program from the same hard disk onto which SyBooks will be installed.

7. Double-click on the *install.me* file that you copied to the hard disk. If you receive the message:

   ```
   Where is HyperCard?
   ```

   Highlight *install.me* and click Open.

8. Follow the instructions on the screen.

9. The installation program is finished when the screen displays the following message:

   ```
   SyBooks 2.2 Installation has completed successfully.
   ```

Post-Installation Procedures

Making SyBooks an Apple Menu Item

1. Open the *SyBooks* folder.

2. Open the *bin* folder.

3. Click on the *sybooks* file.

4. From the File menu, choose the Make Alias command.

5. Drag the *sybooks alias* file to the *Apple Menu Items* folder located in the *Systems* folder.

6. Rename the *sybooks* alias file *SyBooks*.

SyBooks is now accessible from the Apple menu.

Starting SyBooks

To start SyBooks, select SyBooks from the Apple menu. Or:

1. Open the *SyBooks* folder.

2. Open the *bin* folder.

3. Double-click on the sybooks file.

When starting SyBooks, you may receive one or more of the following messages at the bottom of your screen:

```
Warning: '<book folder name>' is not a valid book
```

This indicates that the named book was not selected by the user for installation. To install a specific book, run *install.me* and select the Custom installation option.

For help with using *Dyna*Text, go to the *Reader Guide* located under the Help menu.

Running SyBooks from the CD-ROM Drive

To run SyBooks from the CD-ROM drive:

1. Insert the SyBooks CD into the CD-ROM drive.

2. Open the SYBOOKS CD.

3. Open the *sybooks* folder.

4. Open the *mac* folder.

5. Open the *bin* folder.

6. Double-click on the *sybooks* file.

Installation Notes and Troubleshooting

For up-to-date information, see the *readme.mac* file in the *<cd_drive>:\sybooks* directory on the CD. The *readme.mac* file contains a directory tree of a valid SyBooks installation.

Memory Errors

If you receive the error message:

```
Can't understand 'createconfig'.
```

or, by extrapolation:

```
Can't understand '<module_name>'.
```

the installer is out of memory. It will be necessary to restart the computer, or power down and restart, before rerunning *install.me*.

Installing SyBooks on UNIX

Before SyBooks can be installed, you must mount the CD-ROM drive to the system on which the installation will occur. Superuser privileges are often required to mount the CD-ROM drive.

NOTE: Mounting commands and mount points vary among different UNIX platforms. For mounting instructions, see your System Administrator or the documentation associated with the UNIX platform on which SyBooks will be installed.

In addition, be aware of the following:

- SyBooks requires running the X Window System. Refer to the SyBooks *Release Bulletin* to ensure that your system is running the correct version of the X Window System and operating system software before continuing with the installation.

- The installation program does not overwrite any previously installed books. During the installation process, you can:

  - Install new collections
  - Install new books in existing collections, if the book and the collection have the same release number
  - Delete previously installed collections from your installation
  - Update the *Dyna*Text Browser version and environment

- SyBooks books must be installed on your UNIX system to be available to users. They cannot be read directly from the CD-ROM.

- For a new installation, SyBooks is installed in a directory of your choosing or in a default directory, *$HOME/sybooks*. The requirements for this directory are:

  ■ You must have write permissions on the parent directory (for example, *$HOME*).

  ■ The child directory (for example, sybooks or the last directory in the alternative path name) cannot already exist. It is created by the SyBooks installation program, which installs SyBooks within it.

- For previously existing SyBooks installations, the installation program uses the value of the SYBROOT environment variable and makes changes in that directory. The SYBROOT and EBTRC environment variables must already be defined in your environment.

- The SyBooks directory path, including the sybooks directory (for example, *$HOME/sybooks*), is referred to in this guide as *<SyBooks_root>*. For example, if you choose to install SyBooks at the default location, *<SyBooks_root>* would represent *$HOME/sybooks*.

Calculating Disk Space Requirements

When you are preparing to install SyBooks, it is important to calculate how much hard disk space is required for the SyBooks configuration you want to install. This section describes how to calculate these space requirements.

NOTE: To ensure sufficient disk space, all size values are rounded to the nearest 1/100 megabyte.

To calculate the disk space requirements for your proposed SyBooks installation, add the values obtained for each of the following steps:

1. **Common files**. Auxiliary files required by the *Dyna*Text Browser and common to all supported UNIX platforms are gathered together in the UNIX tar file, common.tar. Therefore, the size of common.tar is a constant value for all UNIX platforms.

   Common files (*common.tar*):   2.32 MB

2. ***Dyna*Text Browser executables**. Table E-1 lists the size of each supported UNIX platform's *Dyna*Text Browser executable. If you plan to install the executable for more than one platform, total the sizes of all the executables to be installed to obtain a final value for this step.

Table E-1: *DynaText Browser Executable Size*

UNIX platform	*Dyna*Text Browser executable size (MB)
SunOS 4.x OpenWindows	4.32
SunOS 4.x Motif	5.63
Sun Solaris 2.x (SPARC) OpenWindows	5.71
Sun Solaris 2.x (SPARC) Motif	7.02
Solaris 2.x (Intel) OpenWindows	2.46
Solaris 2.x (Intel) Motif	3.77
IBM AIX 3.2	3.31
SGI IRIX 5.2	3.42
HP HP-UX 9.0	3.08
Novell UnixWare 1.1	3.91
AT&T System 3000	3.91
Digital UNIX	2.72

**
 *Dyna*Text Browser executable(s):**   MB

3. **Online book collections**. Each online book collection's auxiliary files require approximately 100KB (0.10MB) of disk space. For example, if the SyBooks CD from which you are installing contains three online book collections, and you plan to install all of them, the combined auxiliary files would require 300KB of disk space (3 collections x 100KB).

Book collections: MB

4. **Online books**. Disk space requirements for each online book on this SyBooks CD are listed in the *SyBooks Contents List* included with this CD. Decide which online books you want to install and add their space requirements to obtain a final value for this step.

Online books: MB

5. ***Dyna*Text/SyBooks documentation collection**. An additional collection containing the online *DynaText Reader Guide* and *SyBooks Frequently Asked Questions* is

automatically installed with every SyBooks installation. Therefore, the disk space requirement for this collection is a constant value for all UNIX platforms.

DynaText/SyBooks documentation: 1.56 MB

6. Add the values for steps 1–5 to obtain the disk space requirements for your SyBooks installation.

Total disk space required: MB

Installing SyBooks

The SyBooks installation program for UNIX is a text-based application. Detailed instructions are provided throughout the installation; you are prompted for information to tailor the SyBooks environment, including:

- The directory in which SyBooks will be installed

- The UNIX platform from which SyBooks will be installed

- The UNIX platforms on which SyBooks will be viewed

- The Sybase books that will be installed

You can terminate the installation at any time during installation prior to the actual writing of data. The location at which SyBooks is to be installed will remain untouched. It is highly recommended that you execute the SyBooks installation program inside an X-window that has scroll bars.

If you have an existing SyBooks installation, you must execute the SyBooks installation program as a SyBooks user to properly install additional books, collections, and executables. That is, the SYBROOT and EBTRC environment variables must be defined in your environment.

To execute the SyBooks installation program for UNIX:

1. Change directories to the *unix* directory on the SyBooks CD. For example, assuming that the CD-ROM drive is mounted as */cdrom*, enter:

    ```
    cd /cdrom/sybooks/unix
    ```

2. Execute the installation program as follows:

    - If you are installing SyBooks from an HP 9000 system running HP-UX, an AT&T system running SVR4, or a Digital UNIX system running OSF/1 version

1.x, execute the installation program from the /cdrom/*sybooks/unix* directory with this command:

```
INSTALL.ME*
```

■ If you are installing SyBooks from any other platform, execute the installation program from the /cdrom/*sybooks/unix* directory with this command:

```
install.me
```

Upon completing successfully, the SyBooks installation program stores a record of the work performed in a log file located in *<SyBooks_root>/config/log.cur*. If the log file from a previous SyBooks installation exists at this location, it is renamed *log.old*. A directory tree of the resulting SyBooks installation is located in the *sybooks/readme.unx* file on the CD.

The DynaText Configuration File: .ebtrc

For each version of the *Dyna*Text Browser installed, the SyBooks installation program for UNIX creates a separate *Dyna*Text configuration file, *.ebtrc*, which tailors the Browser to the system on which it is installed. Each *.ebtrc* file is stored in the *<SyBooks_root>/<plat-form _name>* directory. For further information about the *.ebtrc* configuration file, refer to the online document *SyBooks Frequently Asked Questions*.

Collection-Level Indexing

Collection-level indexes are required for cross-collection searches (that is, searches across all installed books within a single collection or multiple collections). The SyBooks installation program for UNIX automatically generates collection-level indexes.

Post-Installation Procedures

Following installation, the System Administrator must perform the following *for each user* who wants to view SyBooks:

1. Create a directory within the user's home directory for private SyBooks annotations. The path and name of this directory must be:

   ```
   ~/sybooks/annot
   ```

2. Set the user's SYBROOT environment variable to point to the directory path where SyBooks is installed. (This is the value of *<SyBooks_root>*.) For example, if SyBooks is installed in */usr/local* and has the default directory name of *sybooks*, set the SYB-ROOT environment variable as follows:

C shell:

```
setenv SYBROOT /usr/local/sybooks
```

Bourne or Korn shell:

```
SYBROOT=/usr/local/sybooks; export SYBROOT
```

3. Set the user's EBTRC environment variable to point to the *.ebtrc* configuration file for the version of *Dyna*Text with which the user will view SyBooks. Set EBTRC as follows:

C shell:

```
setenv EBTRC $SYBROOT/<platform_name>/.ebtrc
```

Bourne or Korn shell:

```
EBTRC=$SYBROOT/<platform_name>/.ebtrc; export EBTRC
```

Refer to the SyBooks Release Bulletin for a list of platform directory names.

If SYBROOT has not been set, or if the .ebtrc file has been moved from its default location, substitute the path associated with <SyBooks_root> in place of SYBROOT.

4. Add the SyBooks executable path to the user's path. This points to the version of *Dyna*Text with which the user will view SyBooks. After installation, SyBooks executables are located in *<SyBooks_root>/<platform_name>/bin*.

5. If your SyBooks installation is distributed over a network, particularly if a user is viewing SyBooks on an X terminal remotely logged into the SyBooks host, you must:

   ■ Set the user's DISPLAY environment variable to point to the user's machine.

   ■ Add the user's machine to the list of those allowed to make connections to your X server.

   To do this, execute the following commands in the rlogin session window on the user's workstation:

C shell:

```
xhost +local_machine_name
setenv DISPLAY local_machine_name:0.0
```

Bourne or Korn shell:

```
xhost +local_machine_name
DISPLAY=local_machine_name:0.0; export DISPLAY
```

Starting SyBooks

When all post-installation steps are complete, use the following command to start SyBooks:

```
sybooks
```

Installation Notes and Troubleshooting

Dyna*Text Browser, Versions 2.0 and 2.3 Compatibility*

SyBooks includes version 2.3 of EBT's *Dyna*Text browser. While version 2.3 of the browser can read online documentation generated for use with earlier versions of the browser, the reverse is not true. Versions of the *Dyna*Text browser earlier than version 2.3 cannot be expected to read online documentation generated for use with version 2.3.

If a version of the *Dyna*Text browser earlier than version 2.3 is currently installed, it is recommended that it be updated to version 2.3. The SyBooks installation program automatically updates earlier versions of the *Dyna*Text Browser that were installed with previous installations of SyBooks.

Updating Annotations from Previous SyBooks Releases

This release of SyBooks does not take advantage of *Dyna*Text's ability to maintain user-created annotations (including bookmarks, internal hypertext links, and margin notes) across successive releases of an online document. However, the SyBooks installation program saves annotations from any previous installation of SyBooks. Old annotations are saved in *<SyBooks_root>/config/annotold.*

Motif Applications and OpenWindows

All versions of *Dyna*Text for UNIX included with SyBooks are Motif applications. Starting Motif applications while running OpenWindows on SunOS 4.x or 5.x operating systems can introduce a variety of problems. The following are problems you can expect when running SyBooks under OpenWindows:

- Double-clicking in any text entry using any mouse button can crash the *Dyna*Text Browser.

- Starting SyBooks can crash the OpenWindows XNEWS server before the *Dyna*Text Browser library window appears.

To resolve these problems, obtain the patches listed in Table E-2 from Sun and install them on the system on which the SyBooks executable is located:

Table E-2: *Sun patches required to resolve Open Windows problems*

Patch number	Patch name
100444-58	OpenWindows 3.0: OpenWindows V3.0 Server Patch 3
100512-04	OpenWindows 3.0: libXt CTE Jumbo Patch

Motif 1.2.2: Errors Mapping Pop-Up Menus

A Motif 1.2.2 bug can prevent *Dyna*Text from mapping pop-up menus. If your UNIX environment supplies Motif 1.2 dynamically linked libraries, or if you are using the toolkit to link to Motif 1.2.2, add the following resources to the *Dyna*Text applications defaults file, Dtext, located in *<SyBooks_root>/<data/X_platform_directory>/defaults/C*:

```
dtext.motif122bug:          TRUE
*whichButton:               5
```

Solaris on Sun Sparc and i86-Based Machines

If revelatory windows appear partially or completely black when using the Solaris version of *Dyna*Text on a Sun Sparc or i86-based workstation, add the following resource to the *.Xebt* file located in each user's home directory:

```
motifResizeBug:             TRUE
```

Translation Table Warnings and the **XKeysymDB** File

On UNIX systems on which Motif is not installed, starting SyBooks can generate many "translation table" warning messages, such as:

```
Warning: translation table syntax error:
Unknown keysym . . .
Warning: . . . found while parsing . . .
```

These messages are merely warnings and do not affect the performance of either SyBooks or the *Dyna*Text Browser.

To resolve this problem, there must be an *XKeysymDB* file in the */usr/lib/X11* directory. An XKeysymDB file is installed with SyBooks and is located in *SyBooks_root/data/misc*.

Perform the following:

- **If an *XKeysymDB* file is not already located in */usr/lib/X11***, copy the XKeysymDB file installed with SyBooks to /usr/lib/X11.

- **If your UNIX environment does not have a */usr/lib/X11* directory**, you must create this directory before copying the XKeysymDB file to it.

- **If an *XKeysymDB* file is already located in */usr/lib/X11***, append the contents of the *XKeysymDB* file installed with SyBooks to the present *XKeysymDB* file in */usr/lib/X11*.

If the UNIX workstation from which SyBooks is started has a usr directory, an *XKeysymDB* file must be located in the */usr/lib/X11* directory. Repeat the steps outlined above for the *XKeysymDB* file on the workstation.

SyBooks on AT&T: "Can't find libXt.so.1" Error

If you get this error when you start SyBooks on an AT&T platform:

```
dynamic linker: ncr/bin/sybooks: can't find libXt.so.1
```

you must create a link called "libXt.so.1" in the */usr/lib* directory pointing to the most recent version of this file (for example, */usr/lib/libXt.so.5.0*).

Unable to View Books

If you can start SyBooks but cannot view books, perform the following steps:

1. Ensure that a map.txt file exists in the following location for each SyBooks collection installed:

   ```
   <SyBooks_root>/<col_name>/ents/map.txt
   ```

2. If the map.txt files are empty or do not exist, create a *map.txt* file for each collection installed containing the following line:

   ```
   -//SYBOOKS//<col_name> Styles//EN $SYBROOT/<col_name>/styles
   ```

   where <col_name> specifies the name of a directory beneath <SyBooks_root> containing a collection's ancillary files and book data. For example:

   ```
   -//SYBOOKS//srv10023 Styles//EN $SYBROOT/srv10023/styles
   ```

This problem is known to occur on AT&T workstations and is due to the erroneous reading of files from the CD during installation.

"Could not open DATA_DIR (check your .ebtrc)" Error

If starting SyBooks generates the following error:

```
Could not open DATA_DIR (check your .ebtrc).
```

ensure that the following conditions have been met:

- The SYBROOT environment variable is set to the directory path where SyBooks is installed.

- The EBTRC environment variable is set to the directory path and file name of the *.ebtrc* configuration file.

- The DATA_DIR value set in the *.ebtrc* configuration file is set to the directory in which *Dyna*Text data files are located (for example, *$SYBROOT/data*).

Finally, set or unset the LANG environment variable as follows:

- If the LANG environment variable is set, unset it.

- If the LANG environment variable is not set, set it to the value *en_us* as follows:

  ```
  setenv LANG en_us
  ```

X Terminal Fonts

If SyBooks is started from an X terminal and *Dyna*Text Browser text does not appear in the same font as on other UNIX platforms, it is possible that all fonts were not installed when the X terminal software was installed.

To resolve this problem, install all the fonts included with the X terminal software.

Book Window Size Too Large

If *Dyna*Text book windows are too large for your monitor, the window's geometry can be adjusted by changing the values in the parameter **fulltext.geometry* in the file *<SyBooks_root>/data/<X_directory>/defaults/C/Dtext.color.*

UNIX Environment-Specific Installation Options

During installation, you are prompted for information about:

- The environment to which your CD-ROM drive is locally attached (from which you are installing SyBooks)

- The environments for which you want to install *Dyna*Text browsers

Table E-3 shows the configurations that correspond to the environment from which you are installing SyBooks. If you install SyBooks for an operating system other than the one on which you are performing the installation, the disk device on which SyBooks is installed must be NFS mounted and accessible directly by the other operating system.

If users are logging in remotely from one operating system to a local operating system on which SyBooks is installed, it is only necessary to install SyBooks for the local operating system. For example, if remote users running Solaris remotely log into a machine running AIX to view SyBooks, it is only necessary to install SyBooks for AIX.

WARNING! If you are running DEC OSF 1 1.x, choose option 4, HP 9000 HP-UX, as the UNIX environment from which you are installing SyBooks. DEC OSF 1 1.x does not interpret file names read from a CD-ROM drive verbatim; choosing HP 9000 HP-UX forces the SyBooks installation program to anticipate the problem and correct for it. If you are running DEC OSF 1 2.x or later, choose option 7, DEC Alpha OSF 1.

Table E-3: *Installation environment options*

Installer Option No.	Machine	Operating system
1	Sun SPARC	SunOS 4.x
2	Sun SPARC	Solaris 2.x
3	IBM RS6000	AIX
4	HP 9000	HP-UX
5	AT&T	AT&T SVR4
6	SGI MIPS	IRIX
7	DEC Alpha	OSF/1
8	Intel x86	Solaris 2.x
9	Intel x86	UnixWare

Table E-4 shows the configurations that corresponds to the browser environments.

Table E-4: *Browser environment options*

Installer option number	Machine	Operating system	SyBooks directory name
1	Sun SPARC	SunOS 4.1.x Motif	sun4m
2	Sun SPARC	SunOS 4.1.x OpenWindows	sun4mol
3	Sun SPARC	Solaris 2.x Motif	sun5m
4	Sun SPARC	Solaris 2.x OpenWindows	sun5mol
5	IBM RS6000	AIX 3.2	ibm
6	HP 9000	HP-UX 9.0	hp
7	AT&T	AT&T SVR4	att

(continues)

Table E-4: *(continued)*

Installer option number	Machine	Operating system	SyBooks directory name
8	SGI MIPS	IRIX 5.2	sgi5
9	DEC Alpha	DEC OSF/1	decosf
10	Intel x86	Solaris 2.x Motif	i86m
11	Intel x86	Solaris 2.x OpenWindows	i86mol
12	Intel x86	UnixWare 1.1	uw

SunOS 4.1.x: Motif vs. OpenWindows Installation

If you are running SunOS 4.1.x using OpenWindows, you can choose between two SyBooks environments during installation:

- Option 1: SunOS 4.1.x running Motif

- Option 2: SunOS 4.1.x running OpenWindows

Depending on the configuration at your site, one choice may yield better visual results than the other. You can install both, then experiment to determine which looks best on your monitor. In either case, you must install the Sun patches discussed earlier in "Motif Applications and OpenWindows."

Exiting and Restarting the Installation Program

You can exit the SyBooks installation program at any user prompt by entering either *Q* or *q*, or at any time by pressing Ctrl-C.

If you exit before all user options have been chosen and confirmed, only a log file located at *$HOME/log.cur* will remain; nothing else in your environment will be affected. If you exit after the final option confirmation, the user-specified SyBooks directory will have been created and populated with directories and files. If you abort the installation, you must rerun it, and it must complete successfully before SyBooks will be properly installed. The installation program must complete without errors and generate the following message:

```
End of SyBooks Installation Program
```

before the SyBooks installation can be considered successful. Each user who wants to view SyBooks must then be configured according to the post-installation instructions described earlier in "Post-Installation Procedures."

Install.me *Installation Program Not Found*

Occasionally, the UNIX shell cannot find the *install.me* installation program, although the program is visible in the file system. Typical error messages generated when this occurs are as follows:

```
csh: Can't find file install.me
csh: ERROR: install.me: command not found
```

If these errors appear, perform the following:

1. Ensure that your CD-ROM drive is mounted correctly.

2. Do one of the following:

    ■ Add "." (the current directory) to your path, or
    ■ Invoke *install.me* using its full path name, as follows:

      ```
      <CD_ROM_mount_point>/unix/install.me
      ```

3. If step 2 fails, ensure that *<CD_ROM_mount_point>/unix* is the current directory, and invoke *install.me* with its own Bourne shell:

      ```
      sh install.me
      ```

"tar: Tape read error" Error

If you receive the following error during installation:

```
tar: Tape read error
```

you must restart the SyBooks installation program for UNIX. This error is generated when either of the following occurs:

*   A read error on the CD-ROM drive

*   A physical problem with the SyBooks CD

Moving SyBooks

To move a SyBooks installation to a different location on the same file system, use the UNIX *mv* command. However, if you want to move SyBooks to a different file system, use the installation program to create a new installation. Do not use the command *cp* or *cp -r*, as this replaces symbolic links with physical files and thus occupies unnecessary disk space.

Installing SyBooks on Microsoft Windows

Before installing SyBooks, be aware of the following:

- You can use the installation program to:

  - Install new collections
  - Install new books in existing collections, if the book and the collection have the same release number
  - Delete previously installed collections and books from your installation, or delete entire installations
  - Update the *Dyna*Text browser and environment

- The minimum system requirements are:

  - A CD-ROM drive
  - A hard disk with about 10MB free space available
  - 4MB RAM

- The operating systems supported are:

  - DOS 4.01 or later and Windows 3.1x
  - Windows 95
  - Windows NT 3.x
  - OS/2 2.x or later (WinOS2)

- The directory path where SyBooks will be installed is referred to in this guide as *<SyBooks_root>*. For example, if you choose to install SyBooks at the default location, *<SyBooks_root>* would represent *C:\sybooks*.

Running SyBooks from the CD

You can run SyBooks from the CD; however you will not be able to use annotations or modify the collections on the CD in any other way. If performance is a concern, you should skip this section and install SyBooks to a hard disk drive.

To run the *Dyna*Text browser from the CD:

1. Insert the SyBooks CD into the CD-ROM drive.

2. Open Windows File Manager and change to the *<cd_drive>:\sybooks\windows\bin* directory.

3. Double-click on the sybooks.exe file.

If you are using Windows 95 with the AutoPlay feature:

1. Insert the SyBooks CD into the CD-ROM drive.

2. Click the right mouse button on the CD-ROM drive icon and select Run from CD.

Installing SyBooks to a Hard Drive

To run the SyBooks installation program for Windows:

1. Insert the SyBooks CD into the CD-ROM drive.

2. Open the Windows File Manager. Change the current drive to the CD-ROM drive, and change the current directory to *<drive_letter>:\pc\install*.

3. Double-click on the *setup.exe* file.

If you are using Windows 95:

1. Insert the SyBooks CD into the CD-ROM drive.

2. Click the right mouse button on the SyBooks CD-ROM drive icon and select Install/Deinstall.

Starting SyBooks

The SyBooks installation program can create a program group and icon for the *Dyna*Text browser. The browser is located at *<SyBooks_root>\bin\sybooks.exe*. By default, a SyBooks icon is created in a group called SyBooks. To start SyBooks:

1. Open the SyBooks group.

2. Double-click on the SyBooks icon.

Installation Notes and Troubleshooting

For up-to-date information, see the *readme.win* file in the *<cd_drive>:\sybooks* directory on the CD. If you are using Windows 95 with the AutoPlay feature, click the right mouse button on the CD-ROM drive icon and select Read Me.

The *readme.win* file contains a directory tree of a valid SyBooks installation. You can use this information to restore the directory structure if you quit installation program during installation or deinstallation.

Compatibility Between DynaText Browser Versions

SyBooks includes version 2.3 of EBT's *DynaText* browser. While version 2.3 of the browser can read online documentation generated for use with earlier versions of the browser, the reverse is not true. Versions of the *DynaText* browser earlier than version 2.3 might not be able to read online documents generated for use with version 2.3.

If a version of the *DynaText* browser earlier than version 2.3 is installed, we recommend that it be updated to version 2.3. The SyBooks installation program updates earlier versions of the *DynaText* browser that were installed with previous installations of SyBooks.

Memory Requirements for Installing SyBooks

Stack Space. If you are using Windows 3.1x or Windows 95, make sure you have enough stack space defined by checking the STACKS setting in the \config.sys file. The statement should say *STACKS=9, 256.*

Conventional Memory. Insufficient conventional memory (under 640KB) might prevent the collection indexing program (mkcolidx.exe) from running during the installation or deinstallation.

Reduce the number of unnecessary device drivers and TSRs loaded during the installation. About 600KB or more of conventional DOS memory should be free.

Systems with 8MB of RAM or Less. Additional operating system swap and page file requirements might be required on systems with 8MB of RAM or less. If you see *Out of Stack Space* error messages during the installation, you should examine the swap and page file settings to see if they need to be increased.

If you are using Windows NT, also make sure that the TEMP environment variable points to a valid drive and directory with sufficient disk space. See the operating system documentation for more information about paging and swap files.

Hard Drive Space Requirements for Installing SyBooks

Installation Drive Requirements. In addition to the space requirements shown during installation, you should have at least an additional 3MB of free space on the installation drive (2MB for compact installations). We recommend that you ensure there is enough space on the drive before running the installation program.

Be aware that other processes might access the installation drive during the installation and consume additional drive space, which might result in a disk-full error. For example, if you are installing SyBooks to the drive used by the operating system for paging and swapping, an additional 6MB of disk space or more might be consumed during the installation. In general, it is not a good idea to attempt to fit SyBooks on a drive that has barely enough space for the installation.

Temporary Space Requirements. The TEMP environment variable should be set to a drive with at least 1MB of free space available for logging installation and deinstallation events and configuration options. If you are using **Windows 3.x** or **Windows 95**, you must:

1. Exit Windows or restart your system in DOS mode.

2. At the DOS prompt, set the TEMP variable. Enter:

   ```
   SET TEMP=<temp_directory>
   ```

3. Restart Windows.

Or, you can put a SET statement in the \autoexec.bat file so that the setting takes effect when you start your computer. If you are using OS/2, put the SET statement in the *\autoexec.bat* file so that the value takes effect when you start a WinOS2 session. If you are using Windows NT, double-click on the System icon in Control Panel to set the TEMP variable.

Installing to an Existing SyBooks Directory

If you are installing to or removing SyBooks from an existing directory, make sure no other processes are accessing the directory when the installation program is running. For example, you must close any instances of the *Dyna*Text browser that are accessing the directory and change directories if any DOS sessions are using the directory as the current directory.

Failure to take these actions might prevent the SyBooks installer from installing files and removing directories. If you notice that the SyBooks directory is not removed after you attempt a full deinstallation, you can delete it or install a new SyBooks installation into the same directory.

In addition, make sure you have full read and write access in the installation directory and *\autoexec.bat* file. If you see path or file access errors during the installation or deinstallation:

- Obtain the necessary privileges and retry the operation, or

- Quit, rerun the installation program, and install SyBooks to a different drive or directory to which you have read and write access.

If a Full installation is selected, all collections and books available on the CD that are already installed on the hard drive are still displayed as available for installation. These collections and books are installed over the corresponding collections and books on the hard drive during the installation. The installation program intentionally overwrites the SyBooks files and directories on the hard drive that might have been invalidly or unintentionally modified.

Installing SyBooks v2.0 and v2.1 CDs

If you are installing several SyBooks CDs, you should install the SyBooks v2.2 CDs after any SyBooks v1.x, v2.0, and v2.1 CDs are installed.

If you have already installed collections from a SyBooks v2.2 CD and need to install collections from earlier SyBooks v2.0 or v2.1 CDs, you can use the SyBooks v2.2 installation program to install these earlier CDs by following these steps:

1. Insert the SyBooks v2.2 CD into the CD-ROM drive.

2. Copy the files in the *<cd_drive>:\sybooks\windows* directory to a diskette or directory on the hard drive.

3. Insert the SyBooks v2.0 or v2.1 CD into the CD-ROM drive.

4. From Windows Program Manager, click on File...Run and enter:

   ```
   <drive>:\<directory>\setup <cd_drive>:
   ```

5. Repeat steps 3 and 4 for each v2.0 or v2.1 CD you want to install.

The SyBooks v2.2 installation program cannot install SyBooks v1.x CDs. You must install the v1.x CDs before installing any other SyBooks CDs.

Attempting to install a SyBooks v1.x, v2.0, or v2.1 CD using the older installation programs over an existing SyBooks v2.2 installation will overwrite the pointers to the collections installed using v2.2. You can restore the pointers by editing the *<SyBooks_root>\bin\dynatext.ini* and *colls?.cfg* files and adding the directory paths and collection aliases to those files. Follow the example of the existing collection pointers in those files.

Installing Across Both CD-ROM and Hard Drives

If you want to conserve hard drive space by installing the browser to the hard drive and reading the collections and books from the SyBooks CD (Compact installation), be aware that only full collections can be read from the CD. That is, you cannot read a partial collection from the CD because the *DynaText* browser requires all files of a single collection to be contained within the collection directory.

Likewise, if you install a partial collection on the hard drive, you cannot read the remainder of the collection from the CD. If your goal is to conserve hard drive space, you should deinstall the partial collection from the hard drive and perform a Compact installation to read the entire collection from the CD.

If a collection that is available on the CD is partially or fully installed on the hard drive, the collection is not displayed when a Compact installation is selected. Likewise, if a collection is being read from the CD, the collection is not displayed as an available collection when a Full or Custom installation is selected.

Installing over Previous Compact Installations

If there is a previous Compact installation on the system that you want to remove, you must run the SyBooks installation program from a drive other than the CD-ROM drive. If you attempt to run the installation program from the CD, a system error might occur during the step in which you must remove the CD during the installation. To copy and run the SyBooks installation program from a different drive:

1. Insert the SyBooks v2.2 CD into the CD-ROM drive.

2. Copy the files in the *<cd_drive>:\sybooks\windows* directory to a diskette or directory on the hard drive.

3. From Windows Program Manager, click on File...Run and enter:

   ```
   <drive>:\<directory>\setup <cd_drive>:
   ```

Installing SyBooks on a Network

If you intend to install SyBooks to or from a network drive, you must map the device to a drive letter before you begin the installation. Universal network connection paths are not supported. The absolute drive letter is used in the *DynaText* configuration files and the browser, and the browser will not work properly if the drive is remapped to a different letter after the installation.

If you attempt to install SyBooks to an NFS-mounted UNIX drive, the browser might not run even though the installation was successful. This configuration is not supported.

During the initial scan for existing installations, only local hard drives are searched. If you want the SyBooks installation program to search all available, mapped network drives, specify *setup/net* when you run the SyBooks installation program. Network CD-ROM drives might be searched if they are attached as a network drive.

If you are connected to several local or network hard drives and the initial scan for existing installations takes too long, you can click the Skip button during the search to bypass the scan. After the scan completes, you can change the installation path to the drive and directory of your choice. Another action you can take before starting the installation to minimize the search time is to set the SYBROOT environment variable to point to the drive and directory of an existing SyBooks installation.

Installing SyBooks on OS/2 (WinOS2)

If you are using OS/2, you should run the SyBooks installation program from a WinOS2 full-screen session or from a windowed Program Manager session. In any case, Program Manager must be running in the same WinOS2 session for any new icons and program groups to be added to the system.

When removing books from a collection and installing new collections and books, the collection indexing program will start in a DOS session off the OS/2 Desktop. The SyBooks installation program will not wait for the collection indexing to end, and will indicate that the installation has completed. You can safely exit the installation program at this point. However, do not attempt to use the *Dyna*Text browser until the DOS collection indexing session completes successfully.

If you are using OS/2 Warp and notice that the DOS collection indexing session is running slowly, it is possible that the WinOS2 session priority is set at a higher level relative to the DOS session. To speed up the collection indexing, either close the WinOS2 session or increase the session priority of the DOS session. See the operating system documentation for more information about session priority.

Installation Progress Estimates

The installation progress meter and time estimates give only an approximate indication of the status of the installation or deinstallation based upon the known SyBooks files and directories found.

The installation program does not take into account any non-SyBooks files or unreferenced files that exist in the installation directory structure. Therefore, it is possible for the time estimations to significantly differ from the actual installation or deinstallation time.

Creating Collection-Level Indexes

Collection-level indexes are provided for the full collections available on the CD. If you perform a Full installation, these collection indexes are installed to the hard drive. If you perform a Custom installation, collection-level indexes are automatically built by the installation program for the partial collections installed.

If you need to build the indexes for the entire set of newly installed partial collections, follow these steps:

1. After the installation program ends, go to a DOS prompt (native DOS or a DOS session).

2. Change to the drive where you installed SyBooks by entering:

   ```
   <drive_letter>:
   ```

3. Change to the SyBooks config directory by entering:

   ```
   cd\<SyBooks_directory>\config
   ```

4. To index the newly installed partial collections, enter:

   ```
   indexall
   ```

If you need to build a single collection index, follow these steps:

1. After the installation program has ended, go to a DOS prompt (native DOS or a DOS session).

2. Change to the drive where you installed SyBooks by entering:

   ```
   <drive_letter>:
   ```

3. Change to the SyBooks directory by entering:

   ```
   cd\<SyBooks_directory>
   ```

4. Look at the collection subdirectories by entering:

   ```
   dir /w.
   ```

   Collection subdirectories begin with three letters and are followed by five digits. For example, for *SyBase Open Client/Server Release 10.0.2*, the collection sub-directory is called *con10021*.

5. Change to the SyBooks binaries directory by entering:

   ```
   cd bin
   ```

6. To index the collection, enter:

    ```
    index <collection_subdirectory>
    ```

7. Repeat steps 3 through 6 for each collection you want to index.

If Indexing Fails

If the *mkcolidx.exe* collection indexing program fails due to insufficient memory:

1. Examine the \config.sys and \autoexec.bat files on the boot drive.

2. Increase the amount of conventional memory available (below 640KB) by temporarily disabling unnecessary device or network drivers and TSRs.

3. Reboot and try indexing the collection. After you build the indexes for the collections, restore the driver and TSR configuration and reboot again, if necessary.

If you are using Windows NT 3.1, the installation program might indicate that collection indexing was performed when, in fact, no collection index was created.

During the installation, the installation program runs *command.com* to start the DOS collection indexing session. Check the system PATH setting to determine whether the DOS command.com is being invoked instead of the Windows NT *command.com*. You can either rename the DOS command.com file (for example, to *command.dos*) or change the order of directories in the path so that the Windows NT *command.com* file is found first. After you install SyBooks, restore the path or DOS *command.com* filename to the original setting.

If you are reading books from the CD, collection-level indexes are provided for the full collections on the CD. You cannot build new collection-level indexes for collections read from the CD.

The DynaText Configuration File: dynatext.ini

The SyBooks installation program for Windows creates a *DynaText* configuration file, *dynatext.ini*, which tailors the browser to the system on which SyBooks is installed. The *dynatext.ini* file is stored in the *<SyBooks_root>\bin* directory. For further information about the *dynatext.ini* configuration file, refer to the online document, *SyBooks Frequently Asked Questions*.

Setting the SYBROOT and SYBVIDEO Environment Variables

The SYBROOT Environment Variable. SyBooks for Windows provides the ability to tailor the default font size for viewing the online documentation. The font size is determined by the SYBVIDEO environment variable. The value of SYBVIDEO indicates the default point size for the body text in the online documentation. The SYBVIDEO value can range from 10 to 20, depending on the screen resolution. If SYBVIDEO is not set, the online documentation will appear in 18-point type.

The SYBVIDEO Environment Variable. The SYBROOT environment variable points to the drive and directory path where you installed SyBooks. SYBROOT is used by the installation program when searching for previous collections. If SYBROOT is not defined, the installation program searches all available hard drives (including network drives) on the system for a previous installation. The search ends when an existing installation is found, or when no installations are found.

Autoexec.bat File and Environment Variables. The SyBooks installation program modifies the *autoexec.bat* file by adding or updating two lines in the file to set the SYBVIDEO and SYBROOT environment variables. A backup file called autoexec.bak is stored in the <SyBooks_root>*config* directory before any modifications are made. Defining these environment variables is optional but recommended. These environment variable settings are removed when you completely deinstall SyBooks, and an *autoexec.bak* backup file is created on the boot drive before any modifications are made.

Setting SYBROOT and SYBVIDEO. The environment variable settings take effect when you restart the system, or whenever those statements are executed.

- If you are using a DOS/Windows 3.1 system, you can exit Windows, enter those statements at the native DOS prompt, then restart Windows to have those settings take effect without having to reboot the machine.

- If you are using a Windows NT system, the environment settings take effect immediately, because the SyBooks installation program notifies Windows *Program Manager* of the environment changes in the Registry.

- If you are using OS/2, the settings take effect whenever a WinOS2 session is started.

Windows NT Registry and Environment Variable Changes

If you are installing SyBooks on a Windows NT system, the SYBVIDEO and SYBROOT environment variables are recorded in the Registry under the HKEY_CURRENT_USER/ Environment key. These environment settings are removed when you completely deinstall SyBooks. You should use the SyBooks installation program to install and deinstall collections and books so that the Registry entries and environment variables are properly maintained. If you need to modify the environment variables in Windows NT, click on the System icon in Control Panel.

Windows 95 Registry and Deinstallation

The Windows 95 Registry is not updated by the SyBooks installation program. Deinstallation of SyBooks using the Windows 95 Add/Remove Programs function is not supported. Deinstallation functions are provided in the SyBooks installation program.

Installing and Deinstalling Icons and Program Groups

If you deinstall an entire SyBooks installation, the program group is removed only if the group name is *SyBooks*. The installer does not remove non-SyBooks program groups that might contain icons for other applications installed on the system.

Windows NT

If you are using Windows NT and the program group is called SyBooks (Common), the group and icon might not be removed. To remove the group or icon, you (or the system administrator) must log onto the system with the necessary privileges to delete the group or icon.

Windows 95

If you are using Windows 95, only one SyBooks icon can exist in a folder. Therefore, if you choose to install a new icon in an existing group that already has a SyBooks icon, the existing icon will be updated and no new icons will be created as a result of the installation.

You might see an error message regarding an icon not found when the installation program attempts to remove the SyBooks icon and group. Ignore the error and continue. If the SyBooks program group is empty, you can remove it by dragging it from Windows Explorer to the Recycle Bin.

Updating Annotations from Previous Installations

This release of SyBooks does not take advantage of *Dyna*Text's ability to maintain user-created annotations (including bookmarks, internal hypertext links, and margin notes) across successive versions of an online book. However, the SyBooks installation program for Windows saves annotations from previous installations. Old annotations are saved in *<SyBooks_root>\config\annotold*.

Moving SyBooks to a Different Location

If you move the entire SyBooks environment to a different location, you must edit the contents of the *DynaText* configuration file, *dynatext.ini,* located in *<SyBooks_root>\bin.* All paths pointing to the previous *<SyBooks_root>* directory must be replaced with paths pointing to the new *<SyBooks_root>* directory.

The *DynaText*-specific environment variables, which you must edit, include:

COLLECTION
SYSCONFIG
DATA_DIR
PRIVATE_DIR
PUBLIC_DIR

Change PRIVATE_DIR and PUBLIC_DIR only if their values include *<SyBooks_root>.* You must also edit these files in *<SyBooks_root>\bin:*

colls1.cfg
colls2.cfg
    .
    .
collsn.cfg

For further explanation of these *DynaText* configuration file variables, refer to the online document *SyBooks Frequently Asked Questions.*

Using the Log for Troubleshooting Installation Errors

If you encounter any problems or errors during the installation, you can consult the log.cur file in the directory pointed to by the TEMP environment variable (before the actual installation has started), or in the *<SyBooks_root>\config* directory, if the installation has started. If you encounter deinstallation problems, consult the *log.cur* file in the directory pointed to by the TEMP environment variable.

Information in the *log.cur* file and other files in this directory can be used for diagnosis and recovery purposes. Try to save these files, especially if you plan to contact Sybase Technical Support for further assistance.

The DynaText Browser

When you start SyBooks, the *Dyna*Text library window appears. The library window is divided into two views: on the left is a *collection* view (listing the available collections, or groups of related books). On the right is a *book* view (listing the titles of books in the selected collection). Selecting a different collection displays the titles of the books in that collection.

To open a book, select its title in the book view. When you open a book, a *Dyna*Text book window appears, containing the contents of the selected book. Like the library window, the book window is divided into two views: on the left is a *table of contents* view, displaying a structural hierarchy of the book. On the right is a *text* view, displaying the contents of the book. When you select a section heading in the table of contents view, the corresponding section appears in the text view.

*Dyna*Text Browser Online Help

SyBooks does not include printed documentation for the *Dyna*Text Browser. However, you can access the *Dyna*Text Browser's online Help through its Help menu. The topics included in the Help menu vary, depending upon where you are when you access Help:

- **Accessed from a library window**, the Help menu displays collection-level help topics.

- **Accessed from a book window**, the Help menu displays book-level help topics.

The complete *Dyna*Text *Reader Guide* is available through both library and book window Help menus using the Windows *Dyna*Text Browser. To open the *Dyna*Text *Reader Guide*, choose Reader Guide from the Help menu.

NOTE: On UNIX platforms, the *Dyna*Text *Reader Guide* cannot be opened from a book window's Help menu; it must be opened from a library window's Help menu.

For further instruction on using the *Dyna*Text Browser, refer to the online *Dyna*Text *Reader Guide*.

For More Information

For more information about topics such as printing sections of the online documentation, locating *Dyna*Text configuration files, and searching in online documents, see the online document *SyBooks Frequently Asked Questions*.

Index

IMPORTANT—READ CAREFULLY BEFORE OPENING

SYBASE, INC. LICENSE AGREEMENT (THIS IS A LICENSE AND NOT A SALE)

<u>SYBASE'S ACCEPTANCE OF YOUR ORDER AND DELIVERY OF THIS SOFTWARE
ARE EXPRESSLY CONDITIONED ON YOUR AGREEING TO THE FOLLOWING LICENSE AGREEMENT.</u>
BY OPENING THIS PACKAGE, YOU INDICATE YOUR AGREEMENT WITH THE FOLLOWING.

1. **LICENSE.** You may use those enclosed software programs (and accompanying documentation) which were ordered by you ("Programs") solely for your internal business purposes. No more than the number of Users for which the license was ordered are authorized to access such Program at any one time. A User is a person (or identifiable unique accessor of information used in place of human interaction) who is authorized by you to access the Program or use a foreground or background process to access a Program.

2. **COPYRIGHT AND OWNERSHIP.** The Programs are owned by Sybase and are protected by United States and Canadian copyright laws and international treaty provisions. You acquire only the right to use the Programs and do not acquire any rights of ownership in the Programs or the media on which they are provided.

3. **COPY RESTRICTIONS AND OTHER RESTRICTIONS.** You may not copy the Programs except to make up to one (1) copy for each User and one (1) copy for backup or archival purposes. You may not copy the written materials and manuals accompanying the Programs assigned, or otherwise conveyed (whether by operation of law or otherwise) to another party without Sybase's prior written consent. You may not use the Programs for timesharing, rental or service bureau purposes. You shall not remove any product identification, copyright notices or other notices or proprietary restrictions from the Programs. Upon reasonable notice to you, Sybase may audit the number of Users using the Programs and the number of copies of the Programs in use by you.

4. **U.S. GOVERNMENT RESTRICTED RIGHTS.** If this license is acquired under a U.S. Government contract, use, duplication or disclosure by the U.S. Government is subject to restrictions as set forth in DFARS 252.227–7013(c)(ii) for Department of Defense contracts and as set forth in FAR 52.227–19(a)–(d) for civilian agency contracts. Sybase reserves all unpublished rights under the United States copyright laws.

5. **TERMINATION.** Either party may terminate this Agreement if the other party breaches any of its obligations hereunder and such breach is not cured within sixty (60) days after written notice. Sybase may terminate this Agreement if you fail to make any payment when due to Sybase and such failure is not cured within fifteen (15) days after written notice. Upon termination, you shall cease using the Programs and shall return to Sybase all copies of the Programs and Documentation in any form.

6. **LIMITED WARRANTY AND LIABILITY.** Sybase warrants that the Programs when properly used, will operate in all material respects in conformity with Sybase published specifications for the applicable version, and the Program media shall be free of defects, for one (1) year from the date of shipment of such version to you. In the event of a failure to meet the foregoing limited warranty, your sole remedy in the event of nonconformity of a Program, at Sybase's option, shall be replacement of the defective materials or a refund of the license fees paid for the affected Program. This limited warranty gives you specific legal rights. **SYBASE DISCLAIMS ALL OTHER WARRANTIES AND CONDITIONS, EXPRESS OR IMPLIED, INCLUDING WITHOUT LIMITATION THE IMPLIED WARRANTIES OR CONDITIONS OF MERCHANTABLE QUALITY AND FITNESS FOR A PARTICULAR PURPOSE, AND WHETHER ARISING BY STATUTE OR IN LAW OR AS A RESULT OF A COURSE OF DEALING OR USAGE OF TRADE, WITH RESPECT TO THE PROGRAMS OR THE DOCUMENTATION. NO WARRANTY IS MADE REGARDING THE RESULTS OF ANY PROGRAM OR INFORMATION CONTAINED THEREIN, THAT ALL ERRORS IN THE PROGRAMS WILL BE CORRECTED, OR THAT THE PROGRAMS' FUNCTIONALITY WILL MEET YOUR REQUIREMENTS. IN NO EVENT WILL SYBASE OR ITS SUPPLIERS BE LIABLE FOR ANY LOSS OR INACCURACY OF DATA, LOSS OF PROFITS OR INDIRECT, SPECIAL, INCIDENTAL OR CONSEQUENTIAL DAMAGES, EVEN IF SYBASE HAS BEEN ADVISED OF THE POSSIBILITY OF SUCH DAMAGES. SYBASE'S TOTAL LIABILITY, IF ANY, ARISING OUT OF OR RELATING TO THIS AGREEMENT SHALL NOT EXCEED THE LICENSE FEES PAID BY YOU FOR THE PROGRAMS. THE FOREGOING RESTRICTIONS, DISCLAIMERS AND LIMITATIONS SHALL APPLY AND REMAIN IN FORCE EVEN IN THE EVENT OF A BREACH BY SYBASE HEREUNDER OF A CONDITION OR FUNDAMENTAL TERM HEREUNDER, OR IN THE EVENT OF A BREACH WHICH CONSTITUTES A FUNDAMENTAL BREACH.**

7. **GOVERNING LAW; COMPLETE AGREEMENT.** THIS AGREEMENT IS GOVERNED BY THE LAWS OF THE STATE OF CALIFORNIA IF THE USER IS LOCATED IN THE UNITED STATES, AND BY THE LAWS OF THE PROVINCE OF ONTARIO IF THE USER IS LOCATED IN CANADA, AND CONSTITUTES THE COMPLETE AGREEMENT BETWEEN THE PARTIES WITH RESPECT TO THE PROGRAMS. The terms of this Agreement supersede the terms of any purchase order, order letter or other document issued or signed by you to authorize its license of the Programs. If any provision of this Agreement is held to be unenforceable, such provision shall be limited, modified or severed as necessary to eliminate its unenforceability, and all other provisions shall remain unaffected.

8. **WAIVERS.** The failure or delay of either party to exercise any of its rights shall not be deemed a waiver thereof and no waiver by either party of any breach of this Agreement shall constitute a waiver of any other subsequent breach.

9. **TRANSLATION.** The parties have requested that this Agreement and all documents contemplated hereby be drawn up in English. Les parties aux presentes ont exigé que cerre entente et tous nutree documents envisagés par les présentes soíent rédigés en anglais.